DEVOTIONAL
{ walk with Jesus }

DEVOTIONAL

{ walk with Jesus }

365 days in the new testament

Contributing editors

Mickey Hodges, John Hoover, Paula Kirk

ZONDERVAN®

WALK THRU THE BIBLE®

TAKE A WALK. CHANGE THE WORLD.

ZONDERVAN

Once-A-Day Walk with Jesus Devotional
Copyright © 2011 by Walk Thru the Bible Ministries

Requests for information should be addressed to:

Zondervan, 3900 *Sparks Dr. SE, Grand Rapids, Michigan 49546*

Library of Congress Cataloging-in-Publication Data

Once-a-day walk with Jesus devotional : 365 days in the New Testament.
    p. cm.
   Copyrighted by Walk Thru the Bible Ministries.
   Includes bibliographical references and index.
   ISBN 978-0-310-44324-7 (softcover : alk. paper)
   1. Bible. N.T. – Devotional use. 2. Devotional calendars. I. Walk Thru the Bible
(Educational ministry)
BS2341.55.O53 2011
242'.2 – dc23
                                               2011035004

Cover design: *Faceout Studio and Jamie DeBruyn*
Interior design: *Sherri Hoffman and Jamie DeBruyn*

Printed in the United States of America

14 15 16 17 18 19 20 /DCI/ 22 21 20 19 18 17 16 15 14 13 12 11 10 9 8 7 6 5 4 3 2

To our friend Joan Holmes,
whose courage, gentleness and perseverance
have touched the lives of all her colleagues at
Walk Thru the Bible for over two decades

"For I know the plans I have for you,"
declares the LORD,
"plans to prosper you and not to harm you,
plans to give you hope and a future."

INTRODUCTION

You are holding a compass designed to guide you on an exciting new adventure. Whether you are a seasoned Bible student or a first-time reader, this tool will lead you on an amazing journey through the life of Jesus and the birth and growth of the early church.

Each day's devotional has been carefully crafted to move the truth off the page and into your life. Along the way you'll discover timeless insights from men and women who walked with God in past generations. These fellow pilgrims will help you apply God's unchanging truth to the challenges of our rapidly changing world.

All of us at Walk Thru the Bible are thrilled to partner with you on this amazing journey. We are honored that you have invited us to walk by your side as you seek to become all our Lord designed you to be.

Walking with you,
Phil Tuttle
President and CEO
Walk Thru the Bible Ministries

ABOUT WALK THRU THE BIBLE

For more than three decades, Walk Thru the Bible has been dedicated to igniting a passion for God's Word worldwide through live events, devotional magazines, and resources designed for both small groups and individual use. Known for innovative methods and high-quality resources, we serve the whole body of Christ across denominational, cultural, and national lines.

Walk Thru the Bible communicates the truths of God's Word in a way that makes the Bible readily accessible to anyone. We are committed to developing user-friendly resources that are Bible centered, of excellent quality, life changing for individuals, and catalytic for churches, ministries and movements; and we are committed to maintaining our global reach through strategic partnerships while adhering to the highest levels of integrity in all we do.

Walk Thru the Bible partners with the local church worldwide to fulfill its mission, helping people "walk thru" the Bible with greater clarity and understanding. Live events and small group curricula are taught in over 45 languages by more than 30,000 instructors in more than 104 countries, and more than 100 million devotionals have been packaged into daily magazines, books, and other publications that reach over 5 million people each year.

Walk Thru the Bible
www.walkthru.org
1–800–361–6131

january1

THE WONDERFUL NAMES OF JESUS

The virgin will conceive and give birth to a son, and they will call him Immanuel (which means "God with us").

MATTHEW 1:23

What if people wore the meaning of their names for all to see? You'd smile to meet David ("beloved"), chuckle at Mary ("stubbornness"), nod with Joanna ("God is gracious").

Matthew 1 begins with a long genealogy of more than 40 names—a few are familiar, many are obscure, but all look forward to the arrival of one central figure: the one named Jesus ("Savior") or Immanuel ("God with us").

Charles Spurgeon was thoroughly captivated—and motivated—by the names of Jesus. What's in a name? Let's let Mr. Spurgeon explain.

WALK WITH CHARLES SPURGEON

"In these days we call children by names which have no particular meaning. But in times past names meant something. Especially is this the case in every name ascribed to the Lord Jesus.

"'He will be called Wonderful Counselor, Mighty God, Everlasting Father, Prince of Peace' (Isaiah 9:6), because he really is all these things.

"His name is Jesus because no other name could fairly describe his great work of saving his people from their sins.

"His name is Immanuel—'God with us'—because there is no pain that tears the heart but what Jesus has been with us in it all. In the fires and in the rivers, in the cold night and under the burning sun, he cries, 'I am with you; do not be dismayed, for I am your God' (Isaiah 41:10)."

WALK CLOSER TO GOD

You can think of Matthew 1 as a long list of names. Or you can view it as the roots of the Savior who came

as Immanuel—to be with you,
as Counselor—to provide wisdom,
as Prince of Peace—to heal a relationship.

He came wearing names that revealed his purpose and character.
Have you come to him with your needs today? ✤

january**2**

IN THE PRESENCE OF THE KING

Where is the one who has been born king of the Jews?

MATTHEW 2:2

How far is it from St. Louis to Kansas City? About 200 miles if you're going in the right direction and about 25,000 miles if you're not!

Whether the goal is to bake a cake, put together a child's Christmas toy, or—like the wise men in Matthew 2—find the Christ-child, the need is the same: good directions, and the willingness to follow them carefully.

F. B. Meyer offers this insight into the importance of hearing—and heeding—God's directions.

WALK WITH F. B. MEYER

"God comes to men in the spheres with which they are most familiar: to the shepherds in the fields, to the wise men by a sign in the heavens.

"God knows just where to find us, and in turn provides all we need to find and worship him.

"When we follow God's guidance, we may be sure that he will not fail to bring us to our goal. He who brings us out will also bring us in.

"The wise men prostrating themselves before the newborn babe were the first of a great procession down through the centuries who have followed them to the same spot.

"We cannot fathom the mystery, but we, like they, can adore and present our gifts, for indeed he is worthy."

WALK CLOSER TO GOD

The road of life can be a baffling route indeed: smooth at times, sometimes full of potholes ... one day a well-marked expressway, the next a maze of detours.

But your heavenly Father has provided a road map—the Bible—to keep you moving in the right direction.

Dotting the pages of the Bible like signposts along the way are promises to encourage you, warnings to protect you and commands to detour you from danger.

By following it daily, you, like the wise men, will come safely to your destination. And you too will fall down and worship. ❖

january3

A HERITAGE IN GOD'S FAMILY

This is my Son, whom I love; with him I am well pleased.

MATTHEW 3:17

In Matthew 3 a man named John burst onto the scene, looking and sounding like Elijah the prophet. According to the Old Testament, that was precisely as it should have been.

Another man, named Jesus, came to be baptized by John. Coincidence? Or was he the long-awaited Messiah ("Anointed One")? The audible voice of God supplied the answer.

Matthew Henry, a prolific eighteenth-century Bible commentator, reveled in the Christian's privileges "in Christ." If you are "in him," you enjoy a rich heritage in God's family, as Mr. Henry explains.

WALK WITH MATTHEW HENRY

"Jesus is God's 'beloved Son,' not only 'with whom' but 'in whom' God is well pleased. God is pleased with all who are in Christ and are united to him by faith. Hitherto God has been displeased with the children of men; but now his anger is turned away, and he has made us 'accepted in the beloved.' Outside of Christ, God is a consuming Fire, but in Christ he is a reconciling Father.

"This is the sum of the whole gospel: God has declared by a voice from heaven that Jesus Christ is his beloved Son. With this we must by faith cheerfully concur and say that he is our beloved Savior, in whom we are well pleased."

WALK CLOSER TO GOD

What is your heavenly heritage? Forgiveness. Acceptance. Salvation. Indescribable wealth in Jesus Christ, all because you are "born again" into God's family, giving you the right to call God your Father. That's your legacy. You are rich in Christ, but do you live as a king's heir?

You are forgiven, but do you nurture feelings of guilt? You are accepted, but do you try to "repay" God for what he has given as a free gift?

It's hard to live like a pauper when you know you're as rich as a king. And focusing on your heritage in the family of God can be exciting.

Don't be surprised if something changes when you do. And don't be content until it does. ♣

january4

GREAT LIGHT IN THE SHADOW OF DEATH

The people living in darkness have seen a great light.

MATTHEW 4:16

Jesus came to bring light into a darkened world, and having been announced by John and tested by Satan, he was ready to begin his public ministry.

But where? Jerusalem, the capital of the nation? Or Samaria, a hotbed of ethnic unrest? Maybe Nazareth, his hometown?

The answer may surprise you!

G. Campbell Morgan probes the significance of Capernaum as the place where Christ's ministry began.

WALK WITH G. CAMPBELL MORGAN

"When God visits his people for redemption, he comes where darkness is greatest, where the people sit in the shadow of death. Both in terms of geography and principle, Jesus did that very thing.

"Capernaum was in a despised region of the land of Palestine known as Galilee of the Gentiles. This portion of the country had been overrun more than any other by foreign invaders. Therefore, it came to be called 'the region and shadow of death.'

"That was Capernaum; and Jesus started his public ministry there.

"He did not commence where people were least likely to need it. Rather, the people who sat in darkness—in the region of the shadow of death—saw the great light."

WALK CLOSER TO GOD

Shine a bright light into an already lighted room, and you have changed nothing. Shine that same light into a dark corner, and you have shattered the darkness.

For you, Capernaum may be as near as your neighborhood, school or office.

Who in your sphere of life sits in ignorance and darkness? Which friends or neighbors of yours are craving the light?

Where the light of the gospel needs to penetrate, there is your Capernaum. ✤

january5

BLESSED ... IN THE EYES OF GOD

Blessed are the poor in spirit, for theirs is the kingdom of heaven.

MATTHEW 5:3

What is happiness? Ask 20 different people to answer that question, and you'll probably get 20 different answers.

But for the citizen of the kingdom of heaven, the path to true happiness is the path of blessedness described by Jesus in Matthew 5:1–11.

As Matthew Henry points out, until you know what true happiness is, you will never discover God's path to find it.

WALK WITH MATTHEW HENRY

"Happiness is the thing people pretend to pursue. But most form a wrong notion of it and miss the way.

"The general opinion is: Blessed are those who are rich and honorable in the world, who spend their days in mirth and their years in pleasure.

"Jesus comes to correct this fundamental error and give us quite another notion of blessedness.

"However paradoxical his teaching may appear to those in the world, to those who are saved it is a rule of eternal truth and certainty by which we must shortly be judged.

"If this, therefore, be the beginning of Christ's doctrine, the Christian's duty must be to take his measure of happiness from those maxims, and to direct his life accordingly."

WALK CLOSER TO GOD

Would you consider yourself truly happy if your life were characterized by meekness ... mercy ... poverty in spirit ... persecution?

You would if you had God's perspective on happiness.

Given the chance, the world will offer you a bogus substitute—a happiness dependent on money, prestige or circumstances.

Christ says true happiness consists of none of these.

But you must decide. Which notion of blessedness will you build your life on today? How do you complete the sentence "Happiness is ..."? ✤

A SOUL FILLED WITH LIGHT FROM HEAVEN

The eye is the lamp of the body. If your eyes are healthy, your whole body will be full of light.
MATTHEW 6:22

Aim at nothing, and you will hit it every time. Aim at something with a whole heart and a clear sense of purpose, and you may be surprised by what you can accomplish.

In short, that's the message of Matthew 6. Call it the principle of focus: single-minded movement toward a goal.

It's what guides the basketball player as he shoots, the archer as he looses the arrow, and the disciple of Jesus Christ as he relates to others in daily life.

Pleasing God seldom happens by accident. But as John Wesley points out, it's not an impossible target to hit, provided your aim is accurate and unwavering.

WALK WITH JOHN WESLEY

"If your eye is single, if God is in all your thoughts, if you are constantly aiming at him who is invisible, if it is your intention in all things small and great to please God and do the will of him who sent you into the world, then the promise will certainly take place: 'Your whole body will be full of light.' Your whole soul shall be filled with the light of heaven—with the glory of the Lord resting upon you.

"In all your actions and conversation, you shall have not only the testimony of a good conscience toward God, but his Spirit will also bear witness with you that your ways are acceptable to him."

WALK CLOSER TO GOD

Aiming to be godly may seem like aiming at an invisible target. But Jesus Christ came to earth to make godliness visible.

What does it mean to become godly?

It means becoming like your teacher, giving your undivided attention to his Word and your unquestioned obedience to his will.

What are your sights set on?

It's easy to tell, for where the eye of your heart is focused, your lips and feet will quickly follow. ✤

IN YOUR FATHER'S THRONE ROOM

Ask and it will be given to you; seek and you will find; knock and the door will be opened to you.

Matthew 7:7

Nothing puts feeling into your prayers like a mighty good reason to pray. But nothing in Christianity is so rare as a praying heart.

Fifteen verses in the Sermon on the Mount concern prayer. Jesus talks about when to pray (Matthew 6:5–8), how to pray (Matthew 6:9–13), and why to pray (Matthew 7:7–11).

Why is prayer so important? The reason is simple: God gives good gifts to his children who ask him.

Augustine spoke often of the privilege of prayer, but he explains that *longing in prayer* and *long prayer* are not necessarily synonymous.

WALK WITH AUGUSTINE

"It was our Lord who put an end to long-windedness, so that you would not pray as if you wanted to teach God by your many words. Piety, not verbosity, is in order when you pray, since he knows your needs.

"Now someone perhaps will say: But if he knows our needs, why should we state our requests even in a few words? Why should we pray at all? Since he knows, let him give what he deems necessary for us.

"Even so, he wants you to pray so that he may confer his gifts on one who really desires them and will not regard them lightly."

WALK CLOSER TO GOD

Prayer is more than heavenly room service to satisfy your heart's desire. Rather, prayer is the workout room of your soul. Asking, seeking and knocking are energetic words. They show sincerity, intensity and wholeheartedness.

Have you ever asked God for great things? Things out of the ordinary? Things that your own ingenuity and energy could never provide?

If not, you've yet to discover the power of prayer. For he has told you to "ask ... seek ... knock," and to expect doors to open as a result. ❖

PANICKY PRAYERS OR UNSHAKABLE TRUST

You of little faith, why are you so afraid?

MATTHEW 8:26

After witnessing three powerful miracles of Jesus in the first half of Matthew 8, the disciples are dropped into the "crucible" in the Sea of Galilee. And their response in that furious storm shows the fickleness of their faith.

Prayers of panic—what child of God hasn't experienced them? Oswald Chambers explains how the way you pray reflects the character of your faith.

WALK WITH OSWALD CHAMBERS

"Our Lord has a right to expect that those who claim to be his should have an understanding confidence in him. But too often our trust is in God up to a certain point; then we go back to the panic prayers of those who do not know God.

"We get to our wits' end, showing that we have not the slightest confidence in him and his government of the world. He seems to be asleep, and we see nothing but breakers ahead.

"'O you of little faith!'

"What a pang must have shot through the disciples. And what a pang will go through us when we suddenly realize that we might have produced downright joy in the heart of Jesus by remaining absolutely confident in Him, no matter what was ahead."

WALK CLOSER TO GOD

It's hard to be a hypocrite in the vortex of a crisis.

There isn't time to paste on a mask or worry about what other people think. When you're confronted by a crisis, the true character of your faith will emerge— unvarnished and unannounced.

But it's never too late to let God still the storm in your heart and teach you to rest confidently in him. He will strengthen your faith as you rely on him.

Give yourself a simple crisis checkup by putting the words *panic* and *pray* in the following statement: When I'm facing a crisis, first I _____, then I _____. ✤

january**9**

ANSWERS FROM THE MASTER PROBLEM SOLVER

When Jesus saw their faith, he said to the man, "Take heart, son; your sins are forgiven".
MATTHEW 9:2

Lingering illness. Guilt. Depression. Financial uncertainty. Loss of a loved one. It doesn't matter how big the problem is, provided you know the infinite problem solver.

The question is not one of ability, as you will see in Matthew 9, but rather one of authority—a willingness on your part to acknowledge who Jesus is as confirmed by his miracles.

Some were indifferent to his claims. Others were infuriated. But as G. Campbell Morgan explains, those who came in believing faith were met at their point of need.

WALK WITH G. CAMPBELL MORGAN

"To the questioning and rebellious heart Jesus proved his authority to forgive sins by an exhibition of his power to heal. The effect was instantaneous and remarkable: The multitudes feared and glorified God.

"Then in rapid succession a ruler, a woman ostracized because of her plague, two blind men, and a mute possessed with a demon crossed his path. He met their varied needs with strong, tender words and spoke to each one a message of peace and courage.

"The Pharisees, madly jealous of his power, attributed it to Satan. But the King, looking upon the crowds, was moved with compassion—the consequence of seeing them in their true condition as distressed and scattered, like sheep without a shepherd."

WALK CLOSER TO GOD

God may not always give you the wisdom to solve your own problem. But you can always be assured that Jesus is strong enough to handle it, compassionate enough to feel it, loving enough to care for it, wise enough to deal with it.

In Matthew 9, six lives were changed after encounters with the problem-solving Savior. Yours will be too when you stop looking at your problem and focus on the problem solver. ✤

january10

SHARING ALL WITH THE MASTER

The student is not above the teacher, nor a servant above his master. It is enough for students to be like their teachers, and servants like their masters. If the head of the house has been called Beelzebul, how much more the members of his household!.

MATTHEW 10:24–25

Jesus told his followers to be as shrewd as snakes and as innocent as doves—rather unflattering similes from Matthew 10. Until you understand his point.

Being Christ's disciple demands a distinctive lifestyle. One that places you squarely in opposition to the world around you. Alexander Maclaren explains how a Christian who lives like the Master will be treated like the Master.

WALK WITH ALEXANDER MACLAREN

"If you are like the Master in conduct, you will be no more popular with the world than he was. As long as Christianity will be quiet, the world is content to let it alone or even to say polite things about it.

"But if Christian men and women live up to their profession, fight drunkenness, go against the lust of great cities, preach peace to a nation howling for war, or apply the golden rule to commerce and social relationships, you will soon hear a different shout.

"The disciple who is truly a disciple must share the fate of the Master."

WALK CLOSER TO GOD

Heavenly Father, give me the courage to be distinctive and to demonstrate my commitment as a disciple of Christ in a way that will cause others to desire a relationship with Christ.

Remind me often that I am in the world but not of the world. Fortify me to command the world's respect through a lifestyle of holiness and consistency, as befitting a follower of your Son. And make me aware of those areas of my life that reflect the world's ways more than yours.

In the name of him who experienced both reception and rejection. Amen. ❖

january11

THE PLACE OF REST IS THE SOURCE OF STRENGTH

Come to me, all you who are weary and burdened, and I will give you rest.

MATTHEW 11:28

Some Christians are experts at making nothing happen ... and doing that very slowly. Others behave as if the work of Christ were their single-handed duty. Both extremes lead to barrenness.

Every day of your life will bring a myriad of demands marked "urgent." Demands that carry the potential to change busyness into barrenness and bring spiritual and emotional burnout.

What can you do to avoid barrenness in your walk with God? J. Hudson Taylor offers wise words for those in danger of growing weary in the work of the Lord.

WALK WITH J. HUDSON TAYLOR

"Never, never did Christ send an over-burdened one to work; never did he send a hungry one, a weary one, a sick or sorrowing one away on any service.

"Yet how many can tell of a time of intense distress because they felt they ought to be speaking to others about their souls, but could not?

"Oh, how different it would have been had they but first come to Jesus and found rest. Then their happy countenance would have said more than the heartfelt words were uttering. No one would then have looked at the face of the speaker and felt, 'What a dreadful religion his must be!'

"For the 'come' is not intended to exclude the 'go,' but to prepare the way for it."

WALK CLOSER TO GOD

There is nothing inherently spiritual about busyness. Christ reserved some of his strongest rebukes for the Pharisees—the spiritual workaholics of his day. They were so busy working for God that they had forgotten to follow him.

Nor is there anything inherently sinful about "unproductive" moments—if they are used to refresh and energize you for renewed service. Even the Creator of the universe set aside his labors for a day of rest.

And the beauty of it all?

While you are at rest, God is at work! ❖

january 12

KINSHIP IN THE FAMILY OF GOD

For whoever does the will of my Father in heaven is my brother and sister and mother.
MATTHEW 12:50

Family life and acceptance are important to each of us. But true kinship does not require a blood relationship.

When Jesus spoke to the crowd in Matthew 12, he told them his disciples were his family—brothers and sisters of *faith* rather than *flesh*.

Listen as Francis of Assisi describes the richness of this family relationship.

WALK WITH FRANCIS OF ASSISI

"We must never desire to be set above others, but to be subject to every human creature for God's sake. And all who do this shall be the brothers and mothers of our Lord Jesus Christ.

"We are his brothers when we do the will of his Father who is in heaven.

"We are his mothers when we bear him in our heart by love and a pure and sincere conscience, and bring him forth in holy deeds which must shine as an example to others.

"O, how glorious and holy and great it is to have a Father in heaven! O, how holy and delightful, pleasing and humble, peaceful and sweet, amiable and above all things to be desired it is to have a brother who laid down his life for his sheep."

WALK CLOSER TO GOD

All the rags-to-riches stories ever told pale by comparison with what God has done for you in making you a full-fledged part of his family.

A son or daughter of his love.

A joint heir with Jesus of all that the Father possesses.

Comfort.

Strength.

Chastening.

Guidance.

They're all part of your family blessings in the household of God.

Think of it: Your Father in heaven cares for you as his very own ... because that's what you are.

So welcome to the family! ❖

january 13

GLORIOUS JEWEL IN THE FATHER'S POSSESSION

The kingdom of heaven is like ... one [pearl] of great value.

MATTHEW 13:45−46

Nothing is quite as unyielding as a price tag. But if something is worth the price, you pay it. After all, objects of genuine value never come cheaply.

In Matthew 13, Jesus employed seven parables to describe the incomparable value of the kingdom of heaven. And, as Matthew Henry explains, a man may gain the whole world, but unless he discovers one pearl of great value, he has failed to find true riches.

WALK WITH MATTHEW HENRY

"Jesus Christ is a Pearl of great price, a Jewel of inestimable value, which will make those who have it rich, truly rich toward God.

"In having him we have enough to make us happy here and forever.

"Those who would have Christ must be willing to part with all for him, leave all to follow him. Whatever stands in opposition to Christ, or in competition with him for our love and service, we must cheerfully quit, though it is precious to us."

WALK CLOSER TO GOD

Items of genuine value are always in danger of being impersonated by imitations and facsimiles.

And counterfeit Christianity—like counterfeit money—looks surprisingly like the real thing.

There is just enough truth in it to make it attractive. And just enough error to ensure that it will never deliver what it promises.

Satan, the master counterfeiter, will dupe you if given the chance. His name even means "adversary" and "accuser."

His game is simple: to offer an attractive alternative to the pearl of great value. Wealth. Education. Personal achievement. Peer acceptance.

He will sell you a "bargain." He will convince you God's kingdom is not worth seeking.

If you let him.

Counterfeit or genuine: Which pearl will you make your own? ❖

MAKING PRAYER A PERSONAL PRIORITY

After he had dismissed them, he went up on a mountainside by himself to pray.
MATTHEW 14:23

Some people load their days with activities, clutter their calendars with appointments and fill the air with music—anything to drown out the sounds of silence. Which is too bad, really.

Because God often speaks in a still, small voice—the kind heard only in moments of silence (see 1 Kings 19:11–13).

You will discover two occasions in Matthew 14 when Jesus left the crowds and retired to a quiet place to pray. John Calvin comments on the importance of the Savior's search for solitude.

WALK WITH JOHN CALVIN

"By going to the mountain he was seeking a time of prayer free from interruption.

"We all know how easily prayer can be quenched by the least distraction.

"Although Christ did not suffer from this weakness, he warned us by his example to be careful to disengage our minds from the snares of the world, so that we may be carried up to heaven.

"The most important thing is solitude. Those who pray with God as their only witness will be more watchful, will pour forth their hearts to him, and will examine themselves more carefully.

"The freedom to pray in all places does not prevent us from praying in secret."

WALK CLOSER TO GOD

Silence. How often do you experience it? What priority do you give it?

Jesus left the accolades of the crowds and climbed a mountain. There he prayed until "shortly before dawn" (Matthew 14:25). Jesus was committed to prayer!

God hears your hurried prayers. But he yearns for you to give him an uncluttered slice of your time, free from the distractions of your busy day.

It will seldom happen by accident. In fact, you may have to turn off your cell phone, walk away from your computer, rearrange your schedule. But what a small price to pay to "be still, and know" God (Psalm 46:10)! ❖

january15

PLACING ALL RESOURCES IN GOD'S HANDS

Where could we get enough bread in this remote place to feed such a crowd?

MATTHEW 15:33

Seven loaves of bread and a few fish. Four thousand hungry men, plus women and children. Put them all together and you have a lot of hungry people!

But add Jesus to the scene, and you have all the ingredients for a miracle.

A world teeming with millions of unreached souls, and a few thousand missionary volunteers. Again, so little in the face of so great a need.

But as J. Hudson Taylor discovered, little is much when God is in it.

WALK WITH J. HUDSON TAYLOR

"What God has given us is all we need; we require nothing more. It is not a question of large supplies—it is just a question of the presence of the Lord.

"Let us look to the Lord's methods. How were the people fed? By the united action of Christ and his disciples. He claimed their all. They gladly gave their all and unhesitatingly obeyed all his directions.

"Let us give up our work, our thoughts, our plans, ourselves, our loved ones, our influence, our all—right into his hand. And then there will be nothing left to be troubled about.

"When all is in his hand, all will be safe; all will be done and well done."

WALK CLOSER TO GOD

Consecration and confidence.

Those are the responses of the disciples who took bread and fish from the Master's hands to feed the multitudes—though they could not explain the source.

With those attitudes you too can boldly share the good news of Jesus Christ with the hungry multitudes in your world. When you commit your life to Christ, you too can have confidence in a God who is big enough, wise enough, rich enough to handle any problem.

At his table there is food to spare. It's your privilege to pass the basket. ❖

january16

WALKING IN THE WAY OF THE CROSS

Whoever wants to be my disciple must deny themselves and take up their cross and follow me.
MATTHEW 16:24

Self-denial. Suffering. Cross-bearing. That's not the kind of lifestyle anyone would normally volunteer for.

But Christ put up with the shame and anguish of the cross that he might bring men and women to himself. So it shouldn't surprise you that he calls you to a similar lifestyle today.

Alexander Whyte provides a helpful insight into the disciple's role as a cross-bearer.

WALK WITH ALEXANDER WHYTE

"There are things in all our lives that chafe and fret and crucify our hearts continually. Those you love best may even be the cause of constant and acute pain.

"There are people with whom you are compelled to stand in the closest of business relationships—people whose tempers and manners and treatment of you continually exasperate you.

"Though no mortal may ever guess you are fast sinking under the weight of such crosses as these, it is no guess with your Savior. He knows all about it.

"No one has ever understood crosses better than Jesus Christ. Be sure he is not far away.

"Every new morning, take up your cross and carry it all day in his strength and under his all-seeing and all-sympathizing eye."

WALK CLOSER TO GOD

What are you willing to put up with to follow Christ? Your neighbor's offenses, your boss's temper, your spouse's indifference, your child's rebellion? Such situations can be the source of intense pain.

But when you respond with a Christlike attitude, your life can be the irresistible evidence that Christ is real.

Does it seem strange to you that God would place before you a task this painful? Then consider once again the work of the cross-bearer you serve and follow, the master you love. ❖

january**17**

MUSTARD-SEED FAITH IN A MIGHTY GOD

If you have faith as small as a mustard seed, you can say to this mountain, "Move from here to there," and it will move. Nothing will be impossible for you.

MATTHEW 17:20

Computer chips. Viruses. Atoms. By anyone's standard, they're not very big. Yet little things can pack a big punch.

Take faith, for instance. According to Jesus in Matthew 17, a mustard-seed amount of faith is enough to move mountains.

Oswald Chambers probes the meaning of faith as the life attitude of the Christian.

WALK WITH OSWALD CHAMBERS

"Faith brings us into right relationship with God and gives God his opportunity. He frequently has to knock the bottom out of our experience to get us into contact with himself.

"God wants you to understand it is a life of faith—not a life of sentimental enjoyment of his blessings—that pleases him.

"Faith by its very nature must be tried. And the real trial of faith is not that we find it difficult to trust God, but that God's character has to be clear in our minds so that we remain true to God whatever he may do.

"'Though he slay me,' announced Job, 'yet will I hope in him' (Job 13:15). This is the most sublime utterance of faith in the whole Bible."

WALK CLOSER TO GOD

Faith. You can't see it, hear it or touch it. But neither can you live without it.

Faith requires a commitment. It is pointless to say, "I have faith in the bank," unless you put your money there.

Likewise, it is meaningless to say, "I have faith in God," unless you trust in him.

And rest in him.

And relax.

Mustard-seed faith in a mighty God—that's how to see him move a mountain of need in your life.

And that's how to bear up under trials until he does it! ♣

january18

GOD FORGAVE MY SIN IN JESUS' NAME

Then Peter came to Jesus and asked, "Lord, how many times shall I forgive my brother or sister who sins against me? Up to seven times?" Jesus answered, "I tell you, not seven times, but seventy-seven times".

MATTHEW 18:21–22

Forgive and forget.

Peter was certainly comfortable with that principle. After all, hadn't Jesus already taught him that if he forgave others when they sinned against him, his heavenly Father would also forgive him? And hadn't the sacrificial system he had grown up with taught him that God forgives the sins of his people?

Yes, Peter was certainly comfortable with forgiveness—seven times. But seventy-seven times?

Unfortunately, all of us since Adam are like Peter in this respect—all except one. John Flavel reminds us to imitate him who is infinite forgiveness.

WALK WITH JOHN FLAVEL

"Imitate our pattern Christ and labor for meek forgiving spirits. I shall only propose two reasons for doing so: for the honor of Christ, and for your own peace. His glory is more than your life, and all that you enjoy in this world. Oh, do not expose it to the scorn and derision of his enemies. Let them not say, 'How is Christ a lamb, when his followers are lions? How is the church a dove, that smites and scratches like a bird of prey?'

"Consider also the quiet of your own heart. What is life worth, without the comfort of life? What comfort can you have in all that you possess in the world as long as you do not have possession of your own soul? If inside you are full of tumult and revenge, the Spirit of Christ will become a stranger to you; that dove delights in a clean and quiet heart. Oh, then imitate Christ in this excellency also!"

WALK CLOSER TO GOD

The rest of the chapter is the parable of the unmerciful servant. The main character refused to forgive as he had been forgiven. Notice that he was "handed ... over to the jailers to be tortured" (Matthew 18:34).

Are you "tortured" by an unforgiving spirit? Ephesians 4:32 has the answer: Meditate on Christ's forgiveness. There is no better way to cultivate your own. ✤

january**19**

GIVING UP YOUR PLACE IN LINE

But many who are first will be last, and many who are last will be first.

MATTHEW 19:30

Ask ten third graders to form a straight line, and chances are good that nine of them will clamor to be first in line.

In the process, they are modeling what society has taught them: Greatness means coming in first.

In Matthew 18:4 and 19:30, Jesus addressed the subject of greatness. And clearly his concept of "coming in first" cut across the grain with the mindset of his day.

John Calvin offers an insightful comment regarding greatness—a preoccupation not limited to the first century.

WALK WITH JOHN CALVIN

"The disciples were too accustomed to the common habits of men. Each one wanted the first place.

"But Christ regarded as worthy the man who forgot his superiority and humbled himself. He declares that they are greatest who abase themselves, lest we should think we lose anything when we willingly surrender all greatness.

"From this we may gather a brief definition of humility: 'He is truly humble who neither claims anything for himself over against God, nor proudly seeks superiority over his brethren, but desires only that Christ the head have preeminence.'"

WALK CLOSER TO GOD

Humility. It's not a highly regarded commodity in a success-oriented world where backstabbing and ladder climbing have become accepted behaviors.

Listen to the world and you will hear the message: "Greatness consists of how many you lead." Listen to God's voice and you will hear just the opposite: "Greatness consists of how many you serve." They can't both be right.

You can push to the head of the line and receive the world's applause. Or you can give up your place in line and hear God's "well done."

The servant of God knows his place. ✤

GOD'S GLORY: THE BUSINESS OF HEAVEN

For the kingdom of heaven is like a landowner who went out early in the morning to hire workers for his vineyard.

MATTHEW 20:1

Ask a person their occupation, and you will learn how they pay their bills.

Ask a person their preoccupation, and you will discover their passion in life.

And if their occupation and their preoccupation are the same, you will find a worker worthy of their hire!

In Matthew 20 Jesus talked about the "business of heaven"—the labor and reward of workers in God's vineyard.

During his brief life, David Brainerd made the pursuit of God's kingdom his daily passion, as revealed by this selection from his diary.

WALK WITH DAVID BRAINERD

"When a soul loves God with a supreme love, he therein acts in conformity to God.

"God's interest and his become one, he longs for God to be glorified, and rejoices to think that God is unchangeably the Possessor of the highest glory and blessedness.

"Those who are totally given to God have the most complete and satisfying evidence of their being interested in all the benefits of Christ's redemption as their hearts are conformed to him.

"And these only are qualified for the employments and entertainments of God's kingdom of glory. None but these have any relish for the business of heaven, which is to give all glory to God, and not to themselves."

WALK CLOSER TO GOD

Coworkers with God. Laborers together in the joyful business of discipling his children.

Does that job description excite you?

It would—if you knew the head of the house!

For to know him is to be like him. And to be like him is to love the business he is about—the business of heaven.

The task is big; the laborers are few; the harvest stands ready; the time is short. Only qualified applicants need apply. ✤

january21

EXCUSES: OBSTACLES TO THE GATES OF HEAVEN

*A man ... said, "Son, go and work today in the vineyard" ... He answered, "I will, sir,"
but he did not go.*

MATTHEW 21:28,30

Ben Franklin was right. There has seldom been a man good at making excuses
who was good at anything else.

Good intentions. Not enough time. Too many responsibilities. The bottom line
in each case is the same: The job just doesn't get done.

The revivalist Charles Finney offers this warning about the danger of coming
to God with excuses rather than repentance.

WALK WITH CHARLES FINNEY

"It seems to be a law of human nature that when a person is accused of wrong,
either by the conscience or any other agent, he must either confess or justify.

"This is the reason why people make so many excuses and why they have so
great a variety.

"But nothing can be more grievous in God's sight than excuses made by those
who know they are utterly false.

"Sinners don't need their excuses. God does not ask for even one. He does not
require you to justify yourself—not at all.

"I can remember the year I lived on excuses and found them to be obstacles in
the way of my conversion. As soon as I let these go completely, I found the gate of
God's mercy wide open.

"And so, sinner, will you."

WALK CLOSER TO GOD

As you read Jesus' parables and Mr. Finney's words, do you grow uncomfortable?

That's God's way of demolishing your carefully constructed refuge of excuses in
order to expose your heart to the truth.

Someday you will face up to your excuses—either in judgment or repentance.
God will see to that.

But why wait? Excuses can be deadly.

"But God, you don't understand ..."

Indeed, he does. And once you realize that, you can't ignore him any longer. ❖

january**22**

DUTY OR DELIGHT: LOVE MAKES THE DIFFERENCE

Love the Lord your God with all your heart and with all your soul and with all your mind.
MATTHEW 22:37

The sergeant growls, "Now, do it! And that's an order!" Muttering to himself, the soldier stoops to the assigned task.

Ironic, isn't it, that the greatest command from our commander-in-chief is a command to love.

"Love the Lord your God ... Love your neighbor as yourself." The law of love supersedes all others. It's that "greatest commandment" of which Jesus speaks in Matthew 22 — and which became the consuming passion of Thomas à Kempis.

WALK WITH THOMAS À KEMPIS

"Blessed is the man who knows what it is to love Jesus, for Jesus desires to be loved alone above all things.

"Love him and keep him for your friend, and he will stand by you when other friends depart.

"When Jesus is present, all is well and nothing seems difficult. But when love for Jesus is absent, everything becomes hard.

"How dry and hard you feel without Jesus! How foolish and empty when you seek anything apart from him!

"He is very poor who lives without Jesus; he is very rich who has him for his friend."

WALK CLOSER TO GOD

Keeping the Great Commandment is as easy as falling in love. And love is the supreme motivation for service.

Washing windows. Cutting lawns. Bathing children. Fixing faucets. You'll seldom find these items written into a marriage contract!

Yet millions of husbands and wives do these and other chores — without being paid a cent!

Why? The law of love.

Encouraging. Nurturing. Testifying. Giving. These are just a few of your responsibilities as a disciple of Jesus Christ.

And whether you view them as a duty or a delight depends on your love for the Savior.

So how's your love life? ❖

january23

HEALER OF THE BROKENHEARTED

Jerusalem, Jerusalem ... how often I have longed to gather your children together ... and you were not willing.

MATTHEW 23:37

Wonder adhesives. Miracle glues. With all of our twenty-first-century know-how, you'd think we could fix anything. But science has yet to discover a product strong enough to mend a broken heart.

For that you'll have to go to the Savior, who specializes in such matters.

He's the one who, in the final days of his life on earth, surveyed the city of Jerusalem—and what he saw made him weep.

Evangelist Dwight L. Moody offers some thoughts about the Savior's tears.

WALK WITH DWIGHT L. MOODY

"From Adam's day to ours, tears have been shed, and a wail has gone up from the brokenhearted.

"And it is a mystery to me how all those broken hearts can keep away from him who has come to heal them.

"Jesus often looked up to heaven and sighed. I believe it was because of so much suffering around him.

"It was on his right and on his left—everywhere on earth. And the thought that he had come to relieve the people of their burdens, yet so few would accept him, made him sorrowful.

"Do you think there is a heart so broken that it can't be healed by him? He can heal them all. But the great trouble is that people won't come."

WALK CLOSER TO GOD

Jesus wept over a city. Not for its buildings, but for its people. People like you—with broken hearts and broken spirits. People in need of repentance and repair.

Though he wept, he can tenderly wipe the tears from your eyes. For he is the mighty physician, capable of healing every wounded heart brought to him. But you must be willing to put yourself under his care.

He has so much to give. But so few are willing to receive. Let the few include you. ❖

SOMEDAY WILL BE THE LAST DAY

And this gospel of the kingdom will be preached in the whole world as a testimony to all nations, and then the end will come.

MATTHEW 24:14

The End. Those words often mark the last page, the last scene, the conclusion. Like the game buzzer when time has expired, they remind us of how finite life is.

Tomorrow will not always be a continuation of today. Some day will mark the last day of life as we now know it—"and then the end will come."

Just before his own earthly life ended, Jesus described "the end" and the events preceding it. F. B. Meyer shows how contemporary these 2,000-year-old warnings are.

WALK WITH F. B. MEYER

"The signs of the times in our own day are much as they were then.

"People still love pleasure rather than God. Those who want to live a godly life must still be prepared to suffer persecution.

"The forms of hatred and dislike of the gospel change, but the hatred of the cross is as deep-rooted as ever.

"There are abroad today the seeds of hurtful and false doctrine. Propagated by the spoken word and written page, they produce unrest in the young and unstable.

"We must judge these damaging teachings, not by their pleasant and innocent appearance, but by their effect on heart and character."

WALK CLOSER TO GOD

Wars. Rumors of war. Famines. Epidemics. Earthquakes. False prophets. Lukewarm love.

Jesus was right: The outlook won't be too comforting just before the end.

But the uplook? Still as bright as the promises of God! And there is good news to share with a dying world.

As a child of God, you have the privilege of introducing others to Jesus. It's as simple as telling someone what you know to be true about him.

But don't put it off. "The End" has a way of coming when you least expect it. ✤

january25

A GLORIOUSLY DIFFICULT LIFE

Therefore keep watch, because you do not know the day or the hour.

MATTHEW 25:13

Christianity is not a rest stop on the way to heaven. Instead, the New Testament pictures it as a walk of perseverance. A race of endurance. A battle of spiritual forces.

In the concluding paragraphs of the Olivet discourse, Jesus underscores the challenging demands of discipleship—the necessity of being watchful in conduct and fervent in service.

Oswald Chambers describes these pursuits as those that demand your "utmost for his highest."

WALK WITH OSWALD CHAMBERS

"The Christian life is gloriously difficult. But the difficulty of it does not make us faint and cave in; it rouses us to overcome. Do we so appreciate the marvelous salvation of Jesus Christ that we give our utmost for his highest?

"Thank God he does give us difficult things to do! His salvation is a glad thing, but it also tests us for all we are worth.

"Jesus is bringing many sons and daughters unto glory, and God will not shield us from the requirements of being his child.

"God's grace turns out men and women with a strong family likeness to Jesus Christ."

WALK CLOSER TO GOD

God is working in you to produce a strong family likeness to Jesus Christ. But are you helping or hindering the process?

Construction projects take time. Are you frequently irritated with God's timetable?

Construction projects involve heat and pressure. Are you seeking the easy way out, stubbornly resisting God's efforts to shape your attitudes and actions?

Construction projects are costly. Are you willing to pay the price following Christ may involve?

Your utmost for his highest may sound like a tall order. But considering what God has invested in your life, it's a fitting way to say, "Thank you!" ✤

january26

THE CHOICE THAT DETERMINES THE COURSE OF LIFE

Then they will go away to eternal punishment, but the righteous to eternal life.

MATTHEW 25:46

Everlasting punishment is the penalty for failing to do what is right in the sight of God. It is the result of—not the remedy for—falling short of God's glory.

But God has provided a path to peace through personal faith in his Son, Jesus Christ. But only you can choose that path, as Jonathan Edwards explains.

WALK WITH JONATHAN EDWARDS

"That you may escape the dreadful and eternal torments, you must embrace him who came into the world for the purpose of saving sinners from such torments. He alone has paid the whole debt due to the divine law, and has exhausted eternal sufferings.

"What great encouragement it is that you are exposed to eternal punishment, that there is a Savior provided who offers to save you from that punishment, and that he will do it in a way which is perfectly in keeping with the glory of God. In fact it is more to the glory of God than it would be if you should suffer the eternal punishment of hell.

"Those who are sent to hell will never pay the whole of the debt which they owe to God. Justice can never be actually satisfied in their damnation; but it is satisfied in Christ. Therefore he is accepted of the Father, and all who believe are accepted and justified in him."

WALK CLOSER TO GOD

The course of your life is determined by the choice you make in life—a choice centering around the person of Jesus Christ.

You can ignore him or embrace him. But you cannot avoid him ... or the consequences of your choice.

Jonathan Edwards preached eloquently of the horrors of hell because he realized what was at stake in the lives of his listeners.

If you haven't as yet realized what is at stake—the "dreadful and eternal torments"—"embrace him who came into the world for the purpose of saving sinners from such torments." ❖

SHARING THE BURDEN OF ANOTHER'S SOUL

My Father, if it is possible, may this cup be taken from me. Yet not as I will, but as you will.
MATTHEW 26:39

Never be afraid to do what God tells you to do; it's always good.

But first be certain your will is in neutral so that God can shift it.

After enjoying a last meal with his disciples, Jesus made his way to the Garden of Gethsemane. He went, not to relax, but to wrestle in prayer. Not to while away the moments, but to urge his disciples to watch with him in prayer.

Alfred Edersheim provides insight into the struggles of the Savior just before his death.

WALK WITH ALFRED EDERSHEIM

"Alone, as in his first conflict with the evil one in the wilderness, the Savior entered into the last contest.

"On his knees, prostrate on the ground, his agony began. His prayer was that — if it were possible — the hour might pass away from him.

"Fallen man is born with the taste of death in his soul. Not so Christ. It was he who had no experience of it. His going into death was his final conflict with Satan for man, and on man's behalf.

"At the close of that hour his sweat — mingled with blood — fell in great drops on the ground. And while he lay in prayer, the disciples lay in sleep."

WALK CLOSER TO GOD

Christ yearned for support in prayer during his darkest hour.

It's possible — even probable — that someone near you is wrestling in prayer to discover God's will or overcome the enemy. That person knows the way ahead may be painful, yet he yearns to do God's will. But the battle for his will is raging and the issue is undecided.

You can slumber indifferently, like the disciples. Or you can kneel at that person's side and share their burden. That's one of the privileges — and responsibilities — of being a brother or a sister in Christ. ❖

january28

TURNING TEARS OF GUILT INTO TEARS OF JOY

Then Peter remembered the word Jesus had spoken: "Before the rooster crows, you will disown me three times." And he went outside and wept bitterly.

MATTHEW 26:75

You have failed someone who was counting on you. Guilt is written all over your face. You lower your head in shame and remorse.

Guilty! That's the unspoken verdict for many individuals who have faced failure in the service of the Lord. But as the apostle Peter discovered and as Hannah Whitall Smith describes, God's forgiveness is as near as a prayer.

WALK WITH HANNAH WHITALL SMITH

"A little girl once asked if the Lord Jesus always forgave us for our sins as soon as we asked him, and I had said, 'Yes, of course he does.'

"*'Just as* soon?' she repeated doubtfully. 'Yes,' I replied, 'the minute we ask, he forgives us.'

"'Well, I cannot believe that,' she replied deliberately. 'I should think he would make us feel sorry for two or three days first. And then I think he would make us ask him a great many times, and not just in common talk. And I believe that is the way he does, and you need not try to make me think he forgives me right at once, no matter what the Bible says.'

"She only said what many Christians think, and what is worse, what a great many Christians act on, for then the emotions of discouragement and remorse make them feel further from God than their sin would have done."

WALK CLOSER TO GOD

When you can no longer lift guilty eyes to God, you can be certain that God is still looking at you. Not with the peeved expression of an irritated parent, but with compassion, love and tenderness.

When you least expect him to forgive, he reaches out in grace—reminding you that you are his own, wiping away the tears of remorse, encouraging you to try again.

If your eyes are clouded with tears of guilt and failure today, run to your Father's waiting arms. He's ready to turn your weeping into tears of joy. ✤

january29

FORGIVENESS: YOURS FOR THE ASKING

"I have sinned," [Judas] said, "for I have betrayed innocent blood" ... So Judas threw the money into the temple and left. Then he went away and hanged himself.

MATTHEW 27:4–5

After a particularly embarrassing moment, the thought might cross your mind: "I wish I could just die."

It's a thought you really don't mean. But for Judas, knowing that he had betrayed the Lord so filled him with remorse that he sought escape through death. Rather than seek forgiveness and a new start, Judas decided to give up and end his own life.

The special circumstances of Judas's life and death provide lessons you can profit from. Alexander Maclaren shares his thoughts on the nature of sin and forgiveness.

WALK WITH ALEXANDER MACLAREN

"I do not suppose that Judas was lost because he betrayed Jesus Christ, but because, having betrayed Jesus Christ, he never asked to be forgiven.

"I pray you to learn this lesson: You cannot think too blackly of your own sins, but you may think too exclusively of them; and if you do, they will drive you to madness or despair.

"My dear friend, there is no remorse which is deep enough for the smallest transgression; but there is no transgression which is so great but that forgiveness for it may come. And we may have it for the asking, if we will go to that dear Christ who died for us.

"If Judas died without hope and pardon, it was not because his crime was too great for forgiveness, but because the forgiveness had never been asked."

WALK CLOSER TO GOD

Judas could not forgive himself. But God could. "[God] does not treat us as our sins deserve or repay us according to our iniquities ... As far as the east is from the west, so far has he removed our transgressions from us" (Psalm 103:10,12).

Forgiveness is yours for the asking when you take God at his word. ❖

PRIDE: THE THIEF OF FAITH

The chief priests, the teachers of the law, and the elders mocked him. "He saved others," they said, "but he can't save himself!".

MATTHEW 27:41–42

Pride. It is a deadly weed that grows rampant on the earth. It is one of the seven things God hates (see Proverbs 6:16–19).

The pride of men nailed Jesus to the cross.

Pride hurled abuses as he suffered and died.

Pride watched with curious detachment as he uttered his final words.

Martin Luther, outspoken critic of the pride and self-righteousness that infected his own day, comments on the cause and condemnation of pride.

WALK WITH MARTIN LUTHER

"Pride is really the haughtiness of Satan against the name and word of God.

"People who claim to be wise in matters of faith pompously exalt themselves, regarding God himself as nothing and all others in comparison to themselves as mere fools. When this happens there is no humility and no fear of God.

"At present there are many such haughty people. They have discovered that they are learned or are otherwise esteemed by the people in points on which they take pride. In fact, they are destitute.

"Such people are enemies of God and must be overthrown, for they have excluded themselves from the kingdom and grace of God."

WALK CLOSER TO GOD

Those who called for Jesus' death were the religious leaders of his day. They were content with the spiritual status quo, proud of their spiritual heritage and blind to their spiritual need.

Pride will cause you to say with the chief priests, "He saved others, but he can't save himself."

Only by abandoning pride can you say with the centurion, "Surely he was the Son of God!" (Matthew 27:54).

Are you too proud to admit you are lost in your sins? Then beware—you are too proud to see the kingdom of heaven.

Is your pride really worth that? ❖

january**31**

PRACTICING THE PRESENCE OF GOD BY FAITH

And surely I am with you always, to the very end of the age.

MATTHEW 28:20

Did you ever play hide-and-seek as a child? Sometimes someone hid so well that you couldn't find them. Or sometimes you just weren't looking in the right place.

When Jesus said he'd always be with us, he wasn't playing games. And he didn't mean maybe or sometimes. If you are a child of God, Jesus is always with you.

Frances Havergal explores why some Christians seem to have trouble with this concept.

WALK WITH FRANCES HAVERGAL

"Some of us think and say a good deal about a sense of his presence. Sometimes we rejoice in it; sometimes we mourn because we don't seem to have it. We pray for it and measure our own position and that of others by it.

"One moment we are on the heights, then in the depths. We have gloom instead of glow because we are turning our attention upon the sense of his presence instead of the reality of it!

"All our disappointment vanishes in the simple faith that grasps his presence. For if Jesus says simply and absolutely, 'I am with you always,' what have we to do with feeling or sense about it? We have only to believe it and to recollect it. And it is only by thus believing and recollecting that we can realize his presence."

WALK CLOSER TO GOD

Jesus doesn't play hide-and-seek with us. He is always available—even when we don't feel that he is. And when you practice his presence by faith, you'll find that feeling will follow.

Do you expect Jesus to go with you everywhere you go? Do you think about whether or not he'll be comfortable everywhere you take him?

Jesus is not someone who lives in a box that you can take out on Sundays and put in storage the rest of the week.

If you're a Christian, he's there! He goes where you go! And that's something to think about. ✤

february1

CALLED TO OBEY WITHOUT DELAY

At once they left their nets and followed him.

MARK 1:18

Procrastination. It's a thief of time and the grave of opportunity.

Two fishermen in Mark 1 were confronted with a command from the Savior: "Follow me."

It was not a particularly convenient command, what with nets to mend, fish to catch, business to tend and families to care for. But there was no time to procrastinate. This was a clear statement of the Master's will for them.

Charles Spurgeon, whose preaching prompted thousands to follow Christ, explains the danger of "later" in the life of a disciple.

WALK WITH CHARLES SPURGEON

"When they heard the call of Jesus, Simon and Andrew obeyed without delay. If we would always, punctually and with determination, immediately put into practice what we hear, it could not fail to enrich us spiritually.

"A person will not lose his loaf once he has eaten it; neither will a believer be deprived of doctrine once he or she has acted on it.

"Most readers and hearers are moved to the point of deciding to amend; but, alas! No fruit comes of it. They wait, they waver, and then they forget.

"That fatal 'tomorrow' is blood-red with the murder of good resolutions. The practice of truth is the most profitable reading of it."

WALK CLOSER TO GOD

Even today, Jesus' call to obedience doesn't always come at a convenient moment. Obedience is often inconvenient; it has a cost.

When we hear a command of Christ, we often hear within us two conflicting voices: one a call to delay, the other a call to obey. You can't answer both calls, for one excludes the other. But you must respond to one of them.

It's not an easy decision; the appeal of both is strong. But remember, for some people, "later" has a way of meaning "never." Disciples obey without delay. ♣

february2

LIFEGIVER, LIGHTBEARER, GREAT PHYSICIAN

News about him spread quickly over the whole region of Galilee.

MARK 1:28

Good news has a way of getting around. If you were to begin a ministry to hurting people, word would spread and you—like Jesus—would never lack an audience.

But the price of serving is often suffering and inconvenience, as Jesus exemplified. And as Eusebius acknowledged 1,700 years ago, you must first count the cost.

WALK WITH EUSEBIUS

"A devoted physician, to save the lives of the sick, sees the horrible danger, yet touches the infected place, and in treating another man's troubles brings suffering on himself.

"But we were not merely sick, or afflicted with horrible wounds and ulcers already festering. We were actually lying among the dead when Christ saved us from the very abyss of death.

"Alone he took hold of our most painful perishing nature. Alone he endured our sorrows. Alone he took upon himself the retribution for our sins.

"When we were lying in tombs and graves, he raised us up, saving us and giving us his Father's blessings without measure.

"He is the Lifegiver, the Lightbringer, our great Physician and King and Lord, the Christ of God."

WALK CLOSER TO GOD

To bring life, Jesus willingly faced death. To offer comfort, he endured suffering. To touch the sorrowing, he shared their sorrow.

Now he calls on you to extend help to those who hurt. By a word. A touch. A smile. An unexpected kindness.

Hurting people aren't hard to find. In fact, those willing to search will find them all around.

Widows and orphans, the sick and bereaved, the lonely and neglected—all need to hear the good news that there is a Great Physician.

But let the word get out that you are looking for those who hurt, and you—like Jesus—may find yourself permanently popular!

So how will you help the hurting today? ✣

february3

RUNNING A RISK TO OFFER A CURE

[The Pharisees] asked his disciples: "Why does he eat with tax collectors and sinners?".

MARK 2:16

A child hovers between life and death as anxious parents wait. The physician is called but refuses to come. "I'm sorry," the doctor explains, "but I don't make house calls."

Ridiculous? Perhaps. But consider this. What if the Great Physician had been unwilling to make a "house call" to planet Earth?

Christ's life calls you to minister to people who may never have visited your church—and possibly never will.

His example calls you to rub shoulders with people who are lost, sick, without hope.

G. Campbell Morgan presses home the importance of making "house calls."

WALK WITH G. CAMPBELL MORGAN

"I believe one of the reasons for the condition of the church is the aloofness of Christians from sinning men and women.

"We still build our sanctuaries, set up our standards, make our arrangements, and say to the sinning ones: 'If you come to us, we will help you!'

"But the way of the Lord is to go and sit where they sit, without looking down on them.

"We may run great risks if we will dare to do it because someone will say that we are consorting with sinning men, and that we are in moral and spiritual peril. I am afraid, however, that the church is not often criticized for this."

WALK CLOSER TO GOD

A doctor takes personal risks when he tends the sick. But they need his help.

You have what the world needs—the good news of sins forgiven.

But it's good news to them only if they've heard it. It's the cure only if they know they are terminally ill.

House calls may be a thing of the past for family doctors. But in God's program they are never out of date.

Make one, and you'll find out why! ❖

february4

LIVING IN THE SPOTLIGHT OF HIGH VISIBILITY

Some of them were looking for a reason to accuse Jesus, so they watched him closely to see if he would heal him on the Sabbath.

MARK 3:2

It's an uneasy feeling ... the feeling of being watched. And evaluated. And talked about.

But it's a feeling Jesus was familiar with. For he attracted the attention of many in Jerusalem, including the Jewish authorities.

Just like Christ, his followers are also on center stage. And as J. C. Ryle comments, that kind of visibility can either move you to action—or immobilize you.

WALK WITH J. C. RYLE

"Christ's people must not expect to fare better than their Master.

"They are always watched by the world. Their conduct is scrutinized. Their ways are noted and diligently observed. They can do nothing without the world noticing it. Their dress, their expenditures, their use of time, their conduct in all areas of life—all are closely observed.

"The thought should make us exercise a holy jealousy over all our conduct.

"It should make us diligent to avoid even the appearance of evil.

"Above all, it should make us pray to be kept pure in our attitudes, speech, and daily conduct.

"That Savior, who himself was watched, knows how to sympathize with his people, and to supply grace to help in time of need."

WALK CLOSER TO GOD

As a servant of Christ you have a life of high visibility. Others are watching your life and evaluating the person you claim to follow.

Like it or not, you may be the best Christian someone knows. Or the worst.

Someone near you may one day say yes to Christ because they saw Christ living in you.

As a Christian, you have no choice about whether or not you will be in the spotlight. But you do have a choice about what that spotlight will reveal to those who watch.

You're on! ✤

february5

A PASSIONATE DEVOTION TO THE WILL OF GOD

His family ... went to take charge of him, for they said, "He is out of his mind".
MARK 3:21

Fanatic! That's a word that evokes the image of a wild-eyed, sign-toting religious zealot, and that is unfortunate.

Jesus' popularity with the common people and his zeal for the business of heaven prompted even his friends and family to conclude that he was beside himself, a fanatic.

But for the Christian there can be no higher compliment, as G. Campbell Morgan explains.

WALK WITH G. CAMPBELL MORGAN

"People today never seem to think that passionate and sacrificial devotion suggests madness in any realm except the spiritual.

"No one suggests that the athlete, who gives himself totally to his sport and sacrifices all for the sake of physical prowess, is beside himself.

"No one imagines that the businessman, who is so devoted to amassing wealth that he shortens his life, is beside himself.

"No! This suggestion is retained only for those whose service for the souls of men and women is sacrificial.

"Let all such servants be comforted. They are in holy comradeship! At the same time, let them determine to be among those who have the highest resemblance to the Son of Man, because they are devoted to the will of God."

WALK CLOSER TO GOD

Lord, show me areas of my life in which—because of my fear of being labeled a fanatic—I have ceased to be excited and moved and compelled by you.

May I always be a fanatic more of heavenly endeavors than of earthly pursuits.

A zealot more for holiness than for hobbies.

An enthusiast more of lost sinners than of sports.

A lover more of Christ than of personal goals.

I pray this in the name of the one whose zeal for his Father's house consumed him. Amen. ❖

february6

A SOIL ANALYSIS OF THE HUMAN HEART

Others, like seed sown on good soil, hear the word, accept it, and produce a crop—some thirty, some sixty, some a hundred times what was sown.

MARK 4:20

You can't sow thistles and expect to reap roses. Nor will oak trees grow in rock-strewn deserts.

What is sown and where it is sown are both crucial elements in producing a harvest.

The divine seed, God's Word, falls on all kinds of ground and produces fruit—little, much or none at all, depending on the condition of the soil.

Alexander Maclaren provides this soil analysis of the human heart.

WALK WITH ALEXANDER MACLAREN

"No one is obliged, either by his temperament or circumstances, to be 'wayside,' or 'stony,' or 'thorny' ground.

"The true acceptance of the Word requires that we do not let it lie only on the surface of our minds, nor be satisfied only to have it penetrate a little deeper and take root in our emotions, or let competing desires grow up unchecked. Instead, we must cherish the word of truth in our deepest hearts, guard it against foes, let it rule there, and mold our conduct to its principles.

"The psalmist said, 'I have hidden your word in my heart' (Psalm 119:11). If we do that we shall be fruitful, because his Word will bear fruit in us.

"There will be increase wherever a heart opens to receive the gospel and keeps it steadfastly.

"Not in equal measure in all, but in each according to faithfulness and diligence."

WALK CLOSER TO GOD

Fruit-bearing requires three things: seed, sower and soil. The first two have already been provided. The perfect seed is the living Word of God. The patient sower is the life-giving Son of God. But as the parable of the sower points out, even that is not enough to guarantee a harvest.

Only you can provide that. And come harvest time, you'll be mighty glad you did!

Barren, rocky, thorny or good. Pick your soil carefully; it could make a hundredfold difference in your life. ✤

february7

LESSONS LEARNED IN THE GALE OF AFFLICTION

They were terrified and asked each other, "Who is this? Even the wind and the waves obey him!".

MARK 4:41

Some things are certain. Like death and taxes—and taxing situations!

Count on it: There will be storms and difficulties in every person's life.

You—like the disciples in Mark 4—may sometimes wonder, "Teacher, don't you care if we drown?"

Yes, he does care. Infinitely. Christ is faithful to see you through difficulties. J. C. Ryle offers some reassuring words for stormy times.

WALK WITH J. C. RYLE

"Here were the twelve disciples in the path of duty. They were obediently following Jesus wherever he went.

"Yet here we see these men in trouble, tossed by a tempest and in danger of being drowned.

"Mark well this lesson. Being in Christ's service does not exempt his servants from storms.

"It will not be strange if we have to endure sickness, losses, and disappointments just like other people. Our Savior has never promised that we shall have no afflictions. He loves us too well to promise that.

"By affliction he teaches us many precious lessons, which otherwise we would never learn. By affliction he shows us our emptiness and weakness, draws us to the throne of grace, purifies our affections, weans us from the world, and makes us long for heaven."

WALK CLOSER TO GOD

It's easy to breathe a prayer of thanks when a storm is over.

But what about when the waves are breaking? When there's water in the boat? When the noise of your circumstance threatens to drown out the prayer on your lips?

If faith in God works, it had better work then!

Be assured, it works.

But, as the disciples learned, there's nothing like a good gale to add zest to your prayers! ❖

february8

THE BEST PLACE TO BE IS THE PLACE GOD CHOOSES

Jesus ... said, "Go home to your own people and tell them how much the Lord has done for you".

MARK 5:19

Children and busy roads don't mix. Why? Because children, if unattended, often play in the road, heedless of danger. So until a child reaches maturity, the parent takes responsibility for the child's protection, guidance and nurture.

Do you sometimes think you know better than your heavenly Father which road is best for you? Listen as J. C. Ryle explains that your Father knows best.

WALK WITH J. C. RYLE

"The place where Christians wish to be is not always the best place for their souls. There are none who need this lesson so much as believers newly converted to God.

"Seeing everything in a new light, yet knowing little of the depths of Satan and the weakness of their own hearts, they are in the greatest danger of making mistakes. With the best intentions they may fall into mistakes about their plans, their choices, or their professions. They forget that what we like best is not always best for our souls.

"Let us pray that God would guide us in all our ways after conversion, and not allow us to err. It may not be quite what we like. But if Christ by his providence has placed us in it, let us not be in a hurry to leave it."

WALK CLOSER TO GOD

Elijah supposed he was the only man left in Israel who worshiped God.

Moses was an obscure shepherd for 40 years before he led God's people out of Egypt.

John lived out his life in exile on a desolate island while he wrote the book of Revelation.

That's because God's best sometimes comes wrapped in unpleasant circumstances and unexpected changes of plan.

Like the man from the region of the Gerasenes in Mark 5, don't hesitate to submit your plans to God's providence. Great things can happen when God's best becomes yours. ✤

TAPPING THE RESERVOIR OF GOD'S POWER

He said to her, "Daughter, your faith has healed you. Go in peace".

MARK 5:34

Jesus felt at home in Jerusalem. Among the crush of people surrounding him, he never forgot his mission. He never lost sight of the lost men and women; the busy, distracted crowds; the lonely, hurting people jostling for space around him.

In Mark 5, an unnamed woman is immortalized. F. B. Meyer explains that she had learned how little it takes to get the Savior's attention when faith is your motive.

WALK WITH F. B. MEYER

"Let those who are conscious of the ravages of evil in their hearts—which is destroying their strength—establish a connection with Christ as slight as the finger's touch of the garment hem, and instantly his power will enter and heal their inward disorder.

"His power is always going forth, and faith receives as much as it desires.

"The reservoir of power is always full, but very few have learned the secret of tapping it! Crowds throng him, but only one touches.

"Proximity to Christ does not necessarily imply the appropriation of Christ. But where there is the faintest touch of faith, there is an instantaneous response.

"There may be great weakness. The fingers may be too nerveless to grasp; they can only touch. But the slightest degree of faith saves, because it is the channel by which Christ enters."

WALK CLOSER TO GOD

You cannot experience the Savior's power by standing on the sidelines. To experience that power, a personal step of commitment is needed, a personal touch of faith.

Faith for salvation. Faith for service. Faith for strength.

Simple faith in a great God. It's not something you'll learn by watching the crowd.

But then, praying in faith has never been a spectator sport. ❖

february10

THE SERVICE OF LOVE IN EVERY SITUATION

A prophet is not without honor except in his own town.

MARK 6:4

No glory. No recognition. No thanks. That's why very few people make a career of being a servant. But servanthood is the calling of every true disciple of Christ.

In Mark 6 Jesus met rejection in Nazareth. There was no honor or welcome for the Savior in his own hometown. And yet his motivation to serve did not spring from a desire for human recognition.

Abraham Kuyper speaks of the proper motive for service.

WALK WITH ABRAHAM KUYPER

"Let your life be one continuous service of love, a service which never grows irksome, a service which will ennoble even the smallest task.

"Do not seek the external, the visible, that which the world chooses as its goal. Seek instead that which is invisible—the hidden power behind the things we see.

"In short, seek the kingdom of God, where God is enthroned and self is denied.

"Seek these things not only in seasons of prayer and worship, but always—in every situation, in every daily task.

"See if God does not give you ample strength for your service of love. See if he does not increase your joy and fill your heart with an exhilarating peace such as you never knew before."

WALK CLOSER TO GOD

Service for God puzzles the world.

Of what other work could it be said that the longer you work, the stronger you become? That the more you give, the more you want to give? That the higher the cause for anxiety, the deeper the cause for peace?

It's clear that serving God may not add up in earthly dollars and "sense."

But it's hard to match the fringe benefits. Or the retirement plan!

Best of all, there are always positions open. And one is tailor-made for you. ✤

february11

STANDING BY FAITH IN THE CRUCIBLE OF CRISIS

[Jesus] said, "Take courage! It is I. Don't be afraid".

MARK 6:50

It's not really unusual when someone drops in unannounced for a meal. But when that "someone" turns out to be 5,000 hungry guests, then you're facing a crisis.

Twice in Mark 6 the disciples faced overwhelming challenges. First beside the sea and later on the sea they ran out of resources long before they ran out of problems.

George Müller, who often tested the resources of God, probes the inconsistency of worry in the life of the believer.

WALK WITH GEORGE MÜLLER

"Ponder these words of Jesus: 'Just believe' (Mark 5:36).

"As long as we are able to trust in God—holding fast in our heart the knowledge that he is able and willing to help those who rest on the Lord Jesus for salvation, in all matters which are for his glory and their good—the heart remains calm and peaceful.

"It is when we let go of faith in his power or his love that we lose our peace and become troubled.

"This very day I am in great trial in connection with my work; yet my soul was calmed and quieted by the remembrance of God's power and love, and the result was peace of soul.

"The very time for faith to work is when sight ceases. The greater the difficulties, the easier for faith."

WALK CLOSER TO GOD

Everything about the disciples' circumstance encouraged them to give up. Yet Jesus wanted them to "take courage" even as hungry stomachs growled and angry winds blew. That's faith—standing strong in the crucible of crisis.

Where faith begins, anxiety ends. It won't make sense to others around you that you can maintain your peace and composure when everyone else is losing theirs.

Perhaps it will make them curious enough to ask you how you do it. What will you tell them? ✤

february 12

THE STRONG BEAT OF A PURE HEART

These people honor me with their lips, but their hearts are far from me.

MARK 7:6

A coat of paint can conceal many a jagged crack. And as the saying goes, you can't judge a book by its cover.

Similarly, the way people act does not necessarily explain the motive behind their action.

Jesus had a way of penetrating to the heart of things, of tearing off the mask to see the motive. As a result, he came into growing conflict with the hypocritical religious leaders of his day.

F. B. Meyer analyzes the heart condition at the root of the Pharisees' problem.

WALK WITH F. B. MEYER

"It is a natural tendency of the human heart to reduce its religious life to an outward and literal obedience, while its thoughts continue unhampered.

"In the life of true holiness, everything depends on the control of the thoughts. 'For it is from within, out of a person's heart, that evil thoughts come' (Mark 7:21).

"And Jesus put evil thoughts first in the black category of the contents of the evil heart.

"That the hands should be often washed, that household vessels should be kept cleansed, that there should be decorum and neatness in the outward life—all these customs are good.

"But you should ask yourself whether you are not more eager for the outward than the inward cleanliness.

"'Create in me a pure heart' (Psalm 51:10) should be your constant prayer."

WALK CLOSER TO GOD

It's easier to maintain clean hands than a pure heart. And because the mind is a private domain, no one may notice whether your thought life is pure or polluted.

No one, that is, except God.

Listen to your heart. What do you hear?

A clean, strong heartbeat of devotion? Or the confused rhythm of a heart far from God?

Right now might be a good time for some cleansing prayer. ✤

february13

SIGHS THAT SPEAK OF SYMPATHY AND POWER

He looked up to heaven ... with a deep sigh.

MARK 7:34

Deeply moved by the needs all around him, Jesus responded in the best way possible—not with fine-sounding words, but with a sigh of compassion followed by meaningful action.

A man who could neither hear nor speak, people who had followed Jesus without eating for three days—each person experienced Jesus' unspoken, yet unmistakable, love.

Jesus sighed. Yet it was no mere sigh of resignation or frustration, as F. B. Meyer makes clear.

WALK WITH F. B. MEYER

"In this passage, along with Mark 8:12, Mark twice calls attention to the Lord's sighs. A sigh is one of the most touching and significant tokens of excessive grief. When our natures are too disturbed to remember to take a normal breath and must compensate for this omission by one deep-drawn breath, we sigh deeply in our spirit.

"'He looked up to heaven ... with a deep sigh.' As the deaf-mute stood before him—an image of all the closed hearts around him, of all the inarticulate unexpressed desires, of all the sin and sorrow of mankind—Jesus' sensitive heart responded with a deep-drawn sigh.

"But there was simultaneously a heavenward look which mingled infinite hope in it. If the sigh spoke of his tender sympathy, the look declared his close union with God, by virtue of which he was competent to meet the direst need.

"Jesus, in doing good, would look to heaven and sigh; but his sighs were followed by the touch and word of power. Let us not be content with a sigh of sympathy and regret."

WALK CLOSER TO GOD

You, like Jesus, can couple a heartfelt sigh with effective action, looking to God for the power to correct that which made you sigh in the first place.

There's a sighing, dying world waiting for someone like you to take compassionate action. What will be your answer: A sigh or a shrug? Or a sigh and service? ❖

february14

A FEELING, HEALING COMPASSION

Jesus called his disciples to him and said, "I have compassion for these people".

MARK 8:1−2

Have you ever happened upon a scene of misfortune that caused you to pity the poor victim? Weep over the victim's plight? Exchange places with the sufferer?

Mark 8 describes a scene in which pity was plentiful, but only compassionate action could meet the needs.

English clergyman John Henry Jowett contrasts pity—which tends to be passive—with compassion—which is active and often costly.

WALK WITH JOHN HENRY JOWETT

"Jesus' compassion was part of his passion. It culminated upon Calvary, but it was bleeding all along the road.

"It was a fellow-feeling with all the pangs and sorrows of the race. Only a pity that bleeds is a pity that heals.

"As in Jesus' day, the multitude is around us still.

"There is the multitude of misfortune, the children of disadvantage. There is the multitude of outcasts, the vast army of modern-day publicans and sinners. There are the bewildering multitudes who have nothing to eat.

"How do I share the compassion of the Lord?

"Do I exercise a sensitive and sanctified imagination, and enter somehow into the pangs of their cravings?

"I must. For my Lord calls me to help."

WALK CLOSER TO GOD

Pity looks and says, "How awful." Compassion weeps and says, "I'll help."

Pity looks on from afar. Compassion rolls up its sleeves and pitches in to help.

Pity waits for a convenient time. Compassion knows no office hours.

Pity is cheap and plentiful. Compassion is rare, priceless and costly.

Jesus said, "I have compassion." What do you have? ✤

february15

WHAT WAY ARE WE TO FOLLOW?

Whoever wants to be my disciple must deny themselves and take up their cross and follow me.
MARK 8:34

When Jesus spoke to his own about the demands of discipleship, the words were strong and foreboding.

"Deny ... take up [your] cross ... follow." Those are the words of Jesus.

"Pamper yourself ... indulge ... grab the gusto." Those are the words of the world.

Augustine reminds all Christians that servanthood involves both a privilege and a price.

WALK WITH AUGUSTINE

"It is good to follow Christ. But we must see by what way we are to follow.

"For when the Lord spoke the words of Mark 8, he had not already risen from the dead. He had not yet suffered, not yet come to the cross, not yet felt the dishonoring, the outrages, the scourging, the thorns, the wounds, the mockeries, the insults, the death.

"Rough may be the way, but follow on. Where Christ has gone is worn smooth.

"Who would not wish to be exalted? Honor is pleasing to all. But humility is the path to it.

"The two disciples disliked taking this step of humility. They sought exaltation, one at the right hand and the other at the left (see Mark 10:37).

"They did not see the cross."

WALK CLOSER TO GOD

Christ's invitation to discipleship is an invitation to die. Die to self. To the world. To personal ambition.

It is a call to follow Jesus in his life. In his death. In his resurrection.

It is a reminder that exaltation and elevation in God's sight are the byproducts of humility.

Small wonder there is so seldom a crowd gathered at the cross. For few are willing to pay the price that discipleship demands.

But it's a price well worth paying, for a life of discipleship is the most fulfilling life of all.

Will you pay the price? ✤

february16

THE POWER TO DO, TO DARE AND TO SUFFER

Jesus [said], "Everything is possible for one who believes".

Mark 9:23

The father's heart was cracking with grief and his mind was wrestling with doubt as his son writhed on the ground in the grip of an impure spirit. "I do believe," he cried, "help me overcome my unbelief!"

If you find yourself discouraged by doubt, remember this father's honest prayer—and these encouraging words from Charles Spurgeon.

WALK WITH CHARLES SPURGEON

"The father said to Jesus, 'If you can do anything, take pity on us and help us.'

"Now there was an *if* in the question. But the poor, trembling father had put the *if* in the wrong place. Christ, without commanding him to retract the *if* kindly puts it in its legitimate position.

"He seemed to say, 'There should be no *if* about my power, nor concerning my willingness; the *if* lies elsewhere. If you can believe, everything is possible for him who believes.'

"We, like this man, often see that there is an *if* somewhere, but we are perpetually blundering by putting it in the wrong place.

"Faith stands in God's power and is robed in God's majesty; it wears the royal apparel and rides on the King's horse, for it is the grace which the King delights to honor. Girding itself with the glorious might of the all-working Spirit, faith becomes, in the omnipotence of God, power to do, to dare, and to suffer. All things, without limit, are possible to the one who believes."

WALK CLOSER TO GOD

Jesus later reminds his disciples that "all things are possible with God" (Mark 10:27).

Even Jesus' closest followers were prone to forget the power they saw him exercise time after time. Like Abraham, they needed to be "fully persuaded that God had power to do what he had promised" (Romans 4:21).

God's Word gives numerous examples of God's power at work in response to a person's faith. So when doubts assail you, remember this: With God, the possibilities are limitless! ♣

february17

HUMILITY THAT LEADS TO HEALING

Anyone who wants to be first must be the very last, and the servant of all.

MARK 9:35

Imagine you're in your favorite store waiting to be "waited on" when someone mistakes you for an employee. Are you flattered or embarrassed? Do you laugh, or are you offended? Being mistaken for a sales clerk can be humorous. It might also be highly revealing!

In Mark 9 and 10, Christ had more to say about serving than he did about being served.

Dwight L. Moody, whose ministry often placed him in prominent positions, shares two examples of the stature of the servant.

WALK WITH DWIGHT L. MOODY

"There is a story told of William Carey, the great missionary, who was at a party attended by the governor-general of India. Also present were some military officers who looked down upon the missionaries with contempt.

"One of those officers said at the table: 'I believe that Carey was a shoemaker, wasn't he, before he took up the profession of a missionary?'

"Mr. Carey spoke up and said: 'Oh, no, I was only a cobbler. I could mend shoes, and wasn't ashamed of it.'

"The one prominent virtue of Christ, next to his obedience, was his humility. And even his obedience grew out of his humility.

"In his lowly birth, his submission to his earthly parents, his contact with the poor and despised, his entire submission and dependence upon his Father, this virtue—consummated in his death on the cross—shines out."

WALK CLOSER TO GOD

Isn't it strange how many vie to be first when, according to Jesus, the prize goes to the one who is last?

William Carey was not ashamed to be a mender of soles and heels, if only by that he might find opportunity to be a mender and healer of souls.

To be called "only a servant"—some would call that an insult. What would you call it? ♣

february18

A PERSONAL PREFERENCE FOR JESUS CHRIST

Peter [said], "We have left everything to follow you!".

MARK 10:28

Bargaining with God is a favorite pastime for many of us: "Lord, I'll follow you if …" "God, I'll put you first when …"

In Mark 10, Peter reminded Jesus of the personal sacrifice involved in being Jesus' disciple: "We have left everything."

Implied is Peter's unspoken concern: "What will we get in return?"

Commitment with strings attached is not new. But as Oswald Chambers points out, it's really not commitment at all.

WALK WITH OSWALD CHAMBERS

"We have become so commercialized that we only go to God for something from him, and not for himself.

"If we only give up something to God because we want more back, there is nothing of the Holy Spirit in our abandonment. It is miserable commercial self-interest.

"That we gain heaven, that we are delivered from sin, that we are made useful to God—these things never enter as considerations into real abandonment, which is a personal sovereign preference for Jesus Christ himself.

"Beware of stopping short of abandonment to God, for most of us know abandonment in word only."

WALK CLOSER TO GOD

Unconditional surrender allows no exceptions.

You cannot be totally available to God *if*…

You cannot surrender to God's will *when*…

You cannot leave all and follow, *provided*…

It just doesn't work that way.

There are many ways to express your level of commitment to Jesus Christ:

"I'm not willing to put you first."

"I'll put you first if …"

"I'll put you first, regardless."

On this commitment scale, where would you place the apostle Peter in Mark 10? Where would you place yourself? ✣

february19

EARTHLY SERVICE IN HEAVENLY PERSPECTIVE

Those who went ahead and those who followed shouted, "Hosanna!" "Blessed is he who comes in the name of the Lord!".

MARK 11:9

The last week of Christ's life began with a hero's welcome … palm branches … hosannas.

Yet by the end of the week, the "key to the city" had become a cross on a hill and the cheering crowds gave way to the jeering mobs.

Why?

Because they forgot Christ's words: "The Son of Man [came] … to give his life as a ransom for many" (Mark 10:45).

Martin Luther, who clearly knew the necessity of Christ's death, sets Jesus' coming to Jerusalem in perspective.

WALK WITH MARTIN LUTHER

"The riding of our blessed Savior into Jerusalem was a poor, humble kind of procession. Christ, king of heaven and earth, was seen sitting upon a lowly donkey.

"This humble transport for so powerful a potentate was a fulfillment of Zechariah's prophecy. Christ had neither money, nor riches, nor earthly kingdom, for he gave those to kings and princes.

"But he reserved one thing for himself, which no human creature or angel could do. Namely, to conquer death and sin, the devil and hell. And in the midst of death to deliver and save those that through his Word believed in him."

WALK CLOSER TO GOD

No one understood Christ's triumph. The celebration was premature, and the empty tomb, not the kingly scepter, would signify his victory.

Now you are sent forth as his servant. Like him, you may be misunderstood and unappreciated. And like the Savior, your reward may not be of this world.

There may be no ticker tape in your future, no cries of "Hurrah!"

But the words "Well done!" falling from the lips of the Savior will make all earthly rewards pale by comparison. ✤

february20

FAITH IN THE FAITHFUL ONE

"Have faith in God," Jesus answered.

MARK 11:22

Faith works no miracles. It never has. But God does. And always will.

God is the provider of power; faith is simply the channel through which his power is released.

In Mark 11 Jesus used the withered fig tree as an object lesson to teach the importance of well-placed faith—faith that is in God, the faithful one.

J. Hudson Taylor, pioneer missionary to China, knew firsthand a lifestyle of faith in a great and faithful God.

WALK WITH J. HUDSON TAYLOR

"We should bring every care for temporal things to him and then be anxious for nothing.

"Is our path dark? He is our sun. Are we in danger? He is our shield.

"If we trust him we shall not be put to shame. But if our faith should fail, *his* will not—'If we are faithless, he remains faithful' (2 Timothy 2:13).

"As the light which shines from the dark waters of the lake is the reflection of the sun's rays, so a person's faith is the impress and reflection of God's faith.

"The one who holds God's faith will not be reckless or foolhardy but will be ready for every emergency.

"The person who holds God's faith will dare to obey him."

WALK CLOSER TO GOD

Do you have a friend who has proved faithful in the past? Then you will have little trouble trusting that friend in the future.

So it is with faith in God—faithfulness begets faith. You trust your trustworthy supplier, not yourself or your feelings.

The living, loving God of creation—the one who made the mountains and therefore has no trouble removing them at the proper time—generates a faith that will not shrink when washed in the waters of affliction, a faith against which mountains of adversity don't stand a chance! ❖

february21

MAKING SO MUCH OUT OF SO LITTLE

Jesus sat down opposite the place where the offerings were put and watched the crowd putting their money into the temple treasury.

MARK 12:41

The Bible has much to say about money matters because, in God's eyes, money matters!

In Mark 12, many rich people were giving huge sums out of their bloated bank accounts. But their "much" seemed as nothing to Jesus when compared with the "all" that the poor widow gave out of her poverty.

Adam Clarke explains how a widow's two small copper coins could add up to more than a rich man's millions.

WALK WITH ADAM CLARKE

"Christ observes all people and all things. All our actions are before his eyes. What we do in public and what we do in private are equally known to him.

"His eye was upon the abundance of the rich who had given much; and he was well acquainted with the poverty and desolate state of the widow who had given her all, though that was only a little in itself.

"Christ sees all the motives which lead people to perform their good deeds. He knows whether they act through vanity, self-love, ambition, hypocrisy . . . or through love, charity, zeal for his glory, and a hearty desire to please him.

"He observes the motivations which accompany our actions—whether we act with care or negligence, with a ready mind or with reluctance."

WALK CLOSER TO GOD

There are many who are willing to give God credit, but few are willing to give him cash!

Many are willing to give him some or even much, but few are willing to give him all.

Many are willing to give a tithe or offering, but few are willing to admit that the balance also belongs to God.

If God rewarded your giving on the basis of motive, not amount, would he make little ado about much or much ado about little?

How you give, not *how much*—that's where a servant's heart is revealed. ❖

february22

COMMOTION, CHANGE AND CONSUMMATION IN HIS PLAN

When you hear of wars and rumors of wars, do not be alarmed. Such things must happen, but the end is still to come ... These are the beginning of birth pains.

MARK 13:7–8

Birth pangs are a bittersweet experience. On the one hand they signal a long-awaited event; on the other, the beginning of hours of intense labor.

So it is with the signs of the times in Mark 13—signs that mark the urgency of the hour.

Though the tendency in every age has been to mistake the birth pangs for the actual moment of birth, J. A. Alexander offers this helpful insight. (And keep in mind that he penned these words more than a century ago!)

WALK WITH J. A. ALEXANDER
"Do not be troubled or filled with concern, as if these commotions necessarily imply some great catastrophe or the final consummation.

"The necessity of this caution—given not only to the first disciples but also to their successors—is abundantly apparent.

"Pious people in every age have concluded that national commotions and collisions were decisive proof that the world was near its end.

"There are no doubt true Christians at this moment drawing such conclusions from the mutiny in India and the war in China, in direct opposition to our Lord's command. The meaning of his words is not that such changes may not be immediately followed by the greatest change of all, but only that they do not guarantee it."

WALK CLOSER TO GOD
The disciples were asking for a sign. Jesus concentrated on the assignment.

Nations will rise and fall, wars will rage, earthquakes will rock, famines will ravage.

But in the midst of it all, there's a job to be done: "The gospel must first be preached to all nations" (Mark 13:10).

Only the servant of God, with his task clearly in view, will be able to watch and pray—and faithfully engage in fruitful service—even as the birth pangs grow. Are you such a servant? ❖

february23

FILLING THE ROOM WITH THE AROMA OF PRAISE

She did what she could. She poured perfume on my body beforehand to prepare for my burial.
MARK 14:8

Whether in words or by actions, true love cannot be contained. It always finds a means of expression.

But you don't always have to talk about love, as Mark 14 illustrates. There a nameless woman expressed her love for the Lord, apparently without uttering a single word.

Scottish minister Robert Murray McCheyne speaks of the woman's act of loving adoration in anointing her precious Savior with a very costly and precious perfume.

WALK WITH ROBERT MURRAY MCCHEYNE

"If we have been saved by Christ, we should pour out our best affections on him.

"It is good to love his disciples, good to love his ministers, good to love his poor. But it is best to love him.

"We cannot now reach his blessed head, nor anoint his holy feet. But we can fall down at his footstool and pour out our affections toward him.

"It was not the ointment Jesus desired, for what does the King of Glory care for a little ointment?

"But it is the loving heart poured out upon his feet; it is the adoration, praise, love, and prayers of a believer's broken heart that Christ cares for.

"The new heart is the alabaster box that Jesus loves—broken and filling the room with the aroma of praise."

WALK CLOSER TO GOD

It's easy to become preoccupied with the work of the Lord and overlook the Lord of the work, to concentrate on the people of God or the business of God and ignore the person of God.

Activity is vital in the life of a servant. But so too is bringing your alabaster box to Jesus, breaking it, pouring out your heart and allowing the sweet fragrance of praise to say as nothing else can, "I love you, Lord."

You need not be eloquent to do that, for God hears the sincere sentiments of his children's hearts. ❖

february24

STRONG ENEMY, SLEEPY SAINTS AND THE MASTER'S SUMMONS

Watch and pray so that you will not fall into temptation. The spirit is willing, but the flesh is weak.

MARK 14:38

Peter, James, and John were involved in serious spiritual combat. But they didn't know it.

Their commander had told them to "watch and pray" so they would not fall victim to the enemy. Instead they slept, giving in to the very temptation they had been warned to avoid.

Temptation is more than something to be met and conquered. As Matthew Poole explains, it is also something to be avoided.

WALK WITH MATTHEW POOLE

"Here Jesus calls his disciples to a greater watching—spiritual watching—that they might not fall under temptation.

"By exhorting them to watch, he directed them to use such means as were within their power to use. By adding prayer, he let them know that it was not in their power to stand without God's help and assistance, and which—upon their praying—would not be denied.

"The spirit is willing, but the body is weak. The spirit is resolved with constancy to perform its duty, but the flesh is apt to faint and fall away when assaulted by temptation.

"Therefore you should earnestly pray for supernatural strength, and be vigilant so you will not be surprised and overcome."

WALK CLOSER TO GOD

Who can calculate the injury inflicted by the enemy on "sleeping" saints?

Christ's summons to watch and pray is just as urgent today as it was then because the battle is just as crucial. The enemy is just as strong. The temptations are just as subtle.

If the disciples had prayed and stayed alert as Christ had commanded, they would not have faced the temptation they did. Their lack of alertness opened the door to unnecessary temptation.

Your need for alertness is just as great. The command to "watch and pray so that you will not fall into temptation" is still applicable.

Are you awake? ❖

february25

THE HEAT OF THE BATTLE OR THE WARMTH OF THE FIRE

Peter followed him at a distance ... There he sat with the guards and warmed himself at the fire.

MARK 14:54

Peter: a servant at last. Unfortunately, he picked the wrong time, the wrong place, and the wrong master!

Christ's call to serve involves a willingness to face persecution. But fear became Peter's master in the face of danger. He chose the guise of a servant in order to escape the hardships of being identified with Christ.

Matthew Henry, one of God's committed servants, suggests where Peter went wrong.

WALK WITH MATTHEW HENRY

"He followed Christ, but it was afar off. Fear and concern for his own safety prevailed.

"It looks bad, and bodes worse, when those who are willing to be Christ's disciples are not willing to be known as such.

"Here begins Peter's denial: For to follow Jesus afar off is to turn away little by little.

"Peter should have gone back up to the court and appeared for his Master. But he went in where there was a good fire and sat with the servants. Not to silence their reproaches, but to screen himself.

"He followed him, led more by his curiosity than by his conscience. He attended as an idle spectator, rather than as a disciple."

WALK CLOSER TO GOD

There is something inconsistent about a servant in the shadows.

A servant more concerned about his own welfare than his master's.

A servant more intent on being comfortable than on being a comforter.

Times of crisis should be the showcase for God's servants. After all, that's what he has uniquely equipped you to handle.

But when the choice falls between the heat of the battle and the warmth of the fire, only you can decide whether you will sit with the servants or stand with the Savior. ✣

february26

THE HEAVENLY STRENGTH OF PATIENT ENDURANCE

"What crime has he committed?" asked Pilate. But they shouted all the louder, "Crucify him!".
MARK 15:14

It's nice to get more than you deserve. But for all the good Jesus did, he received a cross.

Servanthood is often like that. In exchange for selflessness and sacrifice, you may receive misunderstanding, jeers, persecution, hatred, perhaps even death.

Abraham Kuyper offers this insight into Christ's greatest act of service for sinful humanity.

WALK WITH ABRAHAM KUYPER

"That heavenly strength which overcame every effort to thrust the Holy One out of the world is endurance.

"This patience is displayed in Jesus' spiritual struggles against Satan. First in the wilderness, then in Pilate's judgment hall, and finally upon the cross, he was steadfast. He endured.

"Satan left nothing untried in his efforts to destroy that glorious, holy, divine life. But the holiness of Jesus was neither marred nor even slightly soiled.

"The full glory of Jesus' endurance is revealed when, on the third morning, he arises from the grave. He endured that last enemy and overcame it—death!

"There is nothing more that Satan can do now against the Christ. And it is Christ who works that same strength in those who are his."

WALK CLOSER TO GOD

Heat and pressure have a way of revealing and proving the quality of a product.

In the same way, the truest test of commitment comes not on the days when everything goes well but on the days when everything goes wrong—when you are misunderstood, ill-treated, wrongly accused.

But the strength that enabled Jesus to endure is available for you as you follow daily in his steps. Draw on it.

And don't be surprised if you prove to be just as durable. ✤

february**27**

TRAGEDY TRANSFORMED INTO ETERNAL TRIUMPH

And when the centurion, who stood there in front of Jesus, saw how he died, he said, "Surely this man was the Son of God!".

MARK 15:39

Mark's account of Jesus' death is an agonizing record of what seems to be a total failure. A mock trial, a brutal crucifixion, cruel taunts, a hurried burial.

And for three days hope died in the disciples' hearts.

A. W. Tozer explains how failure in the eyes of the world may be success in God's eyes.

WALK WITH A. W. TOZER

"The current mania of people seeking to succeed in the world is a good thing perverted.

"The desire to fulfill the purpose for which we were created is, of course, a gift from God. But sin has twisted this impulse about and turned it into a selfish lust for first place and top honors.

"When we come to Christ, we enter a different realm, one infinitely higher than and altogether contrary to that of the world.

"Our Lord died an apparent failure, discredited by the leaders of established religion, rejected by society, and forsaken by his friends. It took the resurrection to demonstrate how gloriously Christ had triumphed and how tragically the world had failed.

"The resurrection demonstrated once and for all who won and who lost."

WALK CLOSER TO GOD

There is no greater success story than the resurrection, for apparent tragedy was transformed into eternal triumph.

That would be good news enough. But there's more! Christ's resurrection makes a similar success story possible in the lives of Christians who know the truth of this verse: "I have been crucified with Christ and I no longer live, but Christ lives in me" (Galatians 2:20).

That's a success story with new chapters being written every day. One of those chapters is reserved just for you.

How will today's page read? ✤

february28

HIS POWER, HIS PRESENCE, HIS PEOPLE

Then the disciples went out and preached everywhere, and the Lord worked with them.
MARK 16:20

When an experienced orator delivers a moving address, no one is surprised. But when fishermen begin to make stirring speeches, that's news.

The resurrection of Christ transformed the disciples from timid men into bold witnesses.

John Calvin examines the transformation of these fugitives-turned-preachers.

WALK WITH JOHN CALVIN

"Every person would have thought that, by his death on the cross, Christ would either be altogether annihilated or so completely overwhelmed that he would never again be mentioned except with shame and loathing.

"The apostles, whom he had chosen to be his witnesses, had deserted him. And such was the contempt in which they were held that they hardly ventured to utter a word in public.

"There is great emphasis therefore in the words, 'The disciples went out and preached everywhere.'

"For it was impossible that so sudden a change should be accomplished in a moment by human power.

"Therefore Mark adds, 'The Lord worked with them,' by which he means that this was truly a divine work."

WALK CLOSER TO GOD

A servant's life isn't difficult. Without the right motivation, it's impossible!

Eleven men were entrusted with the good news of a risen Christ—a worldwide assignment that was humanly impossible.

That was by design.

For without the power and presence of Christ, their efforts were doomed from the start.

Even today, God is looking for servants through whom he can do a divine work, people willing to exchange their weakness and timidity for his strength and boldness.

Someone like you. ✤

march1

GREATNESS FROM GOD'S POINT OF VIEW

For he will be great in the sight of the Lord.

LUKE 1:15

John the Baptist obviously never read Dalius Carnegius's book, *How to Win Jews and Influence Greeks*. He didn't fit in with the crowd. In fact, everything about him seemed to smack of the peculiar.

His clothes were made of camel skins. His diet was strictly organic. And his behavior was decidedly antisocial. But the impact of John's ministry is undeniable.

You'll discover a clue to John's greatness in the words Matthew Poole wrote over 300 years ago.

WALK WITH MATTHEW POOLE

"We have a natural ambition to be great in the sight of men. But true greatness is to be great in the sight of God.

"In God's sight, a great man is one of whom God makes great use, especially in turning many souls to himself.

"Consider John. His father was an ordinary priest. He had no palace, no stately habitation. Nature was his cook. Yet Christ said of him, 'Among those born of women there is no one greater than John' (Luke 7:28).

"Where was his greatness but in this: He was a great and faithful preacher of God's message, and God blessed his labors to convert souls.

"They are great who do much of the work for which God has sent them into the world, and do much good in their generation."

WALK CLOSER TO GOD

The world views greatness as rising above the crowd, but God's perspective is just the opposite. In his eyes greatness is stooping to serve the crowd and daring at all times to obey God. That's a greatness all can achieve, if they choose to.

Your determination to do God's will may not be understood by the people around you. The things you do and say, the company you keep, your zeal for the things of God—none of these will fit the status quo.

But take comfort from the fact that you—like John—won't get lost in the crowd. ✤

GOD'S WAYS WITH THE PROUD AND THE LOWLY

[God] has brought down rulers from their thrones but has lifted up the humble.

LUKE 1:52

Mary learned firsthand the unpredictable character of God's gracious dealings. A young girl of humble means, she seemed an unlikely choice for the momentous role she would soon play in giving birth to the Son of God.

In her song of praise, Mary acknowledged the greatness of her God and the marvelous—yet mysterious—ways of his goodness. As Matthew Henry notes, he is the God of life-changing, world-shaking surprises.

WALK WITH MATTHEW HENRY

"Proud people expect to carry all before them, to have their way and their will. But God scatters them in the imagination of their hearts, breaks their measures, blasts their projects, and brings them low, by those very counsels with which they thought to advance and establish themselves.

"The mighty think to secure themselves by might, but he puts them down. On the other hand, those of low degree, who despaired of ever advancing themselves, and thought no other than of being ever low, are wonderfully exalted.

"God takes pleasure in disappointing the expectations of those who promise themselves great things in the world, and in outdoing the expectations of those who promise themselves but a little.

"As a righteous God, it is his glory to abase those who exalt themselves, and strike terror on the secure. And as a good God, it is his glory to exalt those who fear him."

WALK CLOSER TO GOD

Reread Matthew Henry's last two paragraphs carefully. Which kind of expectations do you hold?

Promise yourself success as a result of your own efforts, and you are sure to be disappointed. Humbly entrust your way to God, and he may surprise you today in a way you least expect.

Great expectations in God—that's one good way to ensure the surprises coming your way are the kind you'll welcome with open arms! ❖

march3

MERCY: NOT RECEIVING WHAT YOU DESERVE

You will ... give his people the knowledge of salvation through the forgiveness of their sins, because of the tender mercy of our God.

LUKE 1:76–78

Mercy—everyone wants it when it is least deserved, yet most hesitate to give it when another asks for it.

In Luke 1 mercy is mentioned five times. The one giving it is God; those least deserving of it are people. And this mercy consists of God becoming a man—the gift of Christ to sinners.

John Flavel explains that believers have the mercy of God in Jesus Christ.

WALK WITH JOHN FLAVEL

"Jesus Christ is an incomparable and matchless mercy. You will find none in heaven or on earth to equal him.

"He is more than all externals, as the light of the sun is more than that of a candle. He is more than life, as the cause is more than the effect. More than all peace, all joy, as the tree is more than the fruit.

"When you compare Christ with things eternal, you will find him better than they. For what is heaven without Christ?

"If Christ should say to the saints, 'Take heaven among you, but I will withdraw from you,' the saints would weep, even in heaven itself, and say, 'Lord, heaven will not be heaven unless you are there, for you yourself are the joy of heaven!'"

WALK CLOSER TO GOD

Justice is receiving what you deserve. Mercy is not receiving what you deserve. Grace is receiving what you do not deserve.

All three come true in Jesus Christ (Luke 1:68–69,77). His life and death provide redemption (that's justice—the price fully paid), remission (that's mercy—the guilt fully removed) and salvation (that's grace—eternal life freely given).

Giving others what's coming to them—that's only natural. Treating others with the mercy they don't deserve—that's supernatural.

Perhaps that's why Shakespeare wrote, "Earthly power doth show like God's when mercy seasons justice." Does that supernatural seasoning flow through your life to others? ♣

march4

SUCCESS OR FAILURE — THIS IS THE TEST

And she gave birth to her firstborn, a son. She ... placed him in a manger, because there was no guest room available for them.

LUKE 2:7

The "No Vacancy" sign was prominently displayed that night in Bethlehem. And 2,000 years later it still hangs in many lives.

Normally, a woman in Mary's condition might expect the simple courtesy of a place to stay. But those were not normal times.

James Hastings paints a word picture of that crowded night in Bethlehem.

WALK WITH JAMES HASTINGS

"It was a time when every available accommodation was called for, and the people of the inn were too busy to recognize that here was a claim which, in their less occupied moments, they never would have denied. And so Christ was simply crowded out. There was no room.

"Without doubt it is the same today. Every chamber of the soul is so filled with human interests that there is little room for Christ. There is little—if any—time for him.

"And this is true because a thousand other things demand our time. Our interest is drawn off in other directions. Our life is crowded with possessions and pleasures until, strange though it seems, there is no room for the Savior ... except in the stable.

"If we are so preoccupied as to have no room for Christ in our life, then our life is a failure. This is the test of everything: room for Christ."

WALK CLOSER TO GOD

There is a way to discover the passions of your life. Simply check your schedule. Find out what consumes your hours.

You'll quickly discover that if something—or someone—is important enough, you'll never allow it—or them—to be crowded out by other interests.

If the innkeeper on that Christmas Eve had known who would be born in his stable, surely the "No Vacancy" sign would have come down.

Can there be any good reason to leave it hanging in your life? ❖

march5

REPENTANCE IS MORE THAN SORROW FOR SIN

Produce fruit in keeping with repentance.

LUKE 3:8

Fruit trees without fruit soon end up as firewood. Their blossoms may be pretty and fragrant, but they provide no nourishment, no seeds, no means of reproduction.

You can tell a tree—and a true Christian—by the fruit you see. Alexander Maclaren provides insight into John's call for the fruit of repentance from his listeners along the Jordan.

WALK WITH ALEXANDER MACLAREN

"John demanded not only repentance, but its fruits. For there is no value in a repentance which does not change the life, even if such a thing were possible.

"Repentance is more than sorrow for sin. Many people have that, yet they rush again into the old mire. To change the mind and the will is not enough; real change is certified by corresponding deeds.

"So John preached the true nature of repentance when he called for its fruits. And he preached the greatest motive he knew when he pressed home on the sluggish consciences of his listeners the close approach of a judgment for which everything was ready, with the axe already lying at the root of the tree."

WALK CLOSER TO GOD

Repentance is more than saying I'm sorry.

Repentance is changing your mind about your actions. It is seeing that what you did was wrong, not just risky. It is turning around in God's strength and moving in a new direction ... God's direction.

True repentance bears visible fruit: compassion, fairness, wholesome speech, contentment (Luke 3:10–14). Take away the fruit, and whatever you have left is not genuine repentance.

But it is cause for alarm. And a change of mind. And a change of direction. Before the axe falls and the root disappears with the fruit. ❖

march6

YOUR SURE DEFENSE WHEN SATAN COMES CALLING

[Jesus] was hungry. The devil said to him, "If you are the Son of God, tell this stone to become bread." Jesus answered, "It is written: 'Man shall not live on bread alone'".

LUKE 4:2–4

Eve lived in a garden filled with good things to eat. Jesus had been in a desert 40 days without food. Yet when the temptation to eat came, the one who needed it most resisted it best.

Under attack, Eve disobeyed God's word not to eat; Jesus used God's word to defend himself.

The Word is still a sure defense against the wily schemes of Satan, as Martin Luther proclaims.

WALK WITH MARTIN LUTHER

"In every temptation simply close your eyes and follow the Word. Outside the Word there is nothing but tribulation and affliction. Through temptations and afflictions God proves the strength and virtue of his Word.

"Satan constantly tempts the heart. Therefore we must overcome the feeling of the flesh and adhere to the Word; for God does not forsake us but, like a mother, lovingly cherishes and carries us. Go to Christ, who is the sacrifice for our sins. In him the Devil, sin, and death have been crucified.

"One way to conquer is to despise the thoughts suggested by Satan. The more you dwell on those thoughts in your mind, the more they oppress you. Once you lose sight of the Word, the ways and means of help are no more. But as soon as you lay hold of some saying of Scripture and rely on it as a holy anchor, the temptations are driven away."

WALK CLOSER TO GOD

The Word of God is a sword with which you can defend yourself (see Ephesians 6:17)—but only if you carry it with you.

That doesn't mean wearing a sheath with your Bible at your side. But it does suggest the need to know the Word of God intimately in your heart and mind.

His Sword is your sure defense when Satan comes calling. Don't leave home without it. ♣

march7

JESUS—HIGH ABOVE US, YET BENDING OVER US

A man ... who was covered with leprosy ... saw Jesus ... and begged him, "Lord, if you are willing, you can make me clean." Jesus reached out his hand and touched the man. "I am willing," he said. "Be clean!".

LUKE 5:12−13

Leprosy! Unclean! Unclean! Virtually incurable in Bible times, this dreaded disease meant that the sufferer became an outcast from family, friends, society—in fact, from everyone except other lepers ... and the Savior!

In Luke 5 Jesus healed a leper with a touch. His act of compassion changed the man's life and, with it, the course of Jesus' public ministry (Luke 5:15).

Alexander Maclaren reflects on the touch of the man from Galilee.

WALK WITH ALEXANDER MACLAREN

"All true sympathy involves a touch.

"Jesus reaches the leper with the touch of a universal love and pity which disregards all that is repellent and overflows every barrier.

"He is high above us and yet bending over us. He stretches his hand from the throne as truly as he put it out when here on earth. And he is ready to take us all to his heart—in spite of our weakness and shortcomings, the leprosy of our many corruptions, and the depth of our sins—and to hold us ever in the strong, gentle clasp of his divine, omnipotent, and tender hand.

"This Christ lays hold on us because he loves us, and will not be turned from his compassion by our most loathsome foulness."

WALK CLOSER TO GOD

Like a leper, you may feel unworthy of God's forgiveness, love and cleansing. And you are.

You may sense that God is grieved by your sin. And he is.

You may feel that your conduct has placed you beyond his reach. But that's where you're wrong!

No sin is too great for him to forgive. No life is too damaged for him to redeem.

Is it possible that the only thing standing between you and the Savior's forgiveness and cleansing is your own self-pity? ✤

march8

THE REFRESHING NATURE OF PRAYER

Jesus went out to a mountainside to pray, and spent the night praying to God.

LUKE 6:12

The end of a hectic day. A rocky mountainside. Undisturbed moments alone. For Jesus it was the perfect time and place to pass the entire night in prayer with his Father.

Charles Spurgeon points out the significance of the time, place, persistence and occasion for this all-night prayer vigil.

WALK WITH CHARLES SPURGEON

"If ever one born of woman might have lived without prayer, it was our perfect Lord. And yet none was ever so much in supplication as he!

"The time he chose was the hour of silence when the crowd would not disturb him and when all but he had ceased to labor. While others found rest in sleep, he refreshed himself with prayer.

"The place was also well selected. He was alone where none would intrude, where none could observe.

"The persistence of his pleadings is remarkable: The long watches were not too long; the cold wind did not chill his devotions; the grim darkness did not darken his faith, or loneliness check his importunity.

"The occasion for this prayer is notable; it was after his enemies had been enraged—prayer was his refuge and solace; it was before he sent for the twelve apostles—prayer was the gate of his enterprise, the herald of his new work.

"The fact of this eminent prayerfulness of Jesus is a lesson for us—he has given us an example that we may follow in his steps."

WALK CLOSER TO GOD

Students of prayer should find it no different. When big decisions confront you, when commitments need to be strengthened, there is no better place to begin than with a quiet time and place for prayer.

As one commentator has wisely observed, "You can do more than pray after you have prayed. But you can do no more than pray until you have prayed." ✤

FREELY GIVING WHAT YOU CAN SUPPLY

Do to others as you would have them do to you.

LUKE 6:31

Today's popular version of the Golden Rule might go something like this: "Do unto others before they undo you!"—a sure sign of a society preoccupied with itself.

Focusing on the needs of others. That's fairly difficult when you're wrapped up in yourself. But for the Christian, the Golden Rule provides a ready remedy, as Matthew Henry explains.

WALK WITH MATTHEW HENRY

"What would we want others to do to us, either in justice or love, if they were in our condition and we in theirs—that is what we must do to them. We must treat them as we should desire and justly expect to be treated ourselves.

"We must give to those in need, to everyone who is a proper object of charity, who lacks necessities which we have the means to supply.

"Give to those who are not able to help themselves. Christ would have his disciples always ready to distribute what is within their power in ordinary cases, and beyond their power in extraordinary ones."

WALK CLOSER TO GOD

Living by the Golden Rule means your treatment of others is based on how you want to be treated in return.

Do you desire good? Of course! Then give good. Do you want others to forgive? Absolutely! Then be quick to forgive.

But here's the hard part: It is immaterial whether others actually treat you well or forgive you promptly. The point of the rule is: How would you *want* to be treated?

The Golden Rule was not given to society in general, which explains its rather tarnished image. Rather, it was issued to the only group of people empowered to keep it: the people of God!

Do you know someone who needs a golden touch today? He or she may be surprised to learn that someone remembers the original rule, which is untarnished and still shines. ✣

march**10**

BELIEVING FAITH MAKES THE DIFFERENCE

When Jesus heard this, he was amazed at him, and turning to the crowd following him, he said, "I tell you, I have not found such great faith even in Israel".

LUKE 7:9

Faith is a concept more easily demonstrated than defined. You exercise faith when you fly in an airplane or visit a doctor. Chances are good that you couldn't land the airplane or diagnose your illness. Yet you rely on the strength and skill of someone who can. And that's faith!

In Luke 7 Jesus commended a Roman officer for his great faith — a commodity so scarce as to amaze even Jesus!

George Whitefield highlights the necessity of believing faith.

WALK WITH GEORGE WHITEFIELD

"I am not against going to church, nor against the creed, the Lord's prayer, or the commandments. But believing is something more than those. It is coming to Jesus, receiving him, rolling ourselves on him, trusting in him.

"I do not know of any one single thing more often repeated in Scriptures than believing. It is described as a coming, trusting, receiving, and relying, under a felt conviction that we are lost, undone, and condemned without him.

"As a good old Puritan observed, we never come to Jesus Christ — the sinner's only hope — until we feel we cannot do without him."

WALK CLOSER TO GOD

Faith in Jesus Christ sets Christianity apart from religion.

Religion is based on what you do for God; Christianity is what God has done for you.

Religion is man's attempt to work his way to heaven; Christianity is God's good news that heaven is a free gift.

Religion involves trying; Christianity involves relying.

Have you come to the point of realizing you can no longer do without the Savior? He's patiently waiting for you to come, receive and trust. He's waiting for you to put your faith in him. ✤

THE FREEING POWER OF FORGIVENESS

Neither of them had the money to pay him back, so he forgave the debts of both.

LUKE 7:42

In Luke 7 Jesus likened the forgiveness of sins to the forgiveness of a large debt. A large debt freely forgiven prompted the debtor's great gratitude for the creditor's great kindness.

Jesus' parables of the two forgiven debtors points to every person's need of forgiveness, as Albert Barnes explains.

WALK WITH ALBERT BARNES

"If it was a mere debt which we owed to God, he might forgive—as this creditor did—without any equivalent. But it is a crime he forgives.

"So our sins against God are called 'debts' figuratively. God cannot forgive us without maintaining his word, the honor of his government, and law—that is, without an atonement.

"It is clear that by the creditor here our Savior meant God, and by the debtors, sinners and the woman present. Simon, whose life had been comparatively upright, was denoted by the one owing fifty denarii; the woman, who had been a shameless sinner, was represented by the one owing five hundred. Yet neither could pay. Both must be forgiven or perish.

"So, however much difference there is among people, all need the pardoning mercy of God, and all, without that, must perish."

WALK CLOSER TO GOD

Imagine the heartache of the one who owes an enormous debt he can never hope to repay but that may come due at any moment. Such is the fate of every individual without the forgiveness offered by Christ.

Who could refuse the offer of one to pay such a debt? Jesus' parable makes clear the freeing power of forgiveness, and the only proper response: love.

The apostle Paul would later give this instruction: "Let no debt remain outstanding, except the continuing debt to love one another" (Romans 13:8). If you are in Christ, then you are freely forgiven. Will you follow yet further by owing only a debt of loving service? ✤

march**12**

PERSONAL ATTENTION FROM
THE GREAT PHYSICIAN

As Jesus was on his way, the crowds almost crushed him. And a woman ... came up behind him and touched the edge of his cloak.

Luke 8:42–44

A doctor's waiting room. A crowded street. The doctor's office admits people one by one. Each is a person—with a face, a medical history and a reason for being there.

By contrast, the street can be an impersonal place. People are just as needy, but no one is concerned enough to do anything about those needs.

Jesus was often surrounded by throngs of people, but as Charles Spurgeon explains, Jesus never viewed his audience as a mass of faceless figures.

WALK WITH CHARLES SPURGEON

"Jesus is passing through the crowd to the house of Jairus, to raise the ruler's dead daughter. But he has so much power and goodness that he works another miracle while on the road.

"It is enough for us, if we have one need set before us, straightway to relieve it; it might even seem unwise to expend our energies by the way.

"Hastening to rescue one, we cannot afford to exhaust our strength upon another in like danger.

"But our Master knows no limit of power or boundary of mission.

"What delightful encouragement this truth gives us!

"If our Lord is so ready to heal the sick and bless the needy, be not slow to put yourself in his way, that he may smile upon you!"

WALK CLOSER TO GOD

Cares. The universal experience of those on planet Earth.

Some cares are as persistent as the woman's 12-year illness. Others are as heartbreaking as Jairus's dying daughter. But all are within the scope of the Great Physician's strength and skill.

Touching the hem of his garment in faithful prayer may be the only thing you have strength left to do.

But as the woman in Luke 8 discovered, it's a touch that won't go unnoticed. ❖

GETTING TO THE SOURCE OF LIFE

He replied, "You give them something to eat".

LUKE 9:13

What if you were close friends with an author whose works you admired? Would you prize his books over his friendship? Of course not.

The disciples were so concerned about finding food for the crowd that they forgot they were in the presence of the bread of life.

Mary Ann Lathbury wrote of our need for daily spiritual food from the Word of God, which reveals the living Word who is the bread of life.

WALK WITH MARY ANN LATHBURY

Break Thou the bread of life,
　　Dear Lord, to me,
As Thou didst break the loaves
　　Beside the sea:
Beyond the sacred page
　　I seek Thee, Lord;

My spirit pants for Thee, O living Word.
Bless Thou the truth, dear Lord,
　　To me—to me,
As Thou didst bless the bread
　　By Galilee:
Then shall all bondage cease,
　　All fetters fall,
And I shall find my peace, My all in all.

Thou art the bread of life,
　　O Lord, to me;
Thy holy Word the truth
　　That saveth me:
Give me to eat and live
　　With Thee above;
Teach me to love Thy truth, For Thou
　　art Love.

WALK CLOSER TO GOD

You wouldn't throw away a book just because you knew the author. In fact, you would probably strive to know him better by reading his works!

So as you read and meditate on God's Word, expect to get closer to your Lord. And the next time you see a loaf of bread, let it be a reminder of your relationship with the one who is the bread of life. ❖

march**14**

THE RIGORS OF FOLLOWING JESUS

Jesus said to him, "Let the dead bury their own dead, but you go and proclaim the kingdom of God".

LUKE 9:60

In Luke 9:23 Jesus made it clear that becoming his disciple involves self-denial—taking up your cross every day and following him.

He never guaranteed five-star accommodations. Sometimes he asked his followers to oppose social customs and traditions. He expected undivided allegiance.

The three men Jesus talked with in Luke 9 all needed to learn that comfort, social acceptance and even family ties become secondary when Jesus is supreme. Matthew Henry explains.

WALK WITH MATTHEW HENRY

"Our religion teaches us to show piety at home and to honor our parents. But we must not make these an excuse from our duty to God.

"If the nearest and dearest relation we have in the world stands in our way to keep us from Christ, it is necessary that we have a zeal that will make us forget that one.

"The disciple is called to be a minister, and therefore must not entangle himself with the affairs of this world (see 2 Timothy 2:4). And it is a rule that, whenever Christ calls us to any duty, we must not consult with flesh and blood (see Galatians 1:15–16).

"No excuses must be admitted against a present obedience to the call of Christ."

WALK CLOSER TO GOD

Physical fitness dominates the activities of many today. But spiritual fitness is far more crucial to the life of the Christian, for when Christ calls you to become his disciple, he summons you to a life of labor not leisure.

Discipleship is likened to the rigors of being a soldier, an athlete and a hardworking farmer (see 2 Timothy 2:3–6). That means being free from distractions, fit for action and steadfast in your labors.

If flabbiness rather than fitness characterizes your Christian life, perhaps you need to exchange a few excuses for some exercise in the service of your Lord. ✤

march15

DISCOVERING THE ONE NECESSARY THING

But few things are needed—or indeed only one. Mary has chosen what is better, and it will not be taken away from her.

LUKE 10:42

How do you show God that you love him? You might answer that question by listing the number of times you've gone to church. Or attended a Bible study. Or taught a class. Or given an offering.

But in the final analysis, your activities for God aren't the best barometer of your adoration. Your attitude is! A. W. Tozer explains that God wants more than just your output.

WALK WITH A. W. TOZER

"Some Christians feel it is a mark of spirituality to attend banquets, seminars, workshops, and conferences week after week.

"This brings up a lesson concerning Martha and Mary. I think it is plain that Martha loved Jesus, but her concept of devotion was activity.

"Mary also loved Jesus but with a different attitude in her devotion. She was fervently occupied in spirit with her love for him.

"Our Lord marked the distinction then, and he marks the distinction today.

"Jesus commended Mary for knowing that one thing is necessary—that God should be loved and praised above all other business which may occupy us bodily, mentally, or spiritually.

"He wants first an inner experience of the heart, and from that will grow the profound and divine activities which are necessary."

WALK CLOSER TO GOD

Slow me down, Lord.

Keep me from becoming so engrossed in working for you that I fail to nurture our relationship.

I have often felt the exhaustion of activity. Let me today experience a bit of the joy Mary felt—the joy of adoration.

Teach me how to say, "I love you, Lord," while standing still. In the name of him who first demonstrated what the service of worship is all about. Amen. ❖

march**16**

THE DANGER OF LIGHT BECOMING DARKNESS

See to it, then, that the light within you is not darkness.

LUKE 11:35

Fear of the dark ranks right up there with snakes, heights and loud noises among common childhood fears. And adults are not immune to them either.

You may take some comfort in the fact that common sense dictates that in life-and-death situations, you need all the light you can get. Anything less is foolhardy.

However, the Pharisees were in the dark about Jesus. G. Campbell Morgan sheds some light on the causes of their spiritual blindness.

WALK WITH G. CAMPBELL MORGAN

"Is it possible for a lighted lamp to be darkness? Yes, it is.

"That lighted lamp is darkness when it is put out of sight, in the cellar or under a bushel. That lighted lamp is light when it is placed on a stand, so that people may see the light.

"Light then is only of value when it is kept shining, and the steps are guided by it.

"Light hidden is darkness. Truth disobeyed is valueless. Knowledge unyielded to is ignorance.

"How often the light within us is darkness!

"The will of the Lord, clearly revealed to us, is apprehended intellectually, but not carried out in practice; then the light is darkness.

"The Word of the Lord, studied and interpreted by the Spirit, is retained in the intellect, but not permitted to be the guiding principle of the will. Then too the light is darkness."

WALK CLOSER TO GOD

The Pharisees responded to Jesus by closing their eyes to the truth. They preferred the comfort of the darkness to the brightness of God's light.

The status quo, after all, is best maintained in the dark. But if you are eager to know God's will—and do it—there's no need to be in the dark.

The Word of God is a source that sheds light on every subject. Let it always be a lamp for your feet and a light on your path (see Psalm 119:105). Don't allow it to go unheeded. ❖

march**17**

MAKING SECURE INVESTMENTS IN AN UNCERTAIN WORLD

But seek his kingdom, and these things will be given to you as well.

LUKE 12:31

Would you be willing to invest in a venture if you knew part of the dividends would be paid not to you but to your brother or sister?

Of course you would—if you're a member of God's family!

God has promised to meet the needs of his children. And frequently the way he does it is by blessing one in order to benefit another.

The twelfth-century saint Bernard of Clairvaux clarifies the way in which God helps those who help their neighbors.

WALK WITH BERNARD OF CLAIRVAUX

"What if, by giving to our neighbor, we find ourselves in want?

"What should we do except go confidently to God, 'who gives generously to all' (James 1:5), and opening his hand fills all things living.

"Without a doubt he who gives most men more than they need will not deny us bare necessities.

"Has he not told us, 'Seek first his kingdom ... and all these things will be given to you as well' (Matthew 6:33)?

"He has bound himself to give all things needful to those people who discipline themselves and love their neighbors.

"Moreover, it is but justice that we should share the blessings of this life with others."

WALK CLOSER TO GOD

Earthly investments are often uncertain at best. There are just too many factors that you cannot control.

That's why God's heavenly investment portfolio looks better than ever. Consider this prospectus:

Your investment is secure, untouchable by thief, worm or rust (see Matthew 6:20).

Interest is compounded eternally. Where your treasure is, there will your heart be also (see Matthew 6:21).

Best of all, you have the joy of seeing God meet the needs of others out of the overflow of your own life (see 1 Thessalonians 3:12).

Seeking the kingdom of God. When you add it up, there's no better way to invest your life! ✤

march18

STICKING TO THE STRAIGHT AND NARROW

Make every effort to enter through the narrow door, because many, I tell you, will try to enter and will not be able to.

LUKE 13:24

Narrow-mindedness is seldom considered a virtue. Yet it's dangerous to be tolerant when the issues are life and death.

Take salvation, for instance. Jesus was narrow-minded about it: "I am the way" (John 14:6).

Peter was equally narrow: "Salvation is found in no one else" (Acts 4:12).

And Paul made it clear that "the gift of God is eternal life in Christ Jesus our Lord" (Romans 6:23).

John Calvin offers these words of warning about broad paths and those who would seek to travel on them.

WALK WITH JOHN CALVIN

"Christ urges his men to enter in by the narrow door. By these words he intended to move his folk away from that foolish curiosity which hinders and complicates.

"Many look around to see whether others are joining them, as if they could only gain salvation in a crowd. But the faithful will not be curious about the crowd of stragglers.

"In this way we avoid our empty hopes letting us down, as if we had imagined that a crowd of companions would help us enter in.

"Many seek for an easy access to life, and constantly indulge themselves. Christ would have his people shake off such soft behavior, for he warns that those will be shut out who devote themselves to any other supposed entrance to life."

WALK CLOSER TO GOD

Jesus took no public opinion poll to determine the crowd's preference in the matter of salvation.

Rather, he proclaimed the way to God. A narrow way. A way few are finding. A way that allows no alternate routes.

Salvation through Jesus Christ. It may sound like a narrow path. And it is. But when a life is at stake, who could deny that it's better to stick to the straight and narrow path?

So who can you lead to that path today? ❖

march**19**

THE PATH TO NOWHERE IN THE KINGDOM OF GOD

For all those who exalt themselves will be humbled, and those who humble themselves will be exalted.

LUKE 14:11

Can you imagine an awards presentation honoring the "Servant of the Year" ... sponsored by the one receiving the award?

Humility and horn blowing. They simply don't mix, according to Jesus in Luke 14.

The servant who seeks to shine the spotlight of recognition on his own achievements has forgotten an important truth.

Promotion in the business of heaven is based on sacrifice for others—not superiority over others, as A. W. Tozer explains.

WALK WITH A. W. TOZER

"Watch out for the danger of arrogance in assuming that you are somebody indeed.

"The Lord will remind you of his own example, and will rebuke and chasten you in his own way.

"The Lord had no hired servants. He bossed no one around, and he never took a tyrannical attitude toward anyone. He never allowed any success or temporary honor to lead him astray.

"I think it is very good spiritual advice that we should never tie ourselves up to public opinion and never consider any honors we may receive as being due us because of our superior gifts.

"Early church fathers wrote that if a man feels he is getting somewhere in the kingdom of God, that's pride. And until that dies, he is getting nowhere!"

WALK CLOSER TO GOD

The world applauds celebrities, but God delights in exalting faithful servants.

Self-acclaim may propel you to a position of worldly prominence—for a time. But the honor it brings is short-lived.

By contrast, consider Jesus' example in the humiliation of the cross. What the public viewed as his hour of shame became instead the occasion for his exaltation.

It might not make good earthly sense to expect exaltation to follow humiliation. But in the kingdom of God, the way up has always been down! ♣

march20

FINDING FORGIVENESS IN THE FATHER'S HEART

I will set out and go back to my father and say to him: Father, I have sinned against heaven and against you.

LUKE 15:18

Confession. Forgiveness. Inseparable halves of the same cleansing transaction. But it takes two willing hearts, as the lost son discovered.

Mired in the pigpen, he came to his senses and began the long trip home to his waiting father—a father only too willing to forgive.

Confession. It's good for the soul and a whole lot more, as Charles Spurgeon notes.

WALK WITH CHARLES SPURGEON

"The grace of God in the heart teaches us that we, as Christians, own the duty of confession to our heavenly Father. We daily offend, and ought not to rest without daily pardon.

"If I have not sought forgiveness and been washed from the offenses against my Father, I shall feel like the prodigal, who, though still a child, was yet far off from his father.

"But if I go to him with a child's sorrow at offending so gracious and loving a parent, and tell him all, and do not rest until I realize that I am forgiven, then I shall feel a holy love for my Father. I shall enjoy peace with God through Jesus Christ my Lord.

"There is a wide distinction between confessing sin as a culprit and confessing sin as a child. The Father's bosom is the place for sorrowful confessions and for cleansing from the daily defilement of our daily walk."

WALK CLOSER TO GOD

The lost son must have wondered what reception awaited him:

"I told you so." "Get out and stay out!" "You're no longer my son."

But his fears were unfounded.

While the son was still far off, his father ran to embrace him.

Nothing is as tragic as a son or daughter unwilling to confess ... unless it is a parent unwilling to forgive. But the child of God never needs to fear what coming home to the heavenly Father will bring. ❖

march21

WORKING HARD AT DOING NOTHING

The Pharisees, who loved money ... were sneering at Jesus. He said to them, "You are the ones who justify yourselves in the eyes of others, but God knows your hearts".

LUKE 16:14–15

A telescope is helpful for studying the moon—if you look through the right end. But turn it around and the perspective becomes distorted.

In Luke 16 Jesus challenged the perspective of the Pharisees in their relationship with God. Charles Finney analyzes their wrong-ended perspective on righteous living.

WALK WITH CHARLES FINNEY

"Many professing Christians judge themselves falsely because they judge by a false standard.

"Like the Pharisees, they employ a merely negative standard.

"Suppose someone lets a house burn down and makes no effort to save it or its occupants. They hope not to be judged harshly, since they did not set the house on fire. They only let it alone.

"All they did was do nothing.

"That is all many persons plead as their religious duty. They do nothing to pluck sinners out of the fire, and they seem to think theirs is a very commendable religion.

"Such was the religion of the Pharisees.

"But was this the religion of Jesus or Paul?"

WALK CLOSER TO GOD

Jesus said, "Unless your righteousness surpasses that of the Pharisees ... you will certainly not enter the kingdom of heaven" (Matthew 5:20).

Harsh words. After all, the Pharisees did the right things. They prayed often and long. Fasted. Tithed. Went to the temple.

But as Christ pointed out, they were doing all the right things for all the wrong reasons (see Luke 11:42).

In short, they were looking at God through the wrong end of the telescope.

It's sad to think where their misguided perspective led them.

But, of course, no one would make that fatal mistake today. Would they? ❖

march**22**

THE MESSAGE OF A MONUMENTAL MISTAKE

Remember Lot's wife! Whoever tries to keep their life will lose it, and whoever loses their life will preserve it.

LUKE 17:32-33

Nostalgia. It's usually a harmless pastime of fond reflection on the good old days.

But for Lot's wife, the old way of life cost her more than she bargained for and turned out to be dearer than life itself.

In Luke 17 Jesus strongly rebuked those who, after coming to him, looked back fondly on their former way of life.

Jonathan Edwards probes Mrs. Lot's attraction to Sodom's lifestyle ... and its tragic consequences.

WALK WITH JONATHAN EDWARDS

"All the enjoyments of Sodom will soon be burned. As it is with all the enjoyments of sin, they are all appointed to the fire. And surely it is not worthwhile to look back upon the things that are perishing.

"Lot's wife looked back because she remembered the pleasant things she left in Sodom.

"So it is very often with some Christians. But when they look back, they put themselves under vast disadvantages. They dreadfully harden their own hearts and stupefy their souls by quenching the Spirit of God.

"They make way for discouragements. They give Satan great advantage to ruin them. Their souls presently become hard like the body of Lot's wife.

"And though they live long after, they never get much further."

WALK CLOSER TO GOD

The call to discipleship is a call to new life. Looking back means something in your old life is of greater value to you than your new life in Jesus Christ. Looking back allows momentary pleasures to compete with the eternal Savior.

God desires your undivided attention and devotion—a truth Lot's wife learned the hard way, and too late.

Don't miss the message of her disastrous and monumental mistake. Looking back can be hazardous to your health! ✣

march23

A HEART IN TUNE WITH THE HEARTBEAT OF GOD

Then Jesus told his disciples a parable to show them that they should always pray and not give up.

LUKE 18:1

Doctors can learn a lot about their patients by listening to their heartbeats. It's an important barometer of health, even when everything else appears normal.

The same could be said of the spiritual health of the Christian. Outwardly, things may seem fine. But the health of the inner life is crucial. The heartbeat must be strong to know God.

Physically weak, David Brainerd possessed a vibrant spiritual health. The words of his diary reveal the powerful, prayerful beating of a heart strong for God.

WALK WITH DAVID BRAINERD

"I withdrew to my usual place of retirement, in great tranquility. I knew only to breathe out my desire for a perfect conformity to him in all things.

"God was so precious that the world with all its enjoyments seemed infinitely vile. I had no more desire for the favor of men than for pebbles.

"At noon I had the most ardent longings after God which I ever felt in my life.

"In my secret retirement, I could do nothing but tell my dear Lord in a sweet calmness that he knew I desired nothing but him, nothing but holiness, that he had given me these desires and he only could give the thing desired.

"I never seemed to be so unhinged from myself, and to be so wholly devoted to God.

"My heart was swallowed up in God most of the day."

WALK CLOSER TO GOD

Father, make my heart strong to know you.

Where my heartbeat is faint, fortify it with your Word.

Where it is erratic, stabilize it with your faithful promises.

Great Physician, give me a heart like David Brainerd's. A heart that will not rest till it finds its rest in you. Amen. ❖

march24

SMALL BEGINNINGS, ETERNAL ENDINGS

The Son of Man came to seek and to save what was lost.

LUKE 19:10

Tax collectors have never been popular. In Jesus' day, Jews who collected taxes for the Roman government were seen as traitorous and corrupt by their fellow countrymen.

Zacchaeus was one such tax collector. He was small in physical stature, and smaller in the eyes of his countrymen because of his loathsome job.

However, Jesus saw in Zacchaeus what other people missed: a curiosity for the things of God.

And as J. C. Ryle comments, God often works in small ways to accomplish great things.

WALK WITH J. C. RYLE

"The ways by which the Holy Spirit leads men and women to Christ are wonderful and mysterious. He is often beginning in a heart a work which shall stand for eternity, when an onlooker observes nothing remarkable.

"In every work there must be a beginning, and in spiritual work that beginning is often very small.

"Do we see a careless brother coming to church and listening to the gospel after a long indifference? When we see such things, let us remember Zacchaeus.

"Let us not look coldly on such a person because his motives are at present very poor and questionable. It is far better to hear the gospel out of curiosity than not to hear it at all.

"Our brother is with Zacchaeus in the tree! Who can tell but that he may one day receive Christ as joyfully?"

WALK CLOSER TO GOD

It may be difficult to see how salvation can result from a man climbing a tree.

That's because you see a man in a tree, but God sees a man lost and searching.

Before you write off a Zacchaeus near you, take another look—this time through the eyes of Jesus.

Those whom the world would label "little" have a way of appearing much larger when seen from the perspective of the seeking Savior. ❖

march25

WHAT DO YOU THINK OF JESUS?

The stone the builders rejected has become the cornerstone.

LUKE 20:17

It may surprise you to learn that the opposite of love is not hate.

Hate at least acknowledges the other person's presence. The opposite of love is something much colder, much crueler. It is indifference.

There was little apathy toward Jesus during his years on earth. He inspired sacrificial devotion, openmouthed wonder and even sinister opposition. "What do you think about the Christ?" was seldom answered with just a shrug.

Yet today's indifference betrays a lack of contact with the Son of God. James Hastings describes this present-day malady.

WALK WITH JAMES HASTINGS

"It may be that our attitude toward Christ is not that of scorn and insulting rejection. It may be that we just treat the Son of God with indifference.

"We may hear his name, but it awakens no interest. We would not cross the street to hear it again. He does not enter into our lives. He is not a partner in our affairs. It is altogether to us as if he had never come into the world.

"We do not invest in him at all. We do not put anything into his enterprises. We do not mix his stock with our financial concerns.

"Multitudes of men and women will not give him even five minutes. The Son of God is come, but they kill him with indifference."

WALK CLOSER TO GOD

Those who have made a difference for Christ down through the centuries were consumed by the thought of Christ.

They were men and women of action, not apathy.

They did more than talk about prayer; they prayed. They did more than yearn to know Christ; they learned.

And that brings up a crucial question: "What do you think about Jesus?" ❖

march26

WHEN SMALL GIFTS BECOME GREAT TREASURES

"Truly I tell you," he said, "this poor widow has put in more than all the others".

LUKE 21:3

How is it possible to add together the offerings of countless rich men and declare the total less than the two small copper coins of a poor widow? How is it possible for so little to amount to so much?

Jesus' arithmetic is not hard to comprehend when you understand, as he did, that the secret of giving is not in the amount that is given, but rather what is given up.

Attitude—not abundance—is the key. Bishop Ambrose discusses the kind of giving that really adds up.

WALK WITH BISHOP AMBROSE

"Liberality is determined not by the amount of our possessions but by the disposition of our giving.

"For by the voice of the Lord, a widow is preferred above all, of whom it was said: 'This poor widow has put in more than all the others.'

"The Lord teaches that none should be held back from giving through shame of their own poverty, nor should the rich flatter themselves that they seem to give more than the poor.

"The piece of money out of a small stock is richer than treasures out of abundance, because it is not the amount that is given but the amount that remains which is considered.

"No one gives more than she who has nothing left for herself."

WALK CLOSER TO GOD

Giving is not a function of cold numbers, but the result of a warm heart.

A small gift humbly given is of greater value than a vast sum given out of pride, compulsion or guilt.

The amount of your gifts may vary with your resources. But the attitude of your gift should remain constant—and commendable—even if you are a poor widow on a two-coin pension.

Peter Marshall said it well: "Help us to give according to our incomes, lest thou, O God, make our incomes according to our gifts." ❖

march27

COMING OUT ON TOP: MEANING OR MIRAGE?

The greatest among you should be like the youngest, and the one who rules like the one who serves ... I am among you as one who serves.

LUKE 22:26–27

Things are not always as they appear.

The man who struggles across the barren desert may see water on the horizon but never reach it because what he sees is a mirage.

In Luke 22 the disciples argued with each other over who deserved the title of "Tops Among the Twelve."

But as Christ pointed out, they were striving after a mirage. W. H. Griffith Thomas explains that true greatness lies in another direction.

WALK WITH W. H. GRIFFITH THOMAS

"Our Lord's claim upon us presses us at every point, and the world and the church wait to see something of the infinite possibilities of the life of the true Christian.

"Four great words of the New Testament surely sum up our responsibility. Be it ours to realize them in all their fullness of meaning. 'I should'; 'I ought'; 'I must'; 'I will.'

"That is, I am inclined to respond; I am impelled to respond; I am compelled to respond; I am determined to respond.

"It is ours to say what David's followers said to their master: 'Your servants are ready to do whatever our lord the king chooses' (2 Samuel 15:14)."

WALK CLOSER TO GOD

Two models of greatness confronted the disciples: one from the world and dependent on achievement and recognition, the other from the Savior and flowing from selfless service.

Who is the greatest? The world would reply, "The one who comes out on top."

Who is the greatest? The Savior would reply, "The one who, by his willing service, helps others come out on top."

One is only a mirage. The other points the way to a greatness that time cannot dim.

Choose carefully which course you follow. After all, no one likes to discover—too late—that they were chasing a mirage. ❖

march**28**

TO TAKE THE CUP AND DRINK IT

And being in anguish, he prayed more earnestly, and his sweat was like drops of blood falling to the ground.

LUKE 22:44

Aside from the crucifixion itself, Gethsemane was the darkest hour of Christ's life.

Friends misunderstood him; armed soldiers came to arrest him; one of his own followers betrayed him; he agonized in the garden alone.

And while three of his trusted disciples slept, he went to his Father in prayer.

Jonathan Edwards describes the prayer that showed the full extent of Jesus' love.

WALK WITH JONATHAN EDWARDS

"When the dreadful cup was before Christ, he did not say 'Why should I go to plunge myself into such torments for worthless, wretched worms that deserve to be hated by me?'

"'Why should I who have been living from all eternity in the enjoyment of the Father's love, cast myself into such a furnace for those who never can pay me for it?'

"'Why should I yield myself to be crushed by the divine wrath for those who have no love for me, and are my enemies? They do not deserve any union with me, and never did, and never will.'

"Such, however, was not the language of Christ's heart in these circumstances.

"On the contrary, he resolved even then, in the midst of his agony, to yield himself up to the will of God, and to take the cup and drink it."

WALK CLOSER TO GOD

A real battle was fought and won in the agony of Gethsemane.

If anyone had the right to sidestep undeserved suffering, Jesus had that right.

Yet he prayed above all for God's will to be done.

To die an undeserved death for undeserving men and women—no one can fully comprehend such love.

But any grateful heart can respond in praise and adoration. A heart, for example, like yours. ❖

march29

VIEWING THE GREATEST VICTORY OF ALL TIME

But the whole crowd shouted, "Away with this man! Release Barabbas to us!".

LUKE 23:18

At first glance it appears the raucous shouts of a bloodthirsty crowd caused Pilate to send Jesus to his death. But in fact, an unseen higher will was at work in and through the human actors in this moving drama.

Alexander Maclaren shares this fascinating sketch of the criminal Barabbas.

WALK WITH ALEXANDER MACLAREN

"This coarse desperado was the people's favorite because he embodied their notions and aspirations, and had been bold enough to do what every one of them would have done if he had dared. He had headed one of the many small riots against Rome. There had been bloodshed in which he had himself taken part.

"Jesus had taught what the people did not care to hear, given blessings which even the recipients soon forgot, and lived a life whose 'splendor of ... holiness' (2 Chronicles 20:21) rebuked the common life of all.

"What chance did truth, kindness and purity have against the sort of bravery that slashes with a sword and is not elevated above the mob by beauty of thought or character? Even now, after nineteen centuries, are the popular 'heroes' of Christian nations saints or teachers or humanitarians, whose Christlikeness is the thing venerated?

"The vote for Barabbas and against Jesus is an instructive commentary on human nature."

WALK CLOSER TO GOD

Popularity is often a fleeting illusion. Today's bestsellers soon sit on the shelf unnoticed. Superstars endure only for a few brief seasons.

Society exalts winners and ignores losers. The world saw only a pitiful loss when Jesus went to the cross. In fact, they were viewing the greatest victory of all time.

When you think about it, who would remember Barabbas today if Jesus had not died and been raised?

Better to be condemned with Jesus than accepted with Barabbas. Wouldn't you agree? ❖

march30

NO ONE BEYOND THE REACH OF PRAYER

Jesus said, "Father, forgive them, for they do not know what they are doing".

LUKE 23:34

When you are suffering from pain and thirst, it's hard to see beyond your own needs.

Yet from the agony of the cross, Jesus looked out, saw his tormentors—and forgave them.

To pray for help in the midst of suffering would be understandable; to pray for those causing the agony surpasses human comprehension.

A. W. Pink sees in Christ's example a parable on prayer—the kind that reaches into hearts considered untouchable.

WALK WITH A. W. PINK

"In praying for his enemies, not only did Christ set before us a perfect example of how we should treat those who wrong and hate us, but he also taught us never to regard anyone as beyond the reach of prayer.

"Christian reader, never lose hope. Does it seem a waste of time for you to continue praying for that man, that woman, that wayward child of yours? Does their case seem to become more hopeless every day? Does it look as though they have gotten beyond the reach of divine mercy?

"Remember then the cross. Christ prayed for his enemies. Learn then not to look on any as beyond the reach of prayer."

WALK CLOSER TO GOD

Remarkable things happened at Calvary.

A hardened criminal found forgiveness. A Roman centurion acknowledged Jesus as the Son of God. Why? What softened their hearts and made them tender toward the truth?

Might it have been Jesus' willingness to forgive their hatred?

Might the prayer on his lips—"Father, forgive them"—have pricked their hearts as nothing else could?

People may run far from God. But they are never beyond the reach of prayer. Look around you. The need for fervent, forgiving prayer has never been greater. ✤

march31

EYES OPEN TO THE SAVIOR

Then their eyes were opened and they recognized him.

LUKE 24:31

What if you learned that the stranger you sat beside today—the one with whom you shared small talk and pleasantries—was in fact the ruler of your country!

Wouldn't you feel excitement, privilege, even joy? And wouldn't you wonder how it was possible not to recognize the one you know so well?

A. B. Bruce provides this analysis of the reasons why the disciples on the road to Emmaus failed to recognize the Messiah who had so recently accompanied them.

WALK WITH A. B. BRUCE

"The two friends who journeyed to Emmaus did not notice any resemblance between the stranger who joined their company and their beloved Lord, of whom they had been thinking and speaking.

"The main cause of this was sheer heaviness of heart. Sorrow made them unobserving.

"It is obvious how men in such a mood should be dealt with. They can get outward vision only by getting the inward eye opened first.

"Jesus accommodated himself to their condition, and led them on from despair to hope.

"Once these thoughts had taken hold, the hearts of the two men began to burn with the kindling power of new truth.

"They looked outward, and lo, the man who had been discoursing with them was Jesus himself!"

WALK CLOSER TO GOD

The disciples were blinded by sorrow, preoccupied with grief.

Yet Jesus neither berated them, nor called for a stiff upper lip. Instead he set their minds and hearts at ease by patiently instructing them from the Old Testament Scriptures.

The Scriptures that spoke of a Savior who could lift burdens and ease sorrows.

What began as sorrow ended with joy: The Lord is risen indeed!

It's a story repeated thousands of times each day.

Why not repeat it to someone you know? ♣

april1

GREAT GRACE DESERVES GREAT GRATITUDE

The Word became flesh and made his dwelling among us ... full of grace and truth.

JOHN 1:14

John 1 describes a transformation that's more amazing than any metamorphosis in the animal kingdom—and infinitely more significant. There you'll read about the incarnation, God coming to earth in human form.

Why would he do that?

Jonathan Edwards probes the meaning of the incarnation and God's matchless, marvelous grace.

WALK WITH JONATHAN EDWARDS

"It was total grace that God gave us his only begotten Son.

"The grace is great because of the excellency of what is given. The gift was infinitely precious because it was a person of infinite glory, one infinitely near and dear to God, one infinitely worthy.

"The grace is great in proportion to the benefit we have in him: deliverance from an infinite, eternal misery, and enjoyment of eternal joy and glory.

"The grace is great in proportion to our unworthiness; instead of deserving such a gift, we merited infinite ill from God's hands.

"The grace in bestowing this gift is most free. It was what God was under no obligation to bestow.

"It was what we did nothing to merit.

"It was given while we were yet enemies, and before we had so much as repented.

"It was from the love of God that saw no excellency in us to attract it.

"And it was given without expectation of ever being repaid for it."

WALK CLOSER TO GOD

"Grace" is something more than prayer before a meal. It is God sending his only Son to die as a criminal so that God's enemies might live.

From the perspective of most human beings, grace is a free gift—undeserved and unearned.

From God's perspective, grace is a priceless sacrifice—costly and precious. Such great grace deserves great gratitude. You may never be able to thank God adequately for what he has done for you in Christ. But it's never too late to start. ❖

april2

THE CHANGE THAT COMES THROUGH CONTACT WITH JESUS

The first thing Andrew did was to find his brother Simon and tell him, "We have found the Messiah." ... And he brought him to Jesus.

JOHN 1:41–42

You can't force other people to read a book you enjoyed or try a tasty new recipe you discovered. Once you've shared the good news, they must respond for themselves.

In John 1 Andrew encountered the Messiah ... and immediately thought of his brother Simon.

But bringing Simon to the Savior and having Simon trust him for salvation were two different things—as Andrew discovered, and as B. H. Carroll explains.

WALK WITH B. H. CARROLL

"We cannot convert a person. That is not a part of our duty. We have reached our limit of responsibility when we have brought another to Jesus. He will attend to his part of it.

"Yet how many believers have tried to do God's work—attempting to make Christians out of other people, and giving formulas for it.

"Our limit is reached when we have brought that person to Jesus; and the sooner we find that out, the better.

"God alone can forgive sins. It is blasphemy for any man to claim that power.

"Andrew brought Simon to Jesus and stopped. That is the limit of our work."

WALK CLOSER TO GOD

It will take more than your own persuasive powers to convince others that Jesus is the Savior.

And that's where Jesus comes in.

His life, his words, his death and resurrection are far more convincing than any human argument.

In order for others to be changed by Christ, they must first come in contact with him.

And that's where you come in!

Get excited enough about something—or someone—and others will show an interest.

Have you accepted your responsibility to bring your neighbor, coworker or relative to Jesus?

Be an Andrew to some Simon today, and see what happens in that person's life— and your own. ✤

april3

LEAVING THE WHEN AND HOW TO GOD

His mother said to the servants, "Do whatever he tells you".

JOHN 2:5

A formal dinner served on paper plates and folding tables would be an affront to the guests and a disgrace to the host.

John 2 records the story of a wedding at which the host faced a disgraceful lack of provisions: there was no more wine.

But Jesus was there. And as Mary knew, he was all that was needed to correct the situation.

Ole Hallesby spotlights Mary's restful faith in her miracle-working son.

WALK WITH OLE HALLESBY

"The mother of Jesus reveals herself as a tried and true woman of prayer.

"She goes to the right place with the need she has become acquainted with. She goes to Jesus and tells him everything.

"Let us notice that she did nothing more.

"She knew that she did not have to help him by suggesting what he should do.

"She knew also that she did not have to influence him or persuade him to give these friends a helping hand. No one is so willing to help as he is!

"Jesus' mother had learned a secret of successful prayer: We should not interfere in our prayers but should leave the when and the how concerning the fulfillment of those prayers entirely to God.

"Most of us have a great deal to learn in this connection."

WALK CLOSER TO GOD

The door of prayer is always open. Therefore, come confidently to "ask ... seek ... knock" (Matthew 7:7), expecting an answer in return.

But in your asking, be careful that you do not tell God how to answer—and how soon.

Mary brought the need to her son Jesus, and Jesus did the answering—in a way that caused wonder and faith.

Let your prayers today be revitalized with the knowledge that God gives the very best to those who leave the choice with him. ❖

CLOSING THE GAP BETWEEN HEAD AND HEART

No one can see the kingdom of God unless they are born again.

JOHN 3:3

Many people are in danger of missing heaven by 18 inches. That's roughly the distance from your head to your heart. And it marks the difference between believing about Jesus Christ, and believing in Jesus Christ.

Nicodemus was a religious leader of his day who had head knowledge rather than heart knowledge about God. Yet he had religious questions he could not answer.

The answers Nicodemus received when he questioned Jesus demanded more than an intellectual nod, as G. Campbell Morgan explains.

WALK WITH G. CAMPBELL MORGAN

"We often hear it said today that there are many excellent people in the world who make no profession of Christianity.

"Nicodemus was that kind of man, particularly on the intellectual side. And it was to him that Christ first declared the necessity of the new birth.

"Nicodemus was a Pharisee, a ruler of the Jews. Narrow, dogmatic, educated and patriotic, he stood high in public position and prestige.

"But he was in danger of missing the kingdom of God.

"Jesus, looking at Nicodemus with all his intellect and strength, began on the level where Nicodemus would be familiar—his knowledge of the Scriptures.

"There he would learn that life comes through the lifting up of the Son of Man—a heavenly fact demanding more than intellectual activity."

WALK CLOSER TO GOD

Facts about the Savior's life are important. But no amount of facts alone will ever get you into the family of God.

For that takes a miracle of rebirth. You must come to the cross in childlike faith, believing in Jesus rather than simply believing about him.

In the words of Jesus, "You must be born again" (John 3:7).

Have you believed in Jesus and closed that gap between your head and your heart? ✦

april5

LAVISH RIVERS OF IRREPRESSIBLE LIFE

The water I give them will become in them a spring of water welling up to eternal life.
JOHN 4:14

"Give me a drink." Was that just a casual request of a thirsty traveler—or something more?

The Samaritan woman in John 4 came to satisfy her physical thirst, but Jesus saw in her life a more dangerous condition: spiritual drought that only he could relieve.

The well of spiritual life is Jesus himself. Oswald Chambers examines the source of water that eternally satisfies.

WALK WITH OSWALD CHAMBERS

"The picture our Lord gives is not that of a channel, but a fountain.

"Be filled, and the sweetness of a vital relationship to Jesus will flow out of the saint as lavishly as it is imparted to him.

"Keep right at the Source, and out of you will flow rivers of living life—irrepressible life.

"We are to be centers through which Jesus can flow as rivers of living water blessing everyone.

"As surely as we receive from him, he will pour out through us.

"Keep at the Source, guard well your belief in Jesus Christ and your relationship to him, and there will be a steady flow for other lives—no dryness and no deadness."

WALK CLOSER TO GOD

It is a simple matter to satisfy physical thirst—for a time. Drink deeply and your thirst will be quenched—temporarily. But again and again the yearning for water will return.

But in the spiritual realm, Jesus offers a fountain that never stops flowing, a river of life that never runs dry, a drink to quench the most desperate longing.

The woman at the well took Jesus at his word and found eternal satisfaction, as he promised. And the overflow of that fountain within her life reached many of those around her.

"Keep at the Source," and through you the fountain of life will satisfy those around you.

Drink deeply. See for yourself. ❖

april6

WHEN THE WORK OF CHRIST SHOCKS US

His disciples ... were surprised to find him talking with a woman.

JOHN 4:27

Jesus cut right through the cultural prejudices of his day. But he was more interested in the salvation of a woman than in avoiding special stigma.

Unfortunately, his disciples misunderstood both his action and his motive.

Try demonstrating sensitivity toward a castoff of society, and you can expect to become the target of verbal abuse—perhaps even from your own side. John Calvin explains why.

WALK WITH JOHN CALVIN

"The disciples' surprise could have come from two causes. Either they were scandalized by the woman's lowness or they thought Jews were polluted if they spoke with Samaritans.

"Although both these feelings arose from a reverence for the Master, they were wrong to marvel as if it were strange that he should honor such a common woman.

"Why did they not look at themselves? They certainly would have found no less cause for surprise that they—worthless fellows, the dregs of the people—should be raised to the highest rank of honor.

"And yet, they did not dare question him.

"We are taught by their example that if the works or words of Christ shock us, we must not grumble; but rather keep quiet until what is hidden from us is revealed from heaven."

WALK CLOSER TO GOD

As a racial entity, the Samaritans have almost ceased to exist. As a spiritual reality, they are everywhere—perhaps as near as next door.

The struggling divorcee, the shut-in senior citizen, the person who belongs to a cult. Others may misunderstand your intent as you reach out with Jesus' love, but the Lord understands.

After all, from a human perspective Jesus didn't have to go through Samaria.

And neither do you. But if he didn't, who would? And if you don't, who will? ✣

april 7

WAITING IN THE STRENGTH OF HOPE

Here [at a pool called Bethesda] a great number of disabled people used to lie — the blind, the lame, the paralyzed.

JOHN 5:3

There are two types of waiting: waiting because you have to and waiting because you want to.

The people around the pool waited because they had to; they needed to bathe in the healing waters. One man had waited years to be healed.

But when approached by Jesus, the man found himself being asked, "Do you want to get well?" (John 5:6).

Joseph Parker probes these two ways of waiting.

WALK WITH JOSEPH PARKER

"The world is a hospital. The person who is in the most robust health today may be struck before the setting of the sun with a fatal disease. In the midst of life we are in death.

"Life is a perpetual crisis; it can be snapped at any moment.

"Blessed is that servant who shall be found waiting, watching, and working when his Lord comes.

"These folk were all waiting, groaning, sighing. A sigh was a prayer, a groan was an entreaty, a cry of distress was a supplication.

"All the people in the porches were waiting. Are we not all doing the same thing?

"We are waiting for help, waiting till our ship comes in, waiting for sympathy, waiting for a friend without whose presence there seems to be nobody on the face of the earth. Waiting.

"One method of waiting means patience, hope, contentment, assurance that God will redeem his promises and make the heart strong; the other method of waiting is fretfulness, impatience, distrust and complaining—and that kind of waiting wears out the soul."

WALK CLOSER TO GOD

Father, teach me what it means to wait on you for my every need.

You have promised to provide in your time. Guard my heart from fretfulness and complaining, and make my heart strong to hope. Amen. ✤

april8

WORDS RESOUNDING WITH THE TESTIMONY OF TRUTH

You study the Scriptures diligently because you think that in them you have eternal life. These are the very Scriptures that testify about me.

JOHN 5:39

In John 5 the Jews had a problem. While clinging zealously to their Old Testament Scriptures, they refused to embrace the person of whom those Scriptures speak so eloquently—and frequently.

J. C. Ryle, who devoted his life to preaching the clear, insistent truths of God's Word, comments on the message of the Old Testament.

WALK WITH J. C. RYLE

"The 'Scriptures' of which our Lord speaks are, of course, the Old Testament.

"And his words show the important truth which too many are likely to overlook: that every part of the Bible is meant to teach us about Christ.

"Christ is not merely in the Gospels and the Epistles. Christ is to be found directly and indirectly in the Law, the Psalms, and the Prophets.

"In the promises to Adam, Abraham, Moses, and David ... in the pictures and emblems of the ceremonial law ... in the predictions of Isaiah and the other prophets ... Jesus, the Messiah, is everywhere to be found in the Old Testament.

"How is it that men see these things so little?

"The plain truth is that the chief seat of unbelief is the heart. Many do not wish to believe, and therefore remain unbelievers. To talk of lacking evidence is childish folly."

WALK CLOSER TO GOD

Searching is more than merely seeing. Many in Jesus' day saw with their eyes what they were unwilling to believe with their hearts.

They knew the Scriptures but refused to acknowledge the Messiah of whom those Scriptures speak: the Messiah whom John the Baptist proclaimed. The big picture of Christ is there in the Old Testament for those willing to see it. And it's difficult—and dangerous—to ignore such compelling evidence.

The psalmist would describe it another way: Foolish! ✣

april9

THE PRIORITY OF BEING IN HIS PRESENCE

Jesus, knowing that they intended to come and make him king by force, withdrew again to a mountain by himself.

JOHN 6:15

John 6 describes one of Jesus' busiest days — a day filled with sermons and miracles.

A crowd of more than 5,000 listened to him preach, saw him multiply the fish and loaves, then clamored to make him king.

And yet in the midst of it all, Jesus withdrew for some quiet moments with the Father.

Andrew Murray knew firsthand the importance of private audiences with the King of kings.

WALK WITH ANDREW MURRAY

"Man needs to be alone with God, to sense again the presence and power of his holiness, of his life, and of his love.

"Christ on earth needed it. He could not live the life of a Son here in the flesh without at times separating himself entirely from his surroundings and being alone with God. And how much more must this be indispensable to us!

"When our Lord Jesus gave the blessed command to enter our inner chamber, to shut the door and pray to our Father in secret, he gave us the promise that the Father would hear such prayers and mightily answer them.

"Alone with God. That is the secret of true prayer, of true power, of real living in face-to-face fellowship with God."

WALK CLOSER TO GOD

Before Jesus chose his 12 disciples, he spent a night — alone — in prayer.

Before Jesus went to the cross, he agonized in Gethsemane — alone — in prayer.

Solitary prayer. There's no better way to wrestle with a decision.

Deal with a temptation.

Refocus priorities.

Cultivate your love for God.

Worship your Lord and Savior.

Try it, and you'll soon discover how habit-forming being alone with God can be. And how it will empower you to reach out to others. ✤

SEEKING GOD FOR WHO HE IS,
NOT FOR WHAT HE PROVIDES

Very truly I tell you, you are looking for me, not because you saw the signs I performed but because you ate the loaves and had your fill.

JOHN 6:26

Life in Christ. It's not the promise of a chicken in every pot and two cars in every garage.

But in Jesus' day—and still today—many have viewed religion from the perspective, "What's in it for me?"

But Jesus rebuked such self-seeking individuals in John 6. And the result of this hard-hitting sermon? Many turned back and no longer followed him.

Albert Barnes examines the motives that would cause people to be such fair-weather followers.

WALK WITH ALBERT BARNES

"To seek him because they had seen miracles and were convinced by them that he was the Messiah would have been proper. But to follow him simply because their wants were supplied was mere selfishness—and selfishness of a gross kind.

"And yet, many seek religion from no better motive than this. They suppose it will add to their earthly happiness. Or they seek heaven only as a place of happiness, and regard religion as valuable only for this. All this is mere selfishness.

"Religion does not forbid regarding our own happiness, or seeking it in any proper way. But when this is the prevailing motive, it is evidence that we have never yet sought God aright.

"If so, we are aiming at the loaves and fishes, and not at the honor of God and the good of his kingdom."

WALK CLOSER TO GOD

It's true that in Christ you have ample reason to be happy. After all, you've received "every spiritual blessing" (Ephesians 1:3)—and many material ones as well (see James 1:17).

Like the fish-filled crowd, you might be tempted to seek Jesus for the supply he provides. But what if there were no feast tomorrow? Would you still pledge allegiance to the living bread?

The psalmist said it well: "Earth has nothing I desire besides you" (Psalm 73:25). What do you say? ❖

april11

FOLLOWING CHRIST FOR THE RIGHT REASONS

From this time many of his disciples turned back and no longer followed him.

JOHN 6:66

Hard sayings have a way of quickly thinning the ranks of lukewarm followers. In John 6 Jesus cut straight to the heart of the matter: "You are looking for me, not because you saw the signs I performed but because you ate the loaves and had your fill" (John 6:26).

Is it because of what you think Jesus can do for you that you call him "Lord"— or because of who he is?

As James Stalker comments, wrong motives for following Christ often flow from faulty expectations about Christ.

WALK WITH JAMES STALKER

"Jesus had heard of the tragic death of John the Baptist and immediately hurried to a desert place with his disciples to talk over the event.

"When moved by compassion for the helpless multitude, Jesus performed the stupendous miracle of feeding five thousand. The effect was overwhelming.

"The crowd became instantaneously convinced that this was none other than the Messiah. Having only one conception of what that meant, they endeavored to take him by force and make him a king, that is, force him to be the leader of a messianic revolt.

"It seemed the crowning hour of success. But to Jesus himself it was an hour of sadness and shame.

"This was all his work had come to? This was the conception they had of him? Were they to try to determine the course of his future action instead of humbly asking what he would have them do?

"They were looking for a 'bread king' who would give them idleness and plenty, mountains of loaves, rivers of milk, every comfort without labor. What he had to give was eternal life."

WALK CLOSER TO GOD

"No one can come to me unless the Father … draws them, and I will raise them up at the last day" (John 6:44).

Father, draw me to Jesus, that I too may know the one who is the resurrection and the life, and that I may find my satisfaction in him, the bread of life. Amen. ❖

FOUNTAIN OF LIFE FOR THIRSTY HEARTS

Let anyone who is thirsty come to me and drink. Whoever believes in me, as Scripture has said, rivers of living water will flow from within them.

JOHN 7:37–38

Bread. Light. Water. Vine. Gate.

Jesus described himself in unusual ways.

Some were difficult for his audience to understand—no doubt because his words carried significance far beyond that of the object he used.

Bernard of Clairvaux composed this hymn of praise to the Christ who is the fountain of life—and much more.

WALK WITH BERNARD OF CLAIRVAUX

> Jesus, Thou joy of loving hearts,
> Thou fount of life, Thou light of men,
> From the best bliss that earth imparts
> We turn unfilled to Thee again.
> Thy truth unchanged hath ever stood;
> Thou savest those that on Thee call;
> To them that seek Thee, Thou art good;
> To them that find Thee, all in all.
> We taste Thee, O Thou living Bread,
> And long to feast upon Thee still;
> We drink of Thee, the Fountainhead,
> And thirst our souls from Thee to fill.
> Our restless spirits yearn for Thee,
> Where'er our changeful lot is cast,
> Glad when Thy gracious smile we see,
> Blest when our faith can hold Thee fast.

WALK CLOSER TO GOD

"I am the light of the world" (John 8:12).

"Let anyone who is thirsty come to me and drink" (John 7:37).

"I am the bread of life" (John 6:35).

Light. Water. Bread. The essentials of spiritual life. All to be found in the person of Jesus Christ.

Are you hungry to know God? In the dark about God's will? Thirsting to find life in all its fullness?

Those who seek will find that Jesus is truly "all in all." ❖

LIGHT FOR LIFE — NOW AND FOREVER

I am the light of the world. Whoever follows me will never walk in darkness, but will have the light of life.

JOHN 8:12

No one would argue the importance of light; no one would doubt that we need light to live. But what do you do with it once you have it?

Jesus came from heaven, calling himself the light of the world. It was not a claim to be ignored by those dwelling in darkness.

How should individuals respond to the light of the world? Matthew Henry points the way.

WALK WITH MATTHEW HENRY

"If Christ is the light, then it is our duty to follow him, to submit ourselves to his guidance, and in everything take directions from him.

"It is not enough to gaze upon this light. We must follow it, believe in it, and walk in it; for it is a light to our feet, not our eyes only.

"It is the happiness of those who follow Christ that they shall not walk in darkness. They shall have the light of life — that knowledge and enjoyment of God which is spiritual life now, and everlasting life in the future.

"Follow Christ, and we shall undoubtedly be guided safely in both worlds. Follow Christ, and we shall follow him to heaven.

"One sun enlightens the whole world; so does one Christ, and there need be no more.

"What a dungeon the world would be without the sun, or the Son!"

WALK CLOSER TO GOD

Imagine what would happen if the sun actually vanished. Earth would be a cold, lifeless planet. But take away the light of the world, and the picture is even darker and colder.

To know God and enjoy him — that truly is "the light of life."

Jesus came to bring light in the midst of darkness. Light for your daily decisions. Light for this life and the next.

Follow him, and you need never stumble in the dark again. And that's a thought that should brighten anyone's day! ❖

FAITH: A RELATIONSHIP, NOT A FORMULA

Jesus said, "If you hold to my teaching, you are really my disciples".

JOHN 8:31

You can find a formula for doing just about anything. For example:

Physics: $E = mc^2$

Politics: "If you can't convince the voters, confuse them."

Finances: "Live within your income, even if you have to borrow to do it."

But the life of faith cannot be reduced to a formula. It is more than just plugging numbers into an equation and getting the right answer.

In John 8, Jesus revealed that faith is a way of life. As Alexander Maclaren explains, faith goes far deeper than mere mental acknowledgment.

WALK WITH ALEXANDER MACLAREN

"The notion that a man who does not contradict the teaching of the New Testament is thereby a Christian is a very old and very dangerous idea.

"There are many who have no better claim to be called Christians than the fact that they never denied anything that Jesus Christ said.

"This kind of faith hardens into mere formalism, or liquefies into mere careless indifference as to the very truth that it professes to believe.

"There is nothing more impotent than creeds which lie dormant in our brains and have no influence on our lives.

"See to it that all your convictions be translated into practice, and all your practice be informed by your convictions."

WALK CLOSER TO GOD

In John 8 those who believed Christ's claims were called to continue in his Word, abide in his teaching, be "at home" in his truth. In that way they would be known as his disciples—learner-friends—followers whose Christianity was no mere formula, but faith on the march.

Read the Bible through once, and you are on your way to mastering the Word.

Continue in the Word, and you are on your way to being mastered by it! ❖

april15

WORKING FAITHFULLY ON THE TASK AT HAND

As long as it is day, we must do the work of him who sent me. Night is coming, when no one can work.

JOHN 9:4

To become a diligent worker, but not a workaholic — that is the challenge of every Christian.

Jesus was a model worker in more ways than one. Tirelessly he went about his Father's business. He first learned good work habits at Joseph's workbench, and he later called hardworking fishermen as some of his first followers. And always the focus of his life was to "do the work of him who sent me."

Listen as James Hastings provides this sound advice on putting all you have into God's work.

WALK WITH JAMES HASTINGS

"A sure method of finding out what God wishes us to do is to work faithfully and conscientiously at the task that falls to our hand, watching ever for the guidance that God will surely send us.

"We shall never miss God's call as long as we are in the path of duty.

"We may not know where God is leading us, but we can be sure that doing our present work as well and as thoroughly as lies within our power is the best possible training for anything the future may hold for us.

"The work that we are doing may seem to us to be useless and unimportant. It is remarkable, however, how things which at the time seemed to be of no importance turn out to be useful, and how the training we have received, unconscious of its value though we were, bears fruit."

WALK CLOSER TO GOD

The church of Jesus Christ today is full of willing people: a few willing to work, the rest willing to let them.

When zest departs in the work of the Lord, labor becomes drudgery.

Don't allow busyness to turn to barrenness. After all, it's not so much how busy you are, but why you are busy. The bee is praised; the mosquito is swatted. Ask God's blessing on your job, and then do it willingly, joyfully and faithfully. ✤

ALL THE REASON IN THE WORLD TO WORSHIP

Then the man said, "Lord, I believe," and he worshiped him.

JOHN 9:38

John 9 describes a story of front-page significance. A man born blind received his sight—a miracle duplicated nowhere in the Old Testament. A miracle that the Pharisees found disturbing.

For the more they investigated, the more they were faced with a decision regarding the sight-giver.

They were unwilling to admit in their unbelief what the man born blind was only too willing to acknowledge, as Matthew Henry describes.

WALK WITH MATTHEW HENRY

"Believing with the heart, the man professed his faith in Christ: 'Lord, I believe you to be the Son of God.'

"He not only gave him the civil respect due to a great man and the acknowledgments owing to a kind benefactor, but he gave him divine honor, and worshiped him as the Son of God come in the flesh.

"None but God is to be worshiped, and by worshiping Jesus, the man acknowledged him to be God.

"True faith will show itself in humble adoration of the Lord Jesus. Those who believe in him will see all the reason in the world to worship him."

WALK CLOSER TO GOD

Who in your opinion is Jesus of Nazareth?

Before you answer, consider the implications of your response.

If you say he is a man (see John 9:11), then how do you explain his miracles?

If you say he is a prophet (see John 9:17), then where did he get his message?

If you say he is a man of God (see John 9:33), then where did he get his authority?

When a head of state enters a room, everyone stands. What if Jesus Christ, the Son of God, were to come into the room? What response would he deserve?

The man born blind saw clearly how to respond (see John 9:38). Let his example be the model for your response throughout the day. ❖

april17

WE KNOW WITH WHOM WE GO

My sheep listen to my voice; I know them, and they follow me.

JOHN 10:27

A musician who ignores the conductor, a soldier who disobeys his commander, a reporter who covers his eyes and ears—such situations are hard to imagine. But no one has any trouble at all thinking about sheep who fail to follow their shepherd. Everybody knows that sheep are just that dumb.

Charles Spurgeon points out why Christ's use of the shepherd-sheep imagery in John 10 is both appropriate and compelling.

WALK WITH CHARLES SPURGEON

"We should follow our Lord as unhesitatingly as sheep follow their shepherd, for he has a right to lead us wherever he pleases.

"We are not our own; we are bought with a price (see 1 Corinthians 6:19–20). Let us recognize the rights of the redeeming blood.

"The soldier follows his captain, the servant his master. Much more must we follow our Redeemer, to whom we are a purchased possession.

"We are not true to our profession of being Christians if we question the bidding of our leader and commander. Submission is our duty; making excuses is not.

"Wherever Jesus may lead us, he goes before us. If we do not know where we go, we know with whom we go. With such a companion, who will dread the perils of the road?"

WALK CLOSER TO GOD

Think back to the familiar phrases of Psalm 23. What does the Good Shepherd whom you follow do for you?

Provision: "He makes me lie down in green pastures" (verse 2).

Refreshment: "He refreshes my soul" (verse 3).

Leadership: "He guides me along the right paths" (verse 3).

Following the Shepherd is not a chore, but the way to an abundant life. When the shepherd calls, be quick to follow. After all, you are his! ✤

DISCIPLINE, DISAPPOINTMENT AND
THE DELAYS OF LOVE

Jesus loved Martha and her sister and Lazarus. So when he heard that Lazarus was sick, he stayed where he was two more days.

JOHN 11:5–6

When news reached Jesus that his friend Lazarus was critically ill, everyone expected Jesus to rush to Lazarus's side.

Instead, Jesus waited—an act of love misunderstood by many of his disciples.

But the pain had a purpose: that God might be glorified through it all. Alexander Maclaren offers these comforting words concerning the love of Christ.

WALK WITH ALEXANDER MACLAREN

"Christ's delays are the delays of love. If we could once get that conviction into our hearts, how quietly we should go about our work!

"What patience we would have if we recognized that the only reason which moves God in his choice of when to fulfill our desires and lift away burdens is our own good!

"Nothing but the purest, simplest love sways him in all that he does.

"Why should it be difficult for us to believe this?

"If we were more akin to looking at life—with all its often unwelcome duty, and its arrows of pain and sorrow—as a discipline, and were to think less about the unpleasantness and more about the purpose of what befalls us, we should find far less difficulty in understanding that his delay is born of love, and is a token of his tender care."

WALK CLOSER TO GOD

God loves his children too much to give them less than his best. His love is evident in different ways. He disciplines. He delays. He disappoints. Not to dishearten us, but to show us that even in the moments of waiting, he is at work.

Can we pierce through our own circumstances to see that truth? In a day when everything from Twitter to Google searches is instant, learning to wait on the Lord may prove to be a challenging assignment.

But then, isn't it worth it all when you know that the best is yet to come? ❖

WORSHIP: ACT OF AWE AND ADORATION

Then Mary took about a pint of pure nard, an expensive perfume; she poured it on Jesus' feet and wiped his feet with her hair.

JOHN 12:3

Worship: The act of centering one's attention on another worthy to receive it.

Mary, the sister of Lazarus, had good reason to adore Jesus. After all, he had raised her brother from the dead. But how could she turn her awe and adoration into action?

In his nineteenth-century masterpiece *The Suffering Savior*, German preacher F. W. Krummacher portrays Mary's worship.

WALK WITH F. W. KRUMMACHER

"The Lord has just placed himself at the table when Mary approaches. She feels impelled to display to him her inmost soul and to manifest her devout attachment to him.

"But how is she to do this? Words seem too poor. She has precious little to give.

"But what she has is an alabaster vessel of pure oil of spikenard, much valued. She brings it with her.

"With the utmost reverence she approaches her divine friend, breaks the vessel, spreads the spikenard on his head and feet, then humbly bends down and wipes the latter with her loosened tresses.

"In this affectionate act, she demonstrates a rare degree of devotion. She desires to worship him. He is always in her thoughts as her sole delight and the supreme object of her affections—all of which she expresses in the act of anointing."

WALK CLOSER TO GOD

Why would Mary willingly go to such lengths—in terms of cost and inconvenience—to magnify her Savior? And why would countless others like her do the same?

In short, why is Jesus worthy of your reverence and worship?

Go back to Calvary. Think of what was broken and poured out for you there.

Then come and pour out your richest offering of praise upon him. He is worthy! ✤

april20

DEATH AND THE "LAW OF INCREASE"

Unless a kernel of wheat falls to the ground and dies, it remains only a single seed. But if it dies, it produces many seeds.

JOHN 12:24

Take one barren field, bury a handful of seed, add a little water and the care of the farmer, and what do you have?

At first, you still have only a barren field.

But after a few months, the field will produce an abundant harvest.

In John 12 we read how Jesus used the simple illustration of a dying seed to explain to his followers the reason behind his death.

And A. B. Bruce provides this timely explanation of the "law of increase"—a law that Jesus' death portrays.

WALK WITH A. B. BRUCE

"Jesus' purpose is to make it clear to his disciples that death and increase may go together.

"Such is true in the case of grain; and the law of increase is equally true in his own case.

"He might have explained it this way: 'A grain of wheat, by dying, becomes fruitful; so I must die in order to become, on a large scale, an object of faith and source of life.'

"'During my lifetime I have had little visible success. Few have believed, many have disbelieved; and they are about to crown their unbelief by putting me to death.'

"'But my death, far from being—as they fancy—my defeat and destruction, will be but the beginning of my glorification.'"

WALK CLOSER TO GOD

The good news of the gospel began with the bad news of a tragic, unjust execution. It began with death.

A grain of wheat—dead and buried, lifeless, fruitless ... or so it would seem.

But three days later, all that changed.

From death sprang eternal life. The seemingly fruitless became the firstfruits of a mighty harvest that is still bearing fruit today.

Thank God right now for the harvest the death of his Son has accomplished in your life. ✤

april21

DRESSING AS THE KING IN A SERVANT'S TOWEL

Jesus knew that the Father had put all things under his power ... so he got up from the meal ... wrapped a towel around his waist ... and began to wash his disciples' feet.

JOHN 13:3–5

Presidents, kings, queens, ambassadors—they're called VIPs. Ordinary people they're not!

So try to imagine an ambassador washing a taxi driver's car. A queen collecting garbage. A king mopping the floor for the janitor.

That will give you an inkling of what Christ stooped to do, and why his model of servanthood made such an impact on his followers.

John Henry Jowett describes the scene we find in John 13.

WALK WITH JOHN HENRY JOWETT

"We might have assumed that divinity would have moved only in planetary orbits, and would have overlooked the petty streets and ways of men.

"But here the Lord of Glory girds himself with the apron of the slave and does menial service.

"That is the test of a growing servant's heart.

"We may be sure that we are growing smaller when we begin to degrade humble services. We are growing larger when we love ministries that never cry or lift their voices in the streets.

"When a man begins to despise the 'towel,' he has forgotten the words of the King who was not ashamed to wear it: 'I have set you an example that you should do as I have done for you' (John 13:15)."

WALK CLOSER TO GOD

You are a child of the King. That makes you part of a royal family. And the tendency is to want to live like royalty, when in fact you have been called to live like Christ.

Jesus had every right to demand the attentions of his followers. Instead, he took up a servant's towel and assumed a servant's role.

It's a humbling experience to follow his example. Especially in a day when humility is already in short supply.

Even so, the Servant-King's command to his followers still stands: "I have set you an example that you should do as I have done for you" (John 13:15). ❖

ONE WAY, HIS WAY — THE ONLY WAY

I am the way and the truth and the life. No one comes to the Father except through me.

JOHN 14:6

Christianity claims to offer the only way of salvation, to the exclusion of others. There are not any number of doors into heaven.

Nor are there any alternate routes into the family of God. Not if you take Jesus at his word (see John 14).

And that excludes many who are sincere — but sincerely wrong, as J. C. Ryle explains.

WALK WITH J. C. RYLE

"It avails nothing that a man is clever, learned, highly gifted, amiable, charitable, kindhearted, and zealous about some sort of religion.

"All this will not save his soul if he does not draw near to God by Christ's atonement and make use of God's own Son as his Mediator and Savior.

"God is so holy that all men are guilty and debtors in his sight. Sin is so sinful that no mortal man can make satisfaction for it. There must be a mediator, a ransom-payer, a redeemer, between us and God, or else we never can be saved.

"There is only one door, one bridge, one ladder, between earth and heaven: the crucified Son of God. Whosoever will enter in by that door may be saved; but to him who refuses, the Bible holds out no hope at all. Earnestness will never take one to heaven."

WALK CLOSER TO GOD

The Jews thought they could attain salvation by keeping the law. Many others, before and since, have worked out their own procedures to gain salvation.

But procedures don't save. Only one person does.

Jesus is the only way to God. Any other imagined approach can only lead to a dead end — literally.

Someone near you needs to know that — someone who has tried many of those dead-end streets.

You won't always be popular for pointing the way. But then, if one person finds the path of life because you cared enough to show it, will it really matter what others say? ❖

april23

VINE-LIFE IS THE ONLY LIFE

Remain in me, as I also remain in you. No branch can bear fruit by itself; it must remain in the vine. Neither can you bear fruit unless you remain in me.

JOHN 15:4

The only part of a vine that bears fruit is the branch. But an unattached branch can never bear fruit.

In capsule form, that is the lesson of John 15. There Christ described the process by which the true vine produces fruit through Christians. J. Hudson Taylor produced much spiritual fruit during his missionary career in China. He shares this personal insight regarding his struggles to understand the life of remaining, or abiding, in Christ—and the delightful discovery he made.

WALK WITH J. HUDSON TAYLOR

"For years I longed to abide, but I thought of it as a very high attainment to which I was unequal, involving spiritual heights to scale for which I did not have the needed strength.

"Abiding is not impossible; the Scriptures command it. And yet it seemed impossible to me until I saw that what I thought of as abiding was feeding, which is a conscious and voluntary act.

"We partake of our food at fixed intervals only, but we live and work in the strength of that food continuously.

"Abiding is not a thing of consciousness, but of fact. Do we cease to abide in our homes when we are asleep at night?

"So abiding in Christ is a state which commitment to Christ in faith achieves, and the reality of that faith is proved by the result—fruit."

WALK CLOSER TO GOD

Vitality and fruitfulness are the results of an abiding relationship with the vine.

But severed from the vine, the branch shrivels and dies. It cannot bear fruit.

Fruitfulness is more than a good idea. It's the Father's expectation for you as one of his children.

And after all, who should know more about turning barren lives into fruitful branches than the Gardener? ✤

april24

COMING FROM GLORY TO DWELL IN OUR HEARTS

But very truly I tell you, it is for your good that I am going away. Unless I go away, the Advocate will not come to you; but if I go, I will send him to you.

JOHN 16:7

It's easy to be confused about something—or someone—you cannot see.

In order to make the unseen clear, Jesus devoted much of his last discourse to the subject of the Holy Spirit—the helper, the third person of the Trinity.

R. A. Torrey explains who the Holy Spirit is and why his coming would be a source of comfort for Jesus' followers.

WALK WITH R. A. TORREY

"If we think of the Holy Spirit only as an impersonal power or influence, then our thought will constantly be, 'How can I get hold of and use the Holy Spirit?'

"But if we think of him in the Biblical way as a divine person—infinitely wise, infinitely holy, infinitely tender—then our thought will constantly be, 'How can the Holy Spirit get hold of and use me?'

"If we think of the Holy Spirit merely as a divine power or influence, there will be the temptation to feel as if we belong to a superior order of Christians.

"But if we think of the Holy Spirit in the Biblical way as a divine being of infinite majesty, coming down from glory to dwell in our hearts and take possession of our lives, it will put us in the dust, and make us walk very softly before God."

WALK CLOSER TO GOD

Christ knew it would be advantageous for his disciples if he returned to the Father, for his departure meant that the helper was coming!

Not an "it" but a "he."

Not an impersonal force, but a personal teacher, guide, consoler, and advocate.

Reread Mr. Torrey's final paragraph above. Then come to God today with soft steps and a grateful heart for the work of the Holy Spirit in your life. ❖

HE IS PRAYING FOR YOU

I have made you known to them, and will continue to make you known in order that the love you have for me may be in them and that I myself may be in them.

JOHN 17:26

"If I could hear Christ praying for me in the next room," declared Robert Murray McCheyne, "I would not fear a million enemies. Yet distance makes no difference; he is praying for me."

In John 17 we learn exactly what Jesus' desires for his followers are, as Ruth Paxson explains.

WALK WITH RUTH PAXSON

"Have you ever pondered the last words of this prayer: '... that I myself may be in them.' These simple but significant words breathe for the deepest desire of Christ's heart in relationship to his own. It is his consuming desire to reincarnate himself in the Christian.

"To be a Christian means to have the divine seed which was planted in our spirit at the new birth blossom out into growing conformity to his perfect life. It is to be daily 'transformed into his image.' Are you being so transformed?

"To be a Christian is to have Christ as the life of our minds, hearts, and wills so that it is he who thinks through our minds, loves through our hearts, and wills through our wills. It is to have Christ filling our life in ever-increasing measure until we have no life apart from him. Does he so fill you?"

WALK CLOSER TO GOD

Christ's prayer that final night before his death was not for the 11 disciples only.

He also had you on his mind. "My prayer is not for them alone," he said. "I pray also for those who will believe in me through their message" (John 17:20).

He prayed that you would be kept from evil, even as you live in an evil world.

He prayed that you would experience his love, even while the world hates you.

He prayed for your unity with other believers in a world marked by strife.

You may not audibly hear his voice. But you can face each day with confidence. He is praying for you! ✤

TRAGEDY AT GETHSEMANE

Jesus ... asked them, "Who is it you want?" "Jesus of Nazareth," they replied. "I am he," Jesus said ... [Then] they drew back and fell to the ground.

JOHN 18:4–6

"Jesus, knowing all that was going to happen to him, went out" (John 18:4).

He—and he alone—knew every step on the road to the cross.

The soldiers coming to seize him thought he was no more than a dangerous rebel who needed to be silenced. But they were unsuspecting participants in a divine drama, as G. Campbell Morgan explains.

WALK WITH G. CAMPBELL MORGAN

"There and then a remarkable thing happened, which was a supreme evidence of his majesty.

"He faced the soldiers and said, 'Who is it you want?' They replied, 'Jesus of Nazareth.'

"He then said, 'I am.' Our versions render it 'I am he.' Quite literally he simply said, 'I am.'

"When he did so, a cohort of Roman soldiers, the temple police, the rulers themselves, and Judas guiding them, drew back and fell to the ground.

"I think that something in the bearing of Jesus as he stood confronting his enemies caused their shrinking and fall. They could not lay a hand on him.

"Right to the very end he revealed the fact that no man could lay hands upon him until his hour was come.

"'I am,' he said, and they drew back and fell. Thus the majesty of Jesus was revealed."

WALK CLOSER TO GOD

Sovereign.

It's a big word to describe a majestic God. The God who knows the end from the beginning.

Human perception could see only tragedy in Gethsemane. Yet the plan of God was unfolding in all its perfection.

The soldiers came to Jesus to arrest him. Instead, his "I am" drove them to fall on their faces.

Let the thought of his "I am" cause you to fall before him as well. ❖

april27

A DEADLY DECISION, YET PART OF GOD'S PLAN

The Jews insisted, "We have a law, and according to that law he must die, because he claimed to be the Son of God".

JOHN 19:7

Pontius Pilate's otherwise obscure career will forever be remembered because of a decision he made: He condemned the Son of God to death.

Yet his deadly decision fulfilled God's will. As Jesus told him, "You would have no power over me if it were not given to you from above" (John 19:11).

Martin Luther reflects on the purpose of God as revealed in the crucifixion of his Son.

WALK WITH MARTIN LUTHER

"The greatest wonder on earth is that the Son of God should die the shameful death of the cross.

"It is astonishing that the Father should say to his only Son, who by nature is God: 'Go, let them hang you on the gallows.'

"The love of the everlasting Father was immeasurably greater toward his only begotten Son than the love of Abraham toward Isaac.

"Yet the Son was cast away like a worm, a scorn of men, an outcast of the people.

"At this the understanding of man stumbles, saying, 'How does he deal so unmercifully with him? He showed himself more kind to Caiaphas, Herod, and Pilate, than toward his only Son.'

"But to true Christians it is the greatest comfort; for we recognize that the merciful Father so loved the world, that he spared not his only begotten Son, but gave him up for us all, that whoever believes in him should not perish but have everlasting life."

WALK CLOSER TO GOD

From the perspective of earth, Pilate condemned an innocent man to death. From the perspective of heaven, "God so loved the world that he gave his one and only Son" (John 3:16).

In spite of the worst that human beings could do, God still brought forth the best. His loving purposes could not be undone.

Divine love is like that—never failing, always pursuing, always prevailing. And think of it—you're part of his plan! ✣

NO NEED FOR ADDITIONS

Jesus said, "It is finished." With that, he bowed his head and gave up his spirit.

JOHN 19:30

Most Christians begin well; but finishing well—or even at all—is another matter entirely.

Jesus was a finisher. He completed the work of redemption that he came to accomplish. He left nothing undone.

In the closing hours of his life he could pray to his Father, "I have brought you glory on earth by finishing the work you gave me to do" (John 17:4).

John Flavel shares this thought on the completed work of Christ.

WALK WITH JOHN FLAVEL

"Did Christ finish his work? How dangerous it is to join anything of our own to the righteousness of Christ, in pursuit of justification before God! Jesus Christ will never endure this; it reflects upon his work dishonorably. He will be all, or none, in our justification.

"If he has finished the work, what need is there of our additions? And if not, to what purpose are they? Can we finish that which Christ himself could not complete?

"Did he finish the work, and will he ever divide the glory and praise of it with us? No, no; Christ is no half-Savior.

"It is a hard thing to bring proud hearts to rest upon Christ for righteousness. God humbles the proud by calling sinners wholly from their own righteousness to Christ for their justification."

WALK CLOSER TO GOD

If these thoughts from the apostle Paul are the expression of your heart, pray them back to God

"I want to know Christ—yes, to know the power of his resurrection and participation in his sufferings, becoming like him in his death ... I do not consider myself yet to have taken hold of it. But one thing I do: Forgetting what is behind and straining toward what is ahead, I press on toward the goal to win the prize for which God has called me heavenward in Christ Jesus" (Philippians 3:10,13–14). ❖

april29

BASING BEHAVIOR ON YOUR BELIEF

Mary Magdalene went to the disciples with the news: "I have seen the Lord!".

JOHN 20:18

Heedless of his reminders that his death would not be permanent, the disciples mourned Jesus for three long days. When Sunday morning dawned, their attitude was no different, until...

Columba, an Irish missionary nearly 1,500 years ago, gives praise to God in this celebration of the first Easter.

WALK WITH COLUMBA

Christ is the Great Redeemer,
    The lover of the pure,
The fount of heavenly wisdom,
    Our trust and hope secure;
The armor of His soldiers,
    The Lord of earth and sky;
Our health while we are living,
    Our life when we shall die.
Down in the realm of darkness
    He lay a captive bound,
But at the hour appointed
    He rose, a victor crowned;

And now, to heaven ascended,
    He sits upon the throne,
In glorious dominion,
    His Father's and His own.
All glory to the Father,
    The unbegotten One;
All honor be to Jesus,
    His sole begotten Son;
And to the Holy Spirit—
    The perfect Trinity.
Let all the world give answer,
    "Amen, so let it be."

WALK CLOSER TO GOD

The resurrection transformed the grief of the disciples into hope and joy. They had seen the Lord! He was alive! Even Thomas—the skeptic of the group—responded, "My Lord and my God!" (John 20:28).

Do these words express your belief—and explain your behavior? ✤

april30

GUARDED AND GUIDED BY THE FATHER'S LOVE

Jesus answered, "If I want him to remain alive until I return, what is that to you? You must follow me".

JOHN 21:22

Peter was unique among the 12 disciples. He had unique potential. Unique problems. Unique personality.

But in John 21, Peter compared himself with another disciple, wondering if the future course of their lives would be similar.

The Lord's reply was simply, "Follow me."

Timothy Dwight offers this insight on the danger of comparing one Christian's lot in life with another's.

WALK WITH TIMOTHY DWIGHT

"How often we find that we never escape certain difficulties. We hope to escape them; we wonder why we do not.

"The Lord's reasoning is clear: We were made for the accomplishment of a special divine purpose—for the showing forth of a divinely formed character and life—and all allotments of experience are wisely fitted to that end.

"The work of Peter as a disciple of Jesus was intended to be different from that of John. He was to show the development of true life in a different way.

"Providential dealing takes all our living, and every part of our experience, into God's plan and purpose.

"It teaches us to trust that the natural movement of our lives is under a supernatural guidance, and that in all things we are guarded and guided by a Father's love."

WALK CLOSER TO GOD

Loving Father, you are the Lord over all, my Creator, my Savior. You know me better than I know myself.

Remind me often that my life is still under construction as you use my particular abilities for your glory.

Help me to see trials as opportunities to become more like the person you want me to be.

Thank you for the daily delight of following you. In the name of Jesus my Lord I pray. Amen. ✤

WAITING ON THE PROMISES

When they arrived, they went upstairs to the room ... They all joined together constantly in prayer.

ACTS 1:13 – 14

A man appears alive to many after his execution, then disappears into the clouds before a group of his closest friends.

Could you keep quiet if you had been part of that group of privileged observers?

Jesus' disciples did keep quiet until the proper time to unleash the Good News. Jesus told them to wait for the Holy Spirit before beginning the missionary enterprise he had committed to them.

Matthew Henry describes how they prayerfully obeyed.

WALK WITH MATTHEW HENRY

"It was now a time of trouble and danger with the disciples of Christ; they were as sheep in the middle of wolves. They had new work, and before they entered into it, they were continuously in prayer to God for his presence with them in it.

"They are in the best frame to receive spiritual blessings who are in a praying frame.

"Christ had promised shortly to send the Holy Spirit—a promise intended not to supersede prayer, but to quicken and encourage it. God will be enquired of for promised mercies, and the nearer the promise seems to be, the more earnestly we should pray for it.

"The disciples did this with one accord. This intimates that they were together in holy love, and that there was no quarrel or discord among them. Those who so keep the unity of the Spirit in the bond of peace are best prepared to receive the comforts of the Holy Ghost."

WALK CLOSER TO GOD

For the disciples, hastily beginning the work of the gospel—apart from the Holy Spirit—might have caused more harm than good. Instead, they prayed and waited for God's timetable to take effect.

Walking with God, rather than running ahead of him. That's still the best way to "work" the will of God in your life today. ✤

NOT A DESTINATION, BUT A BEGINNING

They devoted themselves to the apostles' teaching and to the fellowship, to the breaking of bread and to prayer.

ACTS 2:42

Perhaps you thought you had "arrived" when you became a Christian. And in a sense, you had!

You arrived at the starting line of a race—a race that requires devotion, as the first converts to Christianity learned (Acts 2:42).

A. W. Tozer echoes this theme in his insightful look at conversion—an event which the Bible portrays more as a place to start than to finish.

WALK WITH A. W. TOZER

"Conversion for the early Christians was not a destination; it was the beginning of a journey.

"And right there is often where the Biblical emphasis differs from our own.

"In our eagerness to make converts, we allow our hearers to absorb the idea that they can deal with their entire responsibility once and for all by an act of believing.

"In the Book of Acts, faith was for each believer a beginning, not a bed in which to lie while waiting for the Lord's triumph.

"Believing was not a once-done act. It was an attitude of heart and mind which inspired and enabled the believer to follow the Lord wherever he went."

WALK CLOSER TO GOD

Whether in the first century or the twenty-first, the hope of heaven comes the same way—through believing faith in the Savior.

That's step one in the lifelong adventure of walking with God. But one step does not make a journey. Indeed, there are many steps to follow.

Instruction in the Word, fellowship with other believers, communication with the Father (see Acts 2:42)—each represents a step in the right direction.

And in the process of learning to walk, you'll discover that following the Lord is the only race in which you grow stronger with each step you take. ❖

THE GREATER BLESSEDNESS OF GIVING

Then Peter said, "Silver or gold I do not have, but what I do have I give you. In the name of Jesus Christ of Nazareth, walk".

ACTS 3:6

There are still some things money can't buy. Like salvation, for instance. And the power of God at work in a life.

The lame man in Acts 3 learned that lesson.

When Peter and John passed by, he begged for alms—but instead he received legs. A miraculous testimony to the God whose power cannot be bought or sold!

Alexander Maclaren examines Peter's words and the message they convey to servants of God.

WALK WITH ALEXANDER MACLAREN

"Peter did not say 'what I do have,' as if what he was offering was inferior to money. Instead he intended a very different tone.

"The expression eloquently magnifies the power which he possessed as far more precious than wealth.

"God gives us all our possessions and spiritual riches as well, not only that we may enjoy them ourselves, but that we may impart them, and so experience the greater blessedness of giving over receiving.

"How often it has been true that a poor church has been a miracle-working church.

"But when a church could not say 'Silver or gold I do not have,' it has also had no power to say 'In the name of Jesus Christ of Nazareth, walk.'"

WALK CLOSER TO GOD

Peter did not have what the lame man expected. But he did have what the lame man needed: the power of God. The same power that transformed Peter from a denier to a declarer of the Savior. Perhaps you hesitate to share your Savior with someone because of what you don't possess: money, status, ability with words.

If so, consider this liberating thought: Even without a coin in your pocket or purse, you possess something that is more precious than gold, and more powerful than dynamite. ✤

may**4**

MAKING THE LIFE OF CHRIST VISIBLE

When they saw the courage of Peter and John ... they were astonished and they took note that these men had been with Jesus.

ACTS 4:13

Peter and John were men of meager means and lowly reputation, men who were at home on the sea and out of place before the educated Jewish leaders of the Sanhedrin.

They had every reason to stand in awe of their accusers. Instead, the Sanhedrin marveled at the boldness of these unlearned men.

Joseph Parker comments on the encounter that transformed these rough fishermen into robust spokesmen for the gospel.

WALK WITH JOSEPH PARKER

"We cannot have personal contact with Christ without people knowing it.

"Once there were some very poor, unlettered men — men who might have been taken from the fishing boat, from the plow, or from some ordinary job.

"And they went before some very great magistrates who did not do manual labor. And these magistrates looked at them and said, 'How ordinary these men are! What disadvantages they must have undergone! And yet there is something about them that makes them special. There is a kind of radiance on all that roughness of exterior.'

"To be with Jesus is an education; to be closeted with Christ is a refining process.

"We ask no other distinction, we long for no greater fame, than to be taken knowledge of that we have been with Jesus."

WALK CLOSER TO GOD

Peter and John impressed the Sanhedrin with their bold stand for the Savior. They had taken Christ's words to heart: "Let your light shine before others, that they may see your good deeds and glorify your Father in heaven" (Matthew 5:16).

They reflected the light of Christ to the Sanhedrin; and, true to his word, God was glorified.

It's seldom hard for others to detect when you have been with the Savior. And that's a nice reflection on him! ♣

A HIGH PRICE FOR A PRECIOUS MESSAGE

The apostles left the Sanhedrin, rejoicing because they had been counted worthy of suffering disgrace for the Name.

ACTS 5:41

At times, the bearer of good news may be in for a rude awakening! Not everyone will receive it as such.

In Acts 5 the apostles were on trial for declaring the gospel of a risen Savior. The threat of personal injury was real. Was the Good News urgent enough to risk even that?

Martin Luther probes the attitude of the disciples—people who were willing to pay a high price to carry a precious message.

WALK WITH MARTIN LUTHER

"See to it when you suffer persecution that you have a genuine divine cause for which you suffer and you are truly convinced of it.

"Then you can have the confidence to say: This cause does not belong to me but to Christ, my Lord. At his word I will take the risk of doing and forsaking whatever I should.

"'Who cares if a foolish emperor fumes in his rage and threatens as long as I am right with God in heaven?' He who comforts you and takes pleasure in you is almighty and eternal. When it is all over, he will still be with you.

"Be grateful and happy in your heart that you are worthy of suffering, like the apostles who went forth leaping for joy over the fact that they were disgraced and beaten."

WALK CLOSER TO GOD

The disciples feared no earthly tyrant because they answered to the God of heaven.

Suffering could not daunt them. Threats could not deter them.

On the contrary, they rejoiced to suffer shame for the one who suffered for them.

Have your attempts at sharing the Good News of Christ resulted in ridicule or rejection? Then you are in good company!

Remember whose cause it is—and whose comfort you are promised—when your "good news" for others turns into "bad news" for you. ✤

THE MESSAGE OF POWER IN A MANNER OF MEEKNESS

Now Stephen, a man full of God's grace and power, performed great wonders and signs among the people.

ACTS 6:8

Acts 6 introduces you to Stephen, a man "full of God's grace and power." A man with an irresistible message.

And yet, when called on to defend the faith with his life, Stephen responded with Christlike humility.

Though his message was full of power, his demeanor was full of meekness—a contrast that Jonathan Edwards helps to explain.

WALK WITH JONATHAN EDWARDS

"The truly humble Christian is clothed with lowliness, mildness, meekness, gentleness of spirit and behavior. These things are just like garments to him.

"Christian humility has no such thing as roughness, or contempt, or fierceness, or bitterness in its nature. It makes a person like a little child, harmless and innocent, that no one needs to fear; or like a lamb, free of all bitterness, wrath, anger, and clamor.

"Yet in searching and awakening the conscience, he should be a son of thunder. He should do it without judging individuals, leaving it to conscience and the Spirit of God to make the particular application.

"But all his conversation should reflect lowliness and good will, love and pity to all mankind.

"He should be like a lion to guilty consciences, but like a lamb to men and women."

WALK CLOSER TO GOD

Gentle as a lamb and powerful as a lion. A seeming contradiction—until you know the Lamb of God who is also the Lion of Judah. Jesus Christ, the one who possesses all power, yet dealt tenderly with those he came to serve, points the way to a witness that is more powerful than words alone.

A witness that is both tender and tough. That speaks the truth in love, and clothes strength in humility.

A witness that others around you need to hear and experience today. ✤

GAZING INTO HEAVEN'S WINDOW

But Stephen, full of the Holy Spirit, looked up to heaven and saw the glory of God, and Jesus standing at the right hand of God.

ACTS 7:55

Stephen's last message provides a moving portrayal of God's dealings on behalf of his people.

The priests and rabbis, no doubt impressed with Stephen's grasp of the Old Testament, were not at all impressed with his application of that truth to their lives: "You are just like your ancestors: You always resist the Holy Spirit!" (Acts 7:51).

Blood boiled. Stones flew. And Stephen's death became a turning point in the history of the New Testament church.

Matthew Henry looks at the significance of Stephen's life to Christians today.

WALK WITH MATTHEW HENRY

"The heavens were opened to give Stephen a view of the happiness he was going to so that he might, in prospect of it, go cheerfully through death.

"Would we by faith look up, we might see the heavens opened.

"Heaven is opened for the settling of a correspondence between God and humans, that his favors and blessings may come down to us, and our prayers and praises may go up to him.

"We may also see the glory of God, as far as he has revealed it in his Word, and the sight of this will carry us through all the terrors of suffering and death."

WALK CLOSER TO GOD

At the moment of his death, Stephen's gaze was fixed in the right place. He looked directly up into heaven and saw Jesus standing at God's right hand. He saw beyond the torment, cursing and physical abuse he was suffering to the heavenly reunion awaiting him with his Savior.

"Look, I see heaven open." It's really not that difficult a sight to see even today—if God's Word is your compass and God's Son is your guide! ✤

SOMETHING MONEY CAN'T BUY

When Simon saw that the Spirit was given ... he offered them money and said, "Give me also this ability".

ACTS 8:18–19

Simon the sorcerer.

He was known in Samaria as "the Great Power." Yet he sought to buy what no amount of money could buy: the power of the Holy Spirit.

Misunderstanding about the Holy Spirit—who he is and why he came—lay at the root of Simon's problem. Gregory of Nazianzus, the fourth-century church father, offers this helpful insight.

WALK WITH GREGORY OF NAZIANZUS

"The deity of the Holy Spirit ought to be clearly recognized in Scripture.

"Look at these facts: Christ is born; the Spirit is his forerunner. Christ is baptized; the Spirit bears witness. Christ is tempted; the Spirit leads him up. Christ ascends; the Spirit takes his place.

"What great things are there in the character of God which are not found in the Spirit? What titles which belong to God are not also applied to him?

"He is called the Spirit of God, the Spirit of Christ, the mind of Christ, the Spirit of the Lord, the Spirit of adoption, of truth, of liberty; the Spirit of wisdom, of understanding, of counsel, of might, of knowledge, of godliness, of the fear of God.

"This only begins to show how unlimited he is."

WALK CLOSER TO GOD

The Holy Spirit is more than a power to be reckoned with. He is a person to indwell you. A Comforter to console you. A Counselor to advise you. An Advocate to defend you. An Intercessor to pray for you. A Guide to direct you.

As you continue your journey through the book of Acts, don't be surprised if you encounter the Holy Spirit frequently.

All the resources of God were available to the New Testament believers in the person of the Holy Spirit. The disciples depended daily on his power and leading. And that power is available to you today! ✣

may9

THE TRANSFORMING POWER OF FORGIVENESS

He [Saul] ... tried to join the disciples, but they were all afraid of him.

ACTS 9:26

Saul of Tarsus, public enemy number one of the church!

Yet God had plans for Saul to become his chosen vessel, to bear his name before the Gentiles, to spread his truth far and wide.

At first the church had grave doubts about Saul. H. A. Ironside shares this illustration of the response only God can produce toward an enemy-turned-brother.

WALK WITH H. A. IRONSIDE

"On the Lord's Day a group of missionaries and believers in New Guinea were gathered together to observe the Lord's Supper.

"After one young man sat down, a missionary recognized that a sudden tremor had passed through the young man's body that indicated he was under a great nervous strain. Then in a moment all was quiet again.

"The missionary whispered, 'What was it that troubled you?'

"'Ah,' he said, 'But the man who just came in killed and ate the body of my father. And now he has come in to remember the Lord with us.'

"'At first I didn't know whether I could endure it. But it is all right now. He is washed in the same precious blood.'

"And so together they had Communion. It is a marvelous thing, the work of the Holy Spirit of God. Does the world know anything of this?"

WALK CLOSER TO GOD

Is it really possible to truly forgive a former enemy who is now your Christian brother or sister?

Consider:

From the cross, Jesus forgave those responsible for putting him there.

The Jerusalem believers forgave the man who formerly sought to destroy them.

A young man in New Guinea found strength to forgive his father's murderer.

Indeed, does the world know anything of this? Do you know anything of this? ✤

TO HEAR IS TO OBEY

While Peter was still thinking about the vision, the Spirit said to him ... "Get up and go downstairs. Do not hesitate to go with them, for I have sent them".

ACTS 10:19–20

Peter could have written a book entitled *The Pitfalls of Disobedience*, for he surely stumbled into many of them! When it was time to think, Peter would talk. When it was time to stand, Peter would run. And when it was time to "get up and go," Peter would stop and ponder.

Even when God chose Peter to take the gospel to the Gentiles, it took three times for his reticent apostle finally to get the message!

John Calvin explains the importance of prompt obedience to the Lord's commands.

WALK WITH JOHN CALVIN

"We must not follow God with a doubting and vacillating mind, but with one that is composed and firm.

"The Lord wishes us to defer to him so much that, when we have heard him, we will have no argument about what we need to do, but will decide without any question that what he commands must be done.

"Certainly his will is worthy to show us the way, when all the doubts have been scattered, and to bring our minds into ready obedience.

"Peter is not permitted to pass judgment on the question, because God is the originator of the business.

"What it amounts to is that we ought to be content merely with God's say-so, so that we may obey his command."

WALK CLOSER TO GOD

There is a time to wait on the Lord and a time to act on his will. God's part is to make his will clear; your part is to do his will promptly.

Disobedience—thinking when you should be doing or questioning when you should be trusting—can only result in delay and disappointment.

To obey or not to obey. Child of God, that's a decision you shouldn't have to think about for very long! ✤

CARRYING CHRIST WITH YOU

The Lord's hand was with them, and a great number of people believed and turned to the Lord.

ACTS 11:21

The disciples must have seemed out of place in the bustling commercial atmosphere of Antioch. But sensing they were there by divine appointment, they dedicated themselves to share their faith. And the result? A secular city turned upside down.

Regardless of your employment situation, the Lord has placed you where you are for a purpose: to introduce others to the Savior. Charles Spurgeon wisely challenges you to use every opportunity.

WALK WITH CHARLES SPURGEON
"Wherever you are called to go, you should make known the gospel of Jesus. Look upon this as your calling and occupation.

"You will not be scattered now by persecution, but should the demands of business carry you into different situations, use that travel for missionary purposes.

"Providence every now and then bids you move your tent; take care that wherever it is pitched you carry with you a testimony for Jesus.

"At times the necessities of health require relaxation, and this may take you to different places of public resort. Seize the opportunity to encourage the churches in such localities by your presence, and endeavor to spread the knowledge of Jesus among those to whom you may be directed.

"The position which you occupy in society is not an accidental one. You are placed where you are that you may be a preserving salt to those around you, a sweet savor of Christ to all who know you."

WALK CLOSER TO GOD
One writer summarizes the challenge this way: "If Christ comes to rule in the hearts of men, it will be because we take him with us on the tractor, behind the desk, or when we're making a sale to a customer."

God knows what he is about when he guides you into a location and a vocation. All that remains is for you to seize the opportunities he has placed within your reach. ✣

SEEING IS NOT ALWAYS BELIEVING

Peter was kept in prison, but the church was earnestly praying to God for him.

ACTS 12:5

If the opponents of the church had known better, they would have left it alone.

Persecution only poured oil on the fire, spreading the gospel all the more. Killing James and imprisoning Peter drove the church to its knees — not in submission, but in prayer.

Yet even the church was surprised by God's miraculous power! A. B. Simpson reflects on the awesome power of prayer.

WALK WITH A. B. SIMPSON

"Prayer is the link that connects us with God. It is the bridge that spans every gulf and bears us over every abyss of danger or need.

"How significant is this picture of the New Testament church: Peter in prison, the Jews triumphant, Herod supreme, the arena of martyrdom awaiting the dawning of the morning.

"'But the church was earnestly praying to God for him.'

"And what is the sequel?

"The prison open, the apostle free, the Jews baffled, the wicked king divinely smitten, and the Word of God rolling on in greater victory.

"Do we know the power of our supernatural weapon? Do we dare to use it with the authority of a faith that commands as well as asks? God grant us holy audacity and divine confidence.

"He is not wanting great men and women, but he is wanting people who will dare to prove the greatness of their God."

WALK CLOSER TO GOD

Which motto summarizes your habits in prayer?

"When all else fails, pray."

"Before doing anything, pray."

The first views prayer as the place of last resort when human abilities have run out. The second realizes that unless God empowers and directs, human strength and wisdom will never suffice.

Are you tired of trying to stand on your own?

Dropping to your knees gives God the opportunity to prove his greatness in your life. ❖

may13

KNOWN BY NAME AND REPUTATION

Then Saul, who was also called Paul, filled with the Holy Spirit, looked straight at [him].
ACTS 13:9

It may surprise you to learn that the apostle Paul is better known by his humble nickname Paul (which means "little one") than by his kingly given name Saul (which means "asked of God").

But as one scholar described it, the day soon came in the Roman Empire when men would call their dogs Nero and their sons Paul!

Alexander Maclaren probes the significance of Paul's change of name and his change of direction and attitude.

WALK WITH ALEXANDER MACLAREN

"From the change of the apostle's name, we may learn that the only way to help people is to get to their level.

"If you want to bless people, you must identify yourself with them. It is no use standing on a pedestal above them, and patronizingly talking down to them. You cannot scold, or bully, or lecture men and women into the acceptance of religious truth if you take a position of superiority.

"The motivation which led to the apostle's change of name from Saul—with its memories of royal dignity—to the Roman name Paul, is this: 'I have become all things to all people so that by all possible means I might save some' (1 Corinthians 9:22).

"The principle demonstrated in this comparatively little matter is the same principle that influenced the Master in the mightiest of all events."

WALK CLOSER TO GOD

No matter what name you answer to, humility must be your "calling card" when you present the gospel.

Even the Son of God "made himself nothing by taking the very nature of a servant, being made in human likeness" (Philippians 2:7), that he might bring men and women to himself.

If your reputation or title gets in the way of another's response to the claims of Christ, it's time for a change—in you!

After all, the only names that really count are the ones written in the book of life. ✤

may14

RESPONDING TO WORDS THAT WOUND

Then some Jews ... won the crowd over. They stoned Paul and dragged him outside the city, thinking he was dead.

ACTS 14:19

There is plenty in the gospel for people to find upsetting. The fact of sin. The ugly specter of the cross. The need for repentance.

So it shouldn't surprise you when your witness produces a "rocky" response.

John Chrysostom, a fourth-century preacher, offers this timeless insight on how to respond to sticks, stones and words.

WALK WITH JOHN CHRYSOSTOM

"Paul's enemies wounded him with stones; there is a wounding with words even worse than stones.

"What then must we do? The same thing Paul did. He did not hate those who cast stones at him; but after they had dragged him out, he entered again into their city to be a benefactor to those who had done him such wrongs.

"If you also endure anyone who harshly insults you and has done you wrong, then you also have been stoned.

"And what had Paul done that he deserved to be stoned? He was bringing men and women away from error, and bringing them to God—benefits worthy of crowns, not of stones.

"Has one insulted you? Hold your peace, and bless if you can.

"Then you also will have preached the Word, and given a lesson of gentleness and meekness."

WALK CLOSER TO GOD

Consider what Paul endured: "Five times I received from the Jews the forty lashes minus one. Three times I was beaten with rods, once I was pelted with stones, three times I was shipwrecked, I spent a night and a day in the open sea" (2 Corinthians 11:24–25).

Paul's example is an encouragement to all who face the sting of stones—or rebukes—in their witness for Christ. When others respond by striking back, rejoice that at least a seed has been planted. And leave it to God that someday a crown will follow! ❖

may15

STANDING FAST FOR OUR FREEDOM IN CHRIST

Then some of the believers who belonged to the party of the Pharisees stood up and said, "The Gentiles must be circumcised and required to keep the law of Moses".

ACTS 15:5

Prejudice is a dirty word. But prejudice is not limited to race. The first church council was called because of the prejudice of one group of Christians. The newly converted Pharisees wanted the Gentiles to participate in ceremonies that foreshadowed the sacrifice of Christ.

But Paul would have none of it. Once Jesus shed his blood, God required no more blood to be shed. And if God no longer required it, how could the Pharisees? Paul's thought is echoed by Charles Hodge.

WALK WITH CHARLES HODGE

"It is a great error in morals, and a great practical evil, to make that sinful which is in fact innocent. Christian love never requires this or any other sacrifice of truth. Paul would not consent, even for the sake of avoiding offense, that eating food offered to idols should be made a sin; he strenuously maintained the reverse. He represents those who thought differently as weak in faith, as being under an error from which more knowledge and piety would free them.

"We should stand fast in the freedom for which Christ has set us free, and not allow our consciences to be burdened by a yoke of slavery to human opinions. There is a strong tendency to treat as matters of conscience things which God has never enjoined.

"It is often necessary to assert our Christian liberty at the expense of incurring censure in order to preserve right principles. Our Savior consented to be regarded as a Sabbath-breaker, a drunkard, and a friend of tax collectors and 'sinners'; but wisdom was proved right by her actions."

WALK CLOSER TO GOD

In a way, we are in a better position to settle such issues than those in Paul's time. We may not have an infallible council, but we have God's infallible counsel—the completed Bible. Praise God that in his Word we have a trustworthy standard to distinguish duty from freedom.

Judgment by the standard of the Bible is required (see 2 Timothy 3:16). But judgment by an arbitrary standard is forbidden (see Matthew 7:1). Have you held some personal traditions and opinions so dear that you have judged others by them? ❖

PAINFUL PARTINGS AND STRUGGLING SAINTS

They had such a sharp disagreement that they parted company.

ACTS 15:39

Contrary to what you may have thought, missionaries are not "super Christians."

Like the rest of us humans, missionaries have been known to quarrel, get tired, experience heartbreak and even make mistakes.

As you will learn from the confrontation between Paul and Barnabas, even the most gifted and dedicated of fellow workers can disagree. What they need at such times is not criticism and condemnation, but rather churches who care, friends who pray and individuals who are quick to forgive.

Martin Luther explores the lesson to be learned from the painful separation of Paul and Barnabas.

WALK WITH MARTIN LUTHER

"Here it appears either Paul or Barnabas went too far. It must have been a violent disagreement to separate two associates who were so closely united. Indeed, the text indicates as much.

"Such examples are written for our consolation: for it is a great comfort to us to hear that great saints, who have the Spirit of God, also struggle. Those who say that saints do not sin would deprive us of this comfort.

"Samson, David, and many other celebrated men full of the Holy Spirit fell into grievous sins. Job and Jeremiah cursed the day of their birth; Elijah and Jonah were weary of life and desired death.

"No one has ever fallen so grievously that he may not rise again. Conversely, no one stands so firmly that he may not fall. If Peter (and Paul and Barnabas) fell, I too may fall. If they rose again, I too may rise again."

WALK CLOSER TO GOD

"God is not human, that he should lie, nor a human being, that he should change his mind. Does he speak and then not act? Does he promise and not fulfill?" (Numbers 23:19).

Fix your gaze upon him, and regardless of who stumbles and falls around you, you can be certain: He stands eternally! ❖

HOW WISE HIS WAY, HOW STRONG HIS WILL

Having been kept by the Holy Spirit from preaching the word in the province of Asia . . .
they tried to enter Bithynia, but the Spirit of Jesus would not allow them to.

ACTS 16:6–7

Paul's ambition was right, but his timing was wrong. He had a good idea: evangelize Asia. But God had a better idea: evangelize Europe!

And once God's will was clear, Paul wasted no time in obeying.

G. Campbell Morgan provides this helpful analysis of how to respond when the what of God's will is clear but the why is not.

WALK WITH G. CAMPBELL MORGAN

"Obedience to the Spirit's guidance when we cannot understand the reason—that experience is not so rare.

"Over and over again in the path of true service a great opportunity is open right before us, and we are not permitted to avail ourselves of it.

"Or we are in the midst of work which is full of real success, and we are called to abandon it. We should never hesitate to do so.

"This wonderful page of apostolic history teaches us that God's outlook is greater and grander than our own. We may always leave the issue to him, and presently we shall learn how wise his way, how strong his will."

WALK CLOSER TO GOD

From Paul's perspective, the closed doors to Bithynia and Asia must have seemed puzzling. But from the perspective of hindsight—a perspective God enjoys from the start—consider what happened: Paul traveled throughout Greece, preaching and establishing churches. Afterward, he returned to Ephesus, the heart of the province of Asia, and preached until "all the Jews and Greeks who lived in the province of Asia heard the word of the Lord" (Acts 19:10).

And Bithynia? Paul may not have returned there personally, but Peter did address his first letter to the Christians in Bithynia (see 1 Peter 1:2). It's a truth you cannot learn too well: Understanding God's plan can wait; obeying God's will cannot. ✣

KEEPING THE SIMPLE TRUTH SIMPLE

"Sirs, what must I do to be saved?" They replied, "Believe in the Lord Jesus, and you will be saved".

Acts 16:30–31

Two notorious "outlaws" in the prison at Philippi were locked in solitary confinement, singing hymns at midnight. Suddenly, without warning, there was a violent earthquake; every prisoner's chains were loosened and every door was opened.

Imagine the dismay of the Philippian jailer. For a man in his position the escape of even one prisoner meant certain death. Yet in his midnight moment of crisis, the jailer discovered someone who specializes in giving life. J. Wilbur Chapman provides this timely comment on the jailer's newfound life.

WALK WITH J. WILBUR CHAPMAN

"God makes it clear that there can be no real life until there is a step taken first of all by faith.

"To make it very clear, the best answer is the one given to the Philippian jailer: 'Believe in the Lord Jesus, and you will be saved.'

"There is something very significant in the way the names of Jesus Christ are used. When he is called Lord, it is to emphasize his kingly office, his reigning power; and what can the meaning be but this, when we are told to believe on him as Lord?

"We must reach the place where we are willing to let him rule and reign in our lives.

"Can you submit to this? He will never make a failure of it.

"Give him absolute control; never take a step without his guidance — this is the secret of grace and joy."

WALK CLOSER TO GOD

The Philippian jailer didn't need a lecture on theology. He just needed a simple, one-sentence sermon: "Believe in the Lord Jesus, and you will be saved."

When the heart is prepared, the odds are good you won't need oratory or arguments to lead another to the Savior.

So keep it short. Clear. Sincere. And when the door swings ajar, be ready to enter! ♣

may**19**

INQUIRING MINDS AND SEARCHING HEARTS

The Berean Jews were of more noble character than those in Thessalonica, for they received the message with great eagerness and examined the Scriptures every day to see if what Paul said was true.

ACTS 17:11

Envy in Thessalonica. Mocking in Athens. Intimidation in Corinth.

But in Berea? A breath of fresh air. The Berean Jews were "of more noble character" than the other Jews Paul encountered.

They were more responsive. More serious about the claims of Christ on their lives. More inquisitive about the implications of what they were hearing.

Johann Peter Lange expands on the attitude that set the Berean Jews apart.

WALK WITH JOHANN PETER LANGE

"Christian nobility of soul exhibits two features: readiness to receive truth and eagerness to examine the evidence.

"True faith is not blind acceptance. It does not dispense with reason, evidence, and argument.

"It is, on the contrary, ready to prove all things with sincerity, to investigate earnestly, to institute a thorough search.

"The people of Berea did not blindly accept Paul's words, but first searched whether he taught the truth.

"They are not criticized for this, but instead are commended for the noble spirit which motivated them."

WALK CLOSER TO GOD

Apart from one verse in Acts 20, the Bereans are not mentioned again in the Bible. But their testimony lives on in the noble character they displayed.

The same character you can demonstrate today in your attitude toward God's Word.

The character you can pray for in the lives of those who hear your witness.

The character you can develop, involving a ready mind and a searching heart.

Does God's truth deserve anything less? ❖

THE DANGER IS REAL

*While Gallio was proconsul of Achaia, the Jews of Corinth made a united attack on Paul
… And Gallio showed no concern whatever.*

ACTS 18:12,17

Apathy suffocates the church of Jesus Christ and paralyzes the work of truth. All that is necessary for evil to prevail is for good people to do nothing. And nothing is precisely what indifference breeds.

What happens when unconcerned listeners encounter uncompromising truth? The apathetic person comes out the loser every time. H. A. Ironside elaborates.

WALK WITH H. A. IRONSIDE

"Gallio the Indifferent! History tells us that he was the brother of Seneca the philosopher, who exclaimed, 'Few men are so agreeable about anything as my brother Gallio is about everything!'

"Yet this amiable man lost a marvelous opportunity to hear the gospel from the lips of Paul, and perhaps lost his soul as well, just because he did not consider eternal things worthy of his attention.

"To him the whole matter was beneath contempt, consisting only, as he supposed, of a quarrel about words and names and Jewish ceremonial observances. So he turned scornfully away without hearing that glad message which God was sending out in grace to a needy world.

"His attitude stands out as a warning to others not to treat lightly the privileges God gives, lest the day of doom find them still in their sins."

WALK CLOSER TO GOD

If someone announced in words both clear and plain, "The building is on fire!" would you respond with a yawn and a shrug? Of course not! Life-threatening situations demand life-saving steps. If the warning is true, then the danger is real. And only prompt action can avert certain disaster.

Think of the gospel as just such a call to action. The danger is real; the penalty for sin is sure; but the lifeboat is standing by in the person of Jesus Christ, the Savior. That's good news indeed for all who take shelter in him. But not for those who—like Gallio—greet him with a yawn and a shrug. ✣

BURNING BOOKS AND BRIDGES

A number who had practiced sorcery brought their scrolls together and burned them publicly.
ACTS 19:19

Would you build a bonfire using two million dollars' worth of kindling?

That's approximately what "fifty thousand drachmas" in Roman times would be worth in today's currency!

The book burning in Ephesus was expensive, and Luke records how the gospel brought about economic disruption in the idolatrous city of Ephesus. But such changes are often necessary when God is at work, as Albert Barnes explains.

WALK WITH ALBERT BARNES

"The Word of God had power in this wicked city, and the power must have been mighty which would make them willing to destroy their property.

"From this instructive passage we may learn that: 1. True religion has the power to break the hold of sinners on unjust and dishonest means of living. 2. Those who have been engaged in an un-Christian and dishonorable practice will abandon it when they become Christians. 3. Their abhorrence of their former course ought to be expressed as publicly as was the offence. 4. The evil practice will be abandoned at any sacrifice, however great. The question is 'what is right?' Not 'what will it cost?'

"If what they did when they were converted was right—and who can doubt it?—it sets forth a great principle on which new converts should act."

WALK CLOSER TO GOD

Cherished dreams. Ingrained habits. Goals for advancement in a career. Previously unquestioned ethics. Sorcery in its many subtle forms. Each may take on a new appearance when seen in the light of God's Word.

Albert Barnes's remarks provide helpful guidelines to show believers how the Word of God prevails in our daily life to replace un-Christian conduct with Christian convictions. ✤

may**22**

WE TAKE CAPTIVE EVERY THOUGHT

You know, my friends, that we receive a good income from this business. And you see and hear how this fellow Paul has convinced and led astray large numbers of people here in Ephesus and in practically the whole province of Asia. He says that gods made by human hands are no gods at all.

ACTS 19:25–26

"Christianity is just a crutch."

Has anyone ever summarily dismissed your faith with those words? To such a critic, Christianity is made foolish because the Christian has a vested interest in believing in God. But according to Matthew Henry, Christians are not the only ones bringing vested interests to the claims of Christ.

WALK WITH MATTHEW HENRY

"It is natural for men to jealously guard, whether right or wrong, the means by which they get their wealth. Many have, for this reason alone, set themselves against the gospel of Christ, because it calls men off from those crafts which are unlawful, however much wealth is to be obtained by them.

"There are those who will haggle for that which is most grossly absurd and unreasonable, and which carries along with it its own conviction of falsehood, if it has but human laws and worldly interests on its side."

WALK CLOSER TO GOD

Is our critic's criticism legitimate? In a word, no. A "vested interest" critic is wielding a two-edged sword. His decision not to believe is not without its motives. Since he rejects Christ because of his own vested interest, his criticism of us is hypocrisy.

"Be prepared to give an answer ... for the hope that you have" (1 Peter 3:15). God commands us to "answer a fool according to his folly, or he will be wise in his own eyes" (Proverbs 26:5). ❖

may23

FUNCTIONING IN A SPHERE OF DIVINE DESIGN

I consider my life worth nothing to me; my only aim is to finish the race and complete the task the Lord Jesus has given me — the task of testifying to the good news of God's grace.

ACTS 20:24

What things can you think of that just might be worth dying for?

Your family. Perhaps a few close friends. Your country.

What about a group of people you've never met?

In effect, that's what Paul told the Ephesian elders. He was prepared to die in order to take the gospel to those who hadn't heard.

What's more, he didn't call such sacrifice a burden; he called it a joy. Let Oswald Chambers probe the basis of Paul's unusual joy.

WALK WITH OSWALD CHAMBERS

"Joy means the perfect fulfillment of that for which I was created and saved.

"The joy of our Lord came in doing what the Father sent him to do. And now he says: 'As the Father has sent me, I am sending you' (John 20:21).

"Have I received a ministry from the Lord?

"If so, I have to be loyal to it, to count my life precious only for the fulfilling of that ministry.

"Think of the satisfaction it will be to hear Jesus say, 'Well done, good and faithful servant!' (Matthew 25:21); to know that you have done what he sent you to do.

"We all have to find our niche in life, and spiritually we find it when we receive our ministry from the Lord.

"In order to do this we must be in close fellowship with Jesus; we must know him as personal Savior — and more."

WALK CLOSER TO GOD

Like a ship out of water or a train off the tracks, you'll find that you don't function well outside the sphere of God's will for your life.

That is by design — his design! A design that promises joy as the by-product of walking in his will.

Joy in serving Jesus.

There's no better way to know you have done what he sent you to do! ❖

THE PRIVILEGE OF PAYING A DEBT

I am ready not only to be bound, but also to die in Jerusalem for the name of the Lord Jesus.
ACTS 21:13

In spite of rumors to the contrary, missionaries are only human. They aren't ten feet tall physically—or spiritually.

Like other Christians, they struggle with illness, attitudes and rebellious children. And their "job description" is basically the same as that of every other Christian: to proclaim the gospel.

David Livingstone describes the attitude that is essential for successful service for the Lord—whether at home or abroad.

WALK WITH DAVID LIVINGSTONE

"People talk of the sacrifice I have made in spending so much of my life in Africa.

"Can that be called a sacrifice which is simply acknowledging a great debt we owe to our God, which we can never repay?

"Is that a sacrifice which brings its own reward in healthful activity, the consciousness of doing good, peace of mind, and a bright hope of a glorious destiny? It is emphatically no sacrifice. Rather it is a privilege.

"Anxiety, sickness, suffering, danger, foregoing the common conveniences of life—these may make us pause, and cause the spirit to waver, and the soul to sink; but let this only be for a moment.

"All these are nothing compared with the glory which shall later be revealed in and through us.

"I never made a sacrifice. Of this we ought not to talk, when we remember the great sacrifice which he made who left his Father's throne on high to give himself for us."

WALK CLOSER TO GOD

Christ gave his life gladly, not considering it too great a sacrifice to die for sinners.

Why then should it be too great a sacrifice to invest your life in spreading his love today?

You don't have to cross an ocean to do that. Your mission field may be as near as your neighbor—a neighbor who needs to hear the news that God has only one Son, the Son he sent as a missionary to all the world. ♣

WILLINGLY LED BY THE SAVIOR'S HAND

"What shall I do, Lord?" I asked. "Get up," the Lord said, "and go into Damascus. There you will be told".

ACTS 22:10

On the road to Damascus, Paul was the zealous leader of a "hunting party."

His prey: followers of Christ.

His license: letters from the high priest.

His intent: death and imprisonment of believers—the destruction of the church.

But before he reached his objective, Paul joined forces with those he had sought to destroy.

Andrew Murray analyzes how Paul the persecutor became Paul the proclaimer of the gospel.

WALK WITH ANDREW MURRAY

"Many have asked what could be the secret of the amazing devotion and power in the life of Paul. The above verse suggests one answer.

"At the time of his conversion, as soon as he knew who it was that called him, he surrendered himself to the will of the Lord. 'What shall I do, Lord?'

"His life was so wonderfully fruitful because he remained true to those words.

"The Lord has a will for each of us, a plan by which he wants us to live. He wants to make his will known to each one.

"He wants us to ask him to reveal his will.

"Such a request sincerely made implies willingness to give oneself to his will and service.

"We may be sure he will answer such prayer. He will lead the child who wants to be led."

WALK CLOSER TO GOD

The Damascus road was more than the place of Paul's conversion. It also marked the place where his will was conquered. His life was no longer his own; he now lived to serve the one who had saved him.

And what was the result? Near the end of his life Paul could say triumphantly, "There is ... the crown of righteousness, which the Lord ... will award to me" (2 Timothy 4:8). God had led him well.

God will do the same in your life when you ask, "What shall I do, Lord?" ❖

may26

A CONSCIENCE TOUCHED BY GOD

Paul ... said, "My brothers, I have fulfilled my duty to God in all good conscience to this day".
ACTS 23:1

The conscience tells you when you have done right or wrong. It may not keep you out of trouble, but at least it lets you know when you are in trouble, so you can deal with the problem.

Everyone has a conscience. But not everyone has a clear conscience. Thomas à Kempis shares these thoughts on how to keep a good conscience toward God.

WALK WITH THOMAS À KEMPIS

"The glory of a good person is the testimony of a good conscience.

"A good conscience is able to bear very much and is very cheerful in adversities. An evil conscience is always fearful and unquiet. Never rejoice except when you have done well. You shall rest sweetly if your heart does not accuse you.

"Sinners never have true joy or feel inward peace, because "'there is no peace,'" says my God, "for the wicked,'" (Isaiah 57:21). The glory of the good is in their consciences, and not in the tongues of others. The gladness of the just is of God, and in God; and their joy is of the truth.

"A person will easily be content and pacified whose conscience is pure. If you consider what you are within, you will not care what others say concerning you. People consider the deeds, but God weighs the intentions.

"To be always doing well and to esteem little of one's self is the sign of a humble soul.

"'For it is not the one who commends himself who is approved, but the one whom the Lord commends,' says Paul (2 Corinthians 10:18). To walk inwardly with God, and not to be kept abroad by any outward affection, is the state of a spiritual person."

WALK CLOSER TO GOD

All it takes to maintain a bad conscience is to do nothing, to ignore the tugging of the Spirit and the still, small voice of God. By contrast, a good conscience is a Christ-cleansed conscience. And that is only a heartfelt prayer away! ✤

may**27**

THE UNLEASHED POWER OF GOD'S WORD

As Paul talked about righteousness, self-control and the judgment to come, Felix was afraid.
ACTS 24:25

The prisoner: Paul. The judge: Felix.

Yet Paul had Felix right where he wanted him!

Sitting in judgment on Paul's case, Felix became the unsuspecting target of Paul's gospel.

The accused stood before the judge — but it was the judge who was convicted! It was a remarkable turn of events that John Calvin explores.

WALK WITH JOHN CALVIN

"Now Felix is forced to realize the effectiveness of the Word of God, a power of which he had no concept. This man, who held the power of life and death over Paul, is trembling all over, as if he were standing before his own judge.

"Forgetting that he is a prisoner bound in chains, Paul exercises the judgment of heaven in the name of Christ. Because he is aware that he must speak in the name of Christ, Paul does not submit to human authority; but, as if from a higher level, he carries out the mission entrusted him by God.

"Let us learn from this what a great influence the Spirit of God exercised not only in Paul's heart but also in his tongue.

"The Word of God has not been bound along with Paul, for not only did he declare it freely and boldly, but it penetrated the hearts of men — proud in their greatness — as if lightning flashed out of heaven."

WALK CLOSER TO GOD

The same Word of God that fortified Paul terrified Felix. Why?

Because "the Word of God is living and active. Sharper than any double-edged sword, it penetrates even to dividing soul and spirit, joints and marrow; it judges the thoughts and attitudes of the heart" (Hebrews 4:12).

Circumstances cannot shackle the power of the Word — a power demonstrated every time a human voice declares it. A voice like yours — telling what you know is true with boldness only the Spirit can give. ✤

THE GUARANTEE OF THE BELIEVER'S RESURRECTION

Instead, they had some points of dispute with him about their own religion and about a dead man named Jesus who Paul claimed was alive.

ACTS 25:19

Believing in Christ's resurrection cost Paul a lot. He was imprisoned, flogged, exposed to death, stoned and shipwrecked. He was in danger from rivers, bandits, Jews, Gentiles and false Christians. He went without sleep, food, drink, warmth and clothing. Besides all that, he, like any good pastor, was "stressed-out" with concern for his flock. Now he was in chains, defending himself before King Agrippa.

R. L. Dabney explains the importance of and evidence for this cardinal doctrine of Christianity.

WALK WITH R. L. DABNEY

"Christ's resurrection is everywhere spoken of in Scripture as a hinge point of the believer's salvation and hope. The apostles everywhere put it forth as the main point of their testimony. It may be proved by the following:

"First, from Old Testament predictions such as Psalm 16:10. This event is one of the criteria predicted for the Messiah. Once you have proved that Jesus is the expected Messiah, you may claim that a resurrection is to be expected for him.

"Second, Christ expressly predicted his own resurrection (see Matthew 20:19; 27:63; and John 10:18). If he is not a monstrous imposter, which his lovely character disproves, we must expect to find it true.

"Third, we have the testimony of many witnesses who saw him after his rising — the eleven, the five-hundred, and last of all Paul. These were competent, honest and credible witnesses. They had everything to lose, and nothing to gain by bearing false testimony on this.

"Fourth, miracles were wrought in its confirmation. The outpouring of the Spirit at Pentecost and all the following outpourings are proofs of it, for they are fruits of his ascension.

"The resurrection of Christ is the guarantee and proof of ours."

WALK CLOSER TO GOD

Yes, believing in Christ's resurrection cost Paul a lot. But not believing in Christ's resurrection will cost so many so much more.

Be like Paul today — talk to someone about that momentous event. ❖

may29

THE ONLY LIFE-AND-DEATH DECISION

Then Agrippa said to Paul, "Do you think that in such a short time you can persuade me to be a Christian?".

ACTS 26:28

People feel intense pressure when they are discussing life-and-death issues—especially if their own lifestyles are at stake. This is why discussions about Christ can be so intense. Christ's message to the unbeliever is, "Your way of life is hellish. I am your only hope." People are intensely uncomfortable with that.

When Paul preached to Agrippa, he turned the pressure to full steam. Agrippa reacted like so many do under the pressure of the truth: He squirmed. He protested. He procrastinated. He escaped.

Matthew Henry explains why.

WALK WITH MATTHEW HENRY

"Agrippa could not but agree that the Old Testament prophecies found their fulfillment in Christ.

"And now that Paul urges him solemnly, he is nearly ready to yield to the conviction of the Spirit.

"He sees a great deal of reason for Christianity. The proofs of it, he admits, are strong; the objections against it, trifling.

"If it were not for his obligations to tradition, his respect for the religion of his fathers and of his country, his regard to his dignity as a king, and his secular interests, he would turn to Christianity immediately. Many are almost persuaded to be saved, who are not quite persuaded.

"They are under strong convictions of their duty, and of the excellency of the ways of God, yet are overruled by some outward circumstances, and do not pursue their convictions."

WALK CLOSER TO GOD

King Agrippa's symptoms: shortsighted vision, a tendency to sacrifice conviction for convenience, and a preoccupation with worldly affairs and popular approval.

The only known cure for such a condition? Taking Jesus Christ—the same Christ whom the apostle Paul proclaimed—at his word.

It was a life-and-death decision—perhaps the very one you are wrestling with today. Agrippa knew the cure, but he wasn't willing to take it. Are you? ✤

may30

READY FOR TEACHABLE MOMENTS

Much time had been lost, and sailing had already become dangerous ... So Paul warned them.
ACTS 27:9

Who needs a Savior when the sun is shining brightly, the sea is calm and the sails are moved by a serene and gentle breeze?

But let the storms of life break loose and trials wash around like high waves, and suddenly the self-sufficient are looking for answers—fast! Answers that the Christian is uniquely prepared to supply, as Joseph Parker explains.

WALK WITH JOSEPH PARKER

"For the Christian to speak when the ship is going merrily over the blue waves is not wrong, but perhaps not best; so the Christian waits.

"The ship comes into difficulty; the sailors begin to look despairingly at the whole situation; illness is about; the air is troubled. Now, if any of you can say a word of comfort, do say it. The Christian is waiting for these times.

"The moment the door stands ajar, he is in; the moment the opportunity shows itself, he seizes it.

"Be wise and do not speak before the time, or your words will be like good seed sown upon the fickle and noisy wind.

"The clock will strike for you—be ready when the hour comes.

"The word will keep; and when it is spoken after long delay, it will come with more thundering resonance, with more penetrating emphasis.

"For that time the Christian witness waits."

WALK CLOSER TO GOD

Death. Lingering illness. Financial reversal. Broken marriage. Runaway child. Loneliness. Loss of job.

The storms of life come with sudden fury. And with them, the realization that someone bigger is needed to cope with life—and death.

People will reach for a Savior when they know they need to be saved. The wise witness is faithful at all times, but watchful for the teachable moments of life.

Will you be ready to speak when they are ready to listen? ❖

may31

GOD'S SERVANTS, GOD'S POSSESSIONS

Once safely on shore ... the islanders showed us unusual kindness ... They honored us in many ways.

ACTS 28:1 – 2,10

Persecution, danger, shipwreck, snakebite, imprisonment. Where did Paul find the strength to face each new challenge?

God specializes in caring for his own as they go about the business of heaven — a truth that J. Hudson Taylor underscores from firsthand experience.

WALK WITH J. HUDSON TAYLOR

"Even in shipwreck and uncertainty, the apostle's heart relied on the truth that he was God's possession, as well as God's servant.

"Long before Paul's day, the assurance given in Deuteronomy 33:12 that 'the beloved of the LORD [will] rest secure in him' had conveyed rest and confidence to many an Israelite.

"Shall we not all rest in the same blessed fact? We are his by creation, his by redemption.

"We value and take care of our own possessions; we cherish and protect our loved ones; how much more does he, whose love and resources so infinitely exceed ours?

"God's love has sustained us. It is unchanging because he is unchanging. He is the great Rock-foundation which alone cannot be shaken.

"We know not what the future may bring with it, but we know him who is the same yesterday, today, and forever. We put our hand afresh in his, and say, 'Lord, lead me on.'"

WALK CLOSER TO GOD

For all the hardships and uncertainties Paul faced, you can certainly say one thing about his life: It wasn't dull!

Yet Paul undoubtedly greeted each new day with the words, "Lord, lead me on."

He trusted God with his future, knowing that he was already there. But above all, Paul was a conqueror in the strength that God supplied (see Romans 8:37).

That same strength is neither diluted nor diminished. And it is yours to draw upon today. ✤

june1

THE GREATEST POWER IN THE UNIVERSE

I am not ashamed of the gospel, because it is the power of God that brings salvation to everyone who believes.

ROMANS 1:16

A 2,000-year-old letter still sends shock waves every time it is read.

Why? Because it leads the reader to "the power of God that brings salvation."

The apostle Paul had never been to Rome—the most important city of his day—but the message of his letter to the believers living there was crucial: how to find peace with God. H. A. Ironside sets the stage for Paul's "letter of life."

WALK WITH H. A. IRONSIDE

"Romans gives us the fullest unfolding of the gospel that we have in the Word of God. It answers every objection of the most astute reasoner. It satisfies the need of every troubled conscience.

"In it we see how God can be just and yet justify the guilty sinner who comes to him in repentance, admitting his need and trusting his grace.

"The Greek philosopher Socrates exclaimed, 'It may be that the deity can forgive sins, but I don't see how!' The Holy Spirit shows here in Romans that God can forgive in righteousness because of the sacrificial work of his Son.

"This is the message which is revealed on the principle of faith to those who believe, whether Jews or Gentiles by birth, according to the words given to Habakkuk so long ago, 'The righteous person will live by his faithfulness' (Habakkuk 2:4)."

WALK CLOSER TO GOD

Socrates was asking the right question: "How can God forgive sins?" Paul supplies the right answer: "Only through his Son Jesus Christ."

Many have looked elsewhere for forgiveness of sins, purpose for living, fellowship with God. Romans points the way to the new life Christ has for all who will come.

Wouldn't you agree that's good news everyone needs to hear? Then don't be ashamed to proclaim what God was not ashamed to provide. ✤

june**2**

PICTURED IN NATURE, PROCLAIMED IN CHRIST

God's invisible qualities — his eternal power and divine nature — have been clearly seen.
ROMANS 1:20

Elizabeth Barrett Browning was right:

> Earth's crammed with heaven,
>> and every common bush aflame with God;
> But only those who see take off their shoes;
>> The rest sit round it and pluck blackberries.

Hebrews puts it this way: "Anyone who comes to him must believe that he exists" (Hebrews 11:6).

A. W. Pink explains how that belief is sparked by seeing the power of the Creator who made the world.

WALK WITH A. W. PINK

"To say that God is visible in nature is true, yet it is a statement which needs qualifying.

"Nature reveals the existence of God, but it tells us little of his character. Nature demonstrates his natural qualities — his power, his wisdom, his unchanging character; but what does it say to us of his moral attributes — his justice, his holiness, his grace, his love? Nature, as such, knows no mercy or pity.

"If a blind saint unwittingly steps off a cliff, he meets with the same fate as if a murderer had stepped off. If I break nature's laws, no matter how sincere may be my subsequent repentance, there is no escaping the penalty.

"In this way we may say that nature conceals as well as reveals God."

WALK CLOSER TO GOD

Creation shows God's grandeur and power; Jesus Christ shows his compassion. What is pictured in nature is proclaimed in Jesus Christ.

Sadly, what most people know of God, they choose to ignore. And though the choice is theirs, the consequences are not.

Consider carefully before you come to the foolish conclusion that "there is no God" (Psalm 14:1). For if you close your eyes to the obvious signs of his existence, you have no one but yourself to blame for the consequences. ✣

june3

GOOD NEWS ABOUT THE LAW

For it is not those who hear the law who are righteous in God's sight, but it is those who obey the law who will be declared righteous.

ROMANS 2:13

High above the gorge, a tightrope walker balances precariously. Every muscle and nerve and thought is trained on just one objective: to stay on the thin strand of wire!

Few would volunteer for such a hazardous high-wire act. Yet many attempt something infinitely more dangerous. They try to find acceptance with God by keeping the law.

And as John Wesley suggests, that's an exercise as unforgiving as a tightrope, for one mistake and the whole effort is futile.

WALK WITH JOHN WESLEY

"When people seek to establish their own righteousness, they do not consider what kind of obedience the law indispensably requires. It must be perfect and complete in every point or it does not answer the demands of the law.

"But which of you is able to perform such obedience? Who can fulfill every jot and tittle of the outward commandments of God, doing nothing which he forbids? Leaving nothing undone which he demands? Speaking no idle word?

"And how much less are you able to fulfill all the inward commandments of God—those which require that every mood and motion should be holiness unto the Lord!

"Are you able to love God with all your heart? To love all mankind as your own soul? To keep every affection, desire, and thought in obedience to his law?"

WALK CLOSER TO GOD

Just as one crack in a mirror makes it a broken mirror, so one violation of God's law makes you a lawbreaker. But there is good news.

Though you cannot keep the law, the law can lead you to someone who can, and did, keep the law on your behalf. And he paid the penalty for the law you break.

That someone is the Savior—Christ the Lord. Is he your Savior? ✢

OUTWARD RITUAL OR INWARD RELATIONSHIP

A person is not a Jew who is one only outwardly ... No, a person is a Jew who is one inwardly.

ROMANS 2:28–29

What you act like on the outside. What you are on the inside. Are they the same? Or different?

The Jews of Paul's day had laws, customs and holidays that reminded them that they were a religious people, a God-centered society.

But they mistook knowing about God for knowing God—a mistake many duplicate today. Outwardly, they honored God with their lips. But inwardly, they dishonored him with their hearts.

W. H. Griffith Thomas offers this caution about confusing head knowledge with heart knowledge in your relationship with God.

WALK WITH W. H. GRIFFITH THOMAS

"Nothing is easier than self-righteousness and self-deception in religion.

"It is possible—without any real change of heart—to know a great deal of Christian truth, to be occupied with Christian work, to be associated with Christian people, to know with great familiarity Christian jargon, to live largely in a Christian atmosphere, yet all the while be without the new life that comes from the Spirit of God.

"The danger of such a position is far greater than that of willful and deliberate sin. Our Lord was constantly warning his hearers against such false assumptions."

WALK CLOSER TO GOD

The Jews thought they were close to God. In reality, they were an eternity away.

Jesus warned, "Many will say to me on that day, 'Lord, Lord ...' Then I will tell them plainly, 'I never knew you. Away from me'" (Matthew 7:22–23). Hard words. Words that remind you that Christianity is more than facts and actions. It involves an inward transformation of heart.

You can fool your friends with the things you know, the words you use, the good works you do. But outward ritual can never replace the inward relationship God wants to have with you today—and every day! ✤

GOD'S LAW: A DIAGNOSTIC TOOL

Therefore no one will be declared righteous in God's sight by the works of the law; rather, through the law we become conscious of our sin.

ROMANS 3:20

A patient with hypertension who dutifully checks his blood pressure morning and evening might still die of a stroke. For simply taking his blood pressure would not solve the problem; it would only reveal a situation in need of treatment.

The Jews made a similar mistake in thinking that the law was the means of their salvation, when in fact it was designed by God to show their need for salvation.

Martin Luther clarifies the issue.

WALK WITH MARTIN LUTHER

"The first understanding of the law should be that we see the inability of human nature to keep it.

"You may do good works outwardly; but God is not satisfied unless they are performed from the heart and out of love, which is not possible unless a man is born anew through the Holy Spirit.

"God, then, wants to achieve no more with the law than getting us to recognize our inability, our frailty, our sickness—to recognize that, so far as we are concerned, we cannot keep one letter of the law. When you feel that, the law has done its work.

"This is what Paul means when he says to the Romans: 'Through the law we become conscious of our sin.'"

WALK CLOSER TO GOD

A wall may appear straight—until you hold a plumb line against it. A garment may look white—until you lay it next to a whiter one. In each case, you need a standard against which all other objects can be compared.

In the realm of righteousness, the standard is God's law. It is there you discover how far you have drifted from God's holiness, how soiled you are with sin. It is there you see an accurate diagnosis of your problem.

It is there you come to realize that you are powerless to save yourself.

Are you ready to acknowledge your predicament? Then you are also ready to receive God's provision. ❖

NO HOPE—EXCEPT IN CHRIST

He did it to demonstrate his righteousness at the present time, so as to be just and the one who justifies those who have faith in Jesus.

ROMANS 3:26

The gospel is so simple that little children can understand it. And yet it is so complex that the Bible uses a word like justification to describe one of its many facets.

Boil it all down and you can simplify the complex into just two words: Jesus Christ. In him all the big words come together to explain the significance of your salvation. Take justification, for example. Charles Spurgeon provides this analysis of its meaning and importance.

WALK WITH CHARLES SPURGEON

"If God is just, then I a sinner—alone and without a substitute—must be punished.

"But Jesus stands in my place and is punished for me. So now, if God is just, then I a sinner—standing in Christ—can never be punished. Jesus has taken the place of the believer and received the full penalty of divine wrath.

"My hope lives not because I am sinless, but because I am a sinner for whom Christ died. My trust is not that I am holy, but that, since I am unholy, he is my righteousness.

"My faith rests not upon what I am, or shall be, or feel, or know, but in what Christ is, in what he has done, and in what he is now doing for me."

WALK CLOSER TO GOD

If you died and awoke at the gates of heaven, and there God confronted you with the question, "Why should I allow you into my heaven?"—what would you say?

"I did my best." "I'm better than most." "I was sincere in my beliefs."

All have sinned. God is just in punishing those who have broken his law. And either Jesus Christ becomes your substitute ... or you feel the force of God's wrath yourself.

"Justified freely by his grace through the redemption that came by Christ Jesus" (Romans 3:24). With that as your passport, you need never fear the reception you'll get in heaven! ✤

june7

THE OVERFLOW OF GOD'S LOVE

David says the same thing when he speaks of the blessedness of the one to whom God credits righteousness apart from works: "Blessed are they whose transgressions are forgiven".

ROMANS 4:6–7

Imagine you owe a vast sum of money ... but then the debt is totally forgiven. How do you react?

Imagine you face a death-row execution ... but then you receive a full pardon. How do you feel?

Joyful. Happy. Relieved beyond measure. A future previously fearful now brims with expectancy.

Getting right with God is cause for unspeakable joy—a joy that David extols in Psalm 32 when he wrote of forgiveness.

C. S. Lewis, who wrote often of his own joyful conversion, provides this analysis of the gift that seems too good to be true.

WALK WITH C. S. LEWIS

"The man who has experienced conversion feels like one who has awakened from nightmare into ecstasy.

"He feels that he has done nothing, and never could have done anything, to deserve such astonishing happiness.

"All the initiative has been on God's side; all has been free, unbounded grace.

"His own puny efforts would be as helpless to retain the joy as they would have been to attain it in the first place. Fortunately, they need not. Bliss is not for sale; it cannot be earned.

"Works have no merit, though of course faith inevitably flows out into works of love. He is not saved because he does works of love; he does works of love because he is saved.

"It is faith alone that has saved him: faith bestowed as the sheer gift of God."

WALK CLOSER TO GOD

Joy—the by-product of God's inexpressible gift.

Joy—the overflow of God's inexhaustible love.

Have you experienced God's grace at work in your life? If so, no one needs to tell you that "the God of hope [can] fill you with all joy" (Romans 15:13). ✣

june8

A PASSING GRADE IN THE SCHOOL OF RIGHTEOUSNESS

For if those who depend on the law are heirs, faith means nothing and the promise is worthless, because law brings wrath.

ROMANS 4:14–15

According to some views, God will grade "on a curve," looking at your life in comparison with others. If the good outweighs the bad, you pass the test of life and get into heaven. However, a passing grade in God's school of righteousness has always been 100 percent. Anything less, and you fail.

Donald Barnhouse provides this insightful look at the folly of trying to "make the grade" on the basis of good works rather than on God's work.

WALK WITH DONALD BARNHOUSE

"We can see where an argument about salvation by works would lead us.

"Suppose a man has made certain sacrifices in his giving to worthy causes. Has he made sacrifices enough? Is there a percentage that may be established?

"If that is so, what about a poor man and a rich man? A poor man may have five children and fifty dollars a week. Is he supposed to give five dollars a week to good Christian causes? And if another man has a thousand dollars a week and only a wife and one child, can he get by with God by giving a hundred dollars a week?

"The absurdities of the comparisons become evident the further we push them to logical conclusions."

WALK CLOSER TO GOD

You may be smarter than most, more generous than many, more honest than some. But when the comparison is made between sinful people and the holy God, your best efforts resemble "filthy rags" (Isaiah 64:6).

God knew that. So he sent his Son to pass the test for you. By placing your confidence in Jesus, his grade becomes yours.

And when the choice is between a perfect score or failure, with eternal consequences, wouldn't you prefer having Christ's grade to your own? ❖

june9

PRECIOUS PRODUCTS OF TRIBULATION

We also glory in our sufferings, because we know that suffering produces perseverance; perseverance, character; and character, hope.

ROMANS 5:3–4

The Christian life is not a parade but a battle in which the opposition is intense and the enemy tenacious. But you can neither be defeated nor disheartened—as long as you remember the one with whom you are at war and the one with whom you are at peace!

Abraham Kuyper probes the power and purpose behind victorious spiritual warfare.

WALK WITH ABRAHAM KUYPER

"When we are attacked, when our opponent takes hold and attempts to throw us, only then does our strength appear.

"Each fierce attack inspires more determined resistance, and we put forth all our strength to remain standing. And thus endurance is born.

"Tribulation and struggle call forth strength to endure; endurance produces the confidence of proven character; and with that new confidence, hope waxes stronger—the hope of never being overcome by an assailant, the hope of winning the crown.

"Thus the child of God, struggling against the forces of evil in and around him, discovers within himself a God-given strength which enables him to endure all assault triumphantly."

WALK CLOSER TO GOD

When called upon to stand, the believer knows where his strength lies.

Paul explained it this way: "I can do all this through him who gives me strength" (Philippians 4:13).

Each "round" with the enemy, each conflict successfully met in the strength of the Lord, only serves to make you stronger for the next. More patient. More experienced. More enduring. More hopeful. More like Christ.

There is no more glorious way to live in this world than to "glory in our sufferings." ❖

WE MUST GO TO JESUS CHRIST

Grace ... reign[s] through righteousness to bring eternal life through Jesus Christ our Lord.
ROMANS 5:21

The church is packed. The organist plays reverently. The smiling groom awaits his bride.

And here she comes down the aisle—dress tattered and torn, face streaked with grime—anything but the picture of beauty.

Yet the groom lovingly cleans her up and then receives her. That's the picture of Christ—who is both groom and groomer—and his church.

The same gift of grace that saves is a gift of righteousness that purifies, as Anne Ross Cousin explains.

WALK WITH ANNE ROSS COUSIN

> Oh! I am my Beloved's,
>   And my Beloved is mine!
> He brings a poor vile sinner
>   Into His "House of wine."
> I stand upon His merit,
>   I know no other stand
> Not e'en where glory dwelleth
>   In Immanuel's land.
>
> The Bride eyes not her garment,
>   But her dear Bridegroom's face;
> I will not gaze at glory,
>   But on my King of Grace—
> Not at the crown He giveth,
>   But on His pierced hand:
> The Lamb is all the glory
>   Of Immanuel's land.

WALK CLOSER TO GOD

The church is the bride of Christ (see Ephesians 5:25–32). And in Christ the bride becomes beautiful with a purity acceptable to God. The dirt of sin and the curse of death cannot be removed in any other way.

Christ is preparing for himself a bride that is cleansed, spotless, holy and without blemish.

Grace leading to righteousness. Unmerited favor leading to upright behavior. They go hand in hand for the one eagerly preparing to meet the Lord. ✤

SIN THAT CRUCIFIES THE LORD AGAIN

For we know that our old self was crucified with him so that the body ruled by sin might be done away with, that we should no longer be slaves to sin.

ROMANS 6:6

In Romans 6, Paul addressed the issue of sin and its relation to the Christian. In Christ you have been set free from the penalty of sin, but you are still in the presence of sin and its deadly influence.

But even though sin continues to beckon, you no longer have to listen, as Charles Spurgeon teaches in this helpful insight.

WALK WITH CHARLES SPURGEON

"All sin is contrary to the designs of eternal love, which has an eye to your purity and holiness. Do not run counter to the purposes of the Lord.

"Be free, and let the remembrance of your past bondage forbid you to enter the net again.

"Christians can never sin cheaply; they pay a heavy price for iniquity.

"Each time you 'serve sin,' you have crucified the Lord afresh, and put him to an open shame. Can you bear that thought?

"Turn to Jesus anew; he has not forgotten his love to you; his grace is still the same. With weeping and repentance, come into his presence and there you shall stand firm."

WALK CLOSER TO GOD

Equipped with new life in Jesus Christ, you no longer have to give in to sin. But that doesn't mean you'll never have to face sin. For God has called you to represent him in a sin-filled world.

Old relationships may lure you. Sinful pleasures may invite you. But in Christ you have the power to say no. And it's important that you do precisely that, for while sin doesn't pay, you will if you fail to draw on his strength.

You'll pay by bearing the effects of sin. You'll pay in the loss of fellowship with him. You'll pay by receiving God's loving but firm discipline. You'll pay with a life that's joyless and empty.

Is it worth all that? ❖

june**12**

CHRIST: THE DEFENDER OF YOUR LIBERTY

You have been set free from sin and have become slaves to righteousness.

Romans 6:18

The battle for your soul may be over, but the battle for your allegiance still rages. But Jesus Christ has conquered the power of sin, and you are free! Free to say no to sin and yes to God.

As John Calvin affirms, that can be very comforting for anyone tired of struggling against sin.

WALK WITH JOHN CALVIN

"The apostle is comforting and strengthening believers, lest they should falter in their zeal and desire for holiness, because they feel their own weakness.

"To prevent discouragement arising from a consciousness of this weakness, he reminds believers that their works are not judged according to the rigid demands of the law.

"The stings of sin continue to harass us, yet they cannot bring us under their power, because we are rendered superior to them by the work of Christ. We are also freed from the rigid demand of the law, because we are in his grace. On this account, believers must fly to Christ and implore his assistance as a defender of their liberty, which he is always ready to do."

WALK CLOSER TO GOD

By his death, Christ broke the power of sin and death. Captives have been liberated. Slaves to sin have been set free to serve a new Master.

Hebrews describes it this way: Christ "shared in their humanity so that by his death he might break the power of him who holds the power of death—that is, the devil—and free those who all their lives were held in slavery by their fear of death" (Hebrews 2:14–15).

No longer afraid of death. No longer bound to sin. No longer giving in to uncleanness. But instead, giving in to God.

Never have you enjoyed anything as free—or as costly. ✤

MY HEART, CHRIST'S HOME

For when we were in the realm of the flesh, the sinful passions aroused by the law were at work in us, so that we bore fruit for death. But now ... we have been released from the law.
ROMANS 7:5–6

An X-ray reveals a serious break in your leg. Do you blame the X-ray for the problem? Do you blame your doctor for informing you of a life-threatening situation? Of course not!

In the same way, the law was designed by God to diagnose the sinful condition of the human race—to make people aware of their need for a Savior.

In *The Pilgrim's Progress*, John Bunyan gives this illustration of the relationship of the law to the gospel of grace, as spoken through the interpreter.

WALK WITH JOHN BUNYAN

"This parlor is the heart of a man who was never cleansed by the sweet grace of the gospel; that dust is his inward corruption that has defiled the whole man.

"He who began to sweep at first is the law, but she who brought the water and did sprinkle it is the gospel.

"Now, so soon as the first began to sweep, the dust did so fly about that you were almost choked therewith. This is to show you that the law, instead of cleansing the heart from sin, does revive, put strength into, and increase it, for it does not give the power to subdue.

"Again, the damsel sprinkling the room with water is to show you what happens when the gospel comes in.

"As the damsel settled the dust by sprinkling the floor with water, sin is vanquished and subdued, and the soul made clean through faith; and consequently made fit for the King of Glory to inhabit."

WALK CLOSER TO GOD

The law merely reveals the soiled condition of the human heart.

What the law of God stirs up, only the grace of God can clean up.

It's enough to make even twenty-first-century pilgrims respond in grateful praise! ✤

june**14**

BATTLING IN A WAR THAT'S ALREADY WON

What a wretched man I am! Who will rescue me from this body that is subject to death? Thanks be to God, who delivers me through Jesus Christ our Lord!.

ROMANS 7:24–25

Without benefit of bullets or bombs, the world, the flesh and the devil have mounted an all-out attack aimed at crippling "everyone who wants to live a godly life in Christ Jesus" (2 Timothy 3:12).

Paul described this "guerrilla warfare" in Romans 7. And as Thomas à Kempis notes, this is one battle that is best fought on your knees.

WALK WITH THOMAS À KEMPIS

"I confess my own unrighteousness; I confess my weakness unto thee, O Lord.

"Often it is a small matter that makes me sad and dejected. I resolve that I will: act with courage, but when even a small temptation comes, I am at once in great distress. It is sometimes a tiny trifle that sparks a great temptation.

"And though I do not altogether consent, yet their continued assaults are troublesome and grievous to me; and it is exceedingly irksome to live thus daily in conflict.

"O Lord, strengthen me with heavenly courage, lest the flesh prevail and get the upper hand."

WALK CLOSER TO GOD

When David met Goliath, he knew God would be victorious, for David knew the battle was indeed the Lord's. Believers face battles daily too. But they're spiritual battles against the giants of Satan and self.

The best defense against the warring flesh is a good offense—a confidence that Satan and his allies are already defeated. The ultimate outcome has already been determined; the cross of Christ has seen to that!

Now you, like Paul, can respond to the question, "Who will rescue me from this body that is subject to death?" with the ringing affirmation, "Jesus Christ our Lord!"

After all, there's nothing like knowing that someone has already won the war to give you strength to face each daily skirmish! ✦

june15

DELIGHTING YOURSELF IN PEACE AND FREEDOM

Therefore, there is now no condemnation for those who are in Christ Jesus.

ROMANS 8:1

Before you believed in Jesus Christ, you were on death row—condemned by God, deserving of his wrath and judgment.

But now, set free by Christ's death in your place, you are serving a life sentence instead—eternal life in his service.

Read thankfully these words spoken by Thomas Chalmers from a Scottish pulpit more than a hundred years ago.

WALK WITH THOMAS CHALMERS

"When a sinner comes to Christ, God reconciles him to himself and remembers his sins no more. They are among the things that are left behind and which ought to be forgotten.

"The believer should feel his conscience relieved from the guilt and dread of his sins. He can look on the account as closed between him and God.

"It is wrong in a believer to live beneath his privileges. How will the spirit of bondage ever be done away with or the joy of the gospel ever be made to spring up in the heart if the believer tries to hang the forgiveness of his sins on anything other than the blood of Jesus?

"Look to Christ lifted up for the offenses of sinners and be encouraged in this thought: Christ has made full payment, and with it God is satisfied.

"If so, you too may be satisfied—delighting yourself greatly in the abundance of peace, and going forth in the light and liberty of this comforting knowledge."

WALK CLOSER TO GOD

Father, often I find myself remembering what you have forgotten and condemning myself for what you have erased.

Teach me never to forget your forgiveness. Because only then will I be at peace with myself—when I remember that I am at peace with you.

I pray in the name of Christ, my deliverer from condemnation. Amen. ✤

june**16**

THE WAY IN WHICH HIS SPIRIT LEADS

Those who are led by the Spirit of God are the children of God.

Romans 8:14

Romans 8 highlights the many facets of life in the Spirit. God has not called you to live for him in a vacuum.

Rather, in the person of the Holy Spirit, he has provided all you need to enjoy daily victory and vitality in your walk with him.

Through the words of Jonathan Edwards, focus today on the importance of the Holy Spirit as your leader.

WALK WITH JONATHAN EDWARDS

"The Spirit leads the children of God by inclining them to do the will of God from a holy, heavenly disposition which the Spirit of God gives them.

"The Spirit inclines and leads them to those things that are excellent and agreeable to God.

"He enlightens them with respect to their duty, by making their eye single and pure, whereby the whole body is full of light.

"The purifying influence of the Spirit corrects the taste of the soul, whereby he savors those things that are holy and agreeable to God.

"Like one with a discriminating taste, he chooses those things that are good and wholesome, and rejects those that are evil.

"And thus the Spirit of God leads and guides; he enables us to understand the commands and counsels of God's Word, and rightly to apply them."

WALK CLOSER TO GOD

Think of the Spirit as your "holy guide" through life.

You are not alone. He is a companion to guide you over each uncertain step. He is already infinitely familiar with the path. He is sent by God, with the mind of God, and knowing the will of God.

All that is necessary is for you to put your hand in his—to acknowledge that he knows the path ahead better than you do and to walk with him, neither lagging behind nor running ahead.

That's your daily privilege as a child of the King! ✤

NO PRICE TOO HIGH FOR SALVATION

For I could wish that I myself were cursed and cut off from Christ for the sake of my people.
ROMANS 9:3

If you heard that a friend was critically ill in the hospital, would you go out of your way to visit and help?

Of course you would. Compassion often causes detours around previously arranged plans.

Paul carried just such a burden of compassion for his "people"—but it was not unique to him. J. Hudson Taylor shares his own burden for Christless people.

WALK WITH J. HUDSON TAYLOR

"We are not exempt from trials, and some of them are very painful and difficult to bear.

"But I shall feel amply repaid if one soul only is, by my witness, rescued from the powers of darkness and brought into the fold of Christ.

"And I trust that not one only, but many, will be turned to righteousness by the Word of God ministered by me.

"Were it at the expense of every source of earthly enjoyment; were health and peace, and comfort and happiness, and even life itself to be sacrificed that we might communicate the blessings of Christianity to others, we ought gladly to make it.

"But there is no surer way of finding happiness than by heartily engaging in the work of the Lord, no more certain way of increasing our own blessings than by endeavoring to communicate them to others."

WALK CLOSER TO GOD

A coworker. A family member. A neighbor.

What would you be willing to endure for the privilege of seeing one of these respond to the good news of sins forgiven?

J. Hudson Taylor gladly faced a foreign culture—and the misunderstandings of many of his fellow Britishers—to share the Good News with China.

Paul was willing to be "cursed" if by that his "people" would accept the gospel of Christ.

What price are you willing to pay that a lost soul might hear God's message of life? ✤

june18

GOD LOVES TO USE THE WEAKEST SAINT

And how can anyone preach unless they are sent? As it is written, "How beautiful are the feet of those who bring good news!".

When God calls for volunteers, do you respond? It may surprise you to learn that God is looking not for the most capable candidates to do his work but for the most faithful.

He doesn't need your talent as much as he does your trustworthiness. He can supply you with everything you need to do all he calls you to do.

Oswald Chambers analyzes the qualifications of God's "sent ones"—qualifications that help to ensure that God gets the credit for whatever is accomplished.

WALK WITH OSWALD CHAMBERS

"The Christian must be sent; he must not merely elect to go. How am I to know I have been sent of God? By the realization that I am utterly weak and powerless, and if I am to be of any use to God, God must do it all the time.

"Is this the humbling certainty of my soul?

"The only way to be sent is to let God lift us right out of any sense of fitness in ourselves and place us where he will.

"The man whose work tells for God is the one who not only realizes what God has done for him but who realizes his own utter unfitness and overwhelming unsuitability—the impossibility of God ever calling him."

WALK CLOSER TO GOD

Of those who were called, "not many ... were wise"—so that the wisdom might come from God; "not many were influential"—so that God might prove to be the source of strength; "not many were of noble birth"—so that the glory might be wholly God's (1 Corinthians 1:26).

Moses, Gideon, Jeremiah and Isaiah considered themselves totally inadequate to do anything of lasting significance for God. But in their weakness, his glorious strength could be clearly seen.

When God has a job to do, only weak people need apply. Weak people who are willing to say, "Here am I. Send me!" (Isaiah 6:8). ♣

ONE IS A MAJORITY WITH GOD

God did not reject his people, whom he foreknew ... What was God's answer to him [Elijah]? "I have reserved for myself seven thousand".

ROMANS 11:2,4

Perhaps you have experienced that sinking feeling that it's you against the world. And frankly, the world seems to have you badly outnumbered.

But an amazing transformation takes place when you realize it's not simply you, but you and God and the remnant God has promised never to be without.

W. H. Griffith Thomas points out how Paul used the life of Elijah to encourage both his countrymen and his fellow believers that God always has a remnant of believers who remain loyal to him.

WALK WITH W. H. GRIFFITH THOMAS

"To support his contention that God has not cast away his people, Paul points out that the same state of affairs existed in the time of Elijah.

"Appearances are not always the same as reality, and there is still a godly remnant, though disregarded by the entire nation.

"When Elijah on Mt. Horeb brought an accusation against his countrymen of such unfaithfulness to God that he alone was left, the divine response quickly showed him that there was a kernel of loyalty.

"In exactly the same way in Paul's day, the mass of people were unfaithful, but there was a remnant of loyal Israelites who had accepted thankfully the divine righteousness by faith.

"Like the quiet group that welcomed the birth of Jesus at Bethlehem, there were many in this remnant who 'waited for the salvation of Israel.'"

WALK CLOSER TO GOD

It's never easy to stand alone for what you believe. But learn a lesson from Elijah: When hostility comes, when you feel like it's you against the world, look up. It may surprise you to see how many others are standing with you. You, like Elijah, are part of an entire army of faith! ❖

june**20**

STANDING BY GOD'S GRACE ALONE

Consider therefore the kindness and sternness of God: sternness to those who fell, but kindness to you, provided that you continue in his kindness.

ROMANS 11:22

Longevity is no guarantee of legitimacy. Tradition alone is no safeguard of the truth. Over a period of time, what is right and true can easily become perverted and powerless.

It happens in the Christian life with surprising regularity. The revolutionary claims of the gospel become routine; holiness becomes humdrum. And when that happens, it's time for God to snap his children out of their spiritual stupor, as Matthew Henry explains.

WALK WITH MATTHEW HENRY

"God is most severe toward those who, in their profession, have been nearest to him, if they rebel against him. Patience and abused privilege turn to the greatest wrath.

"It is possible for churches that have long stood by faith to fall into such a state of infidelity as to be their ruin. Their unbelief not only provoked God to cut them off, but by this they cut themselves off.

"You do not stand in any strength of your own. You are no more than the grace of God makes you.

"Continue in his goodness, in a dependence upon and compliance with the free grace of God. Be careful to keep up your interest in God's favor by being continually careful to please him and equally fearful of offending him. The sum of your duty, the condition of your happiness, is to keep yourself in the love of God. 'Come trembling to the LORD and to his blessings' (Hosea 3:5)."

WALK CLOSER TO GOD

Serving God should be the pattern of your existence. But in the process, never let it become routine—ordinary, stale, monotonous. Greet each new day as a fresh challenge to display the goodness of God to a waiting world.

Just as there was no stale manna for Israel in the wilderness, so keep your faith fresh through daily feeding on the bread of life. Then you, as Mr. Henry suggests, will be "continually careful to please [God] and equally fearful of offending him." ✤

june21

THE RICH AND UNSEARCHABLE WISDOM OF GOD

Oh, the depth of the riches of the wisdom and knowledge of God! How unsearchable his judgments, and his paths beyond tracing out!.

ROMANS 11:33

As Paul explains God's plan for the Jews and Gentiles, many questions surface. Questions for which God has answers, but which his children sometimes lack the understanding to grasp.

In such cases, often the best answer God can supply is "Father knows best."

And the proper response of his children? Allow Martin Luther to answer.

WALK WITH MARTIN LUTHER

"God's ways are what he intends to do, and that cannot be discovered by human reason or thought.

"Therefore, people had better not dictate to God in the presumption of what is right or wrong, or how a divine act ought to be performed.

"On the contrary, people should humble themselves before God and confess that they know nothing of these matters, and can neither advise nor teach anything concerning them.

"They should glorify God by acknowledging that, as their God and Creator, he knows and understands better what he is about and how he ought to govern than do we as his creatures."

WALK CLOSER TO GOD

Who knows better what makes watches "tick" than the watchmaker himself? Who understands better the business of heaven and earth than the Creator of both?

God is in control. He knows what he is doing and how best to accomplish his purposes.

Moses, who talked with God face to face for 40 years, discovered that "the secret things belong to the LORD our God, but the things revealed belong to us and to our children forever, that we may follow all the words of this law" (Deuteronomy 29:29).

That means God is looking not for your opinion but for your obedience.

And obedience is something you should never have any question about. ✣

june**22**

THE SACRIFICE THAT LIVES AND BREATHES

Therefore, I urge you, brothers and sisters, in view of God's mercy, to offer your bodies as a living sacrifice, holy and pleasing to God—this is your true and proper worship.

ROMANS 12:1

Today it's considered a "sacrifice" to forego a second dessert or give a dollar to charity.

Contrast that with an Old Testament sacrifice, which was precious, personal and costly.

There is nothing cheap about the sacrifice Paul calls for in Romans 12. Far more than a dead animal or a hard-earned buck, it involves your very life.

Listen as John Henry Jowett explains.

WALK WITH JOHN HENRY JOWETT

"The Lord wants my body. He needs its members as ministers of righteousness. He works in the world through my brain, and eyes, and ears, and lips, and hands, and feet. And the Lord wants my body as a 'living sacrifice.' He asks for it when it is thoroughly alive!

"We so often deny the Lord our bodies until they are infirm and sickly, and sometimes we do not offer them to him until they are quite worn out. It is best to offer our bodies to the Lord when they are strong and vigorous and serviceable, and when they can be used in the strenuous places of the field.

"And so let me have a daily consecration service, and let me every morning present my body a living sacrifice to God. Let me regard it as a most holy possession, and let me keep it clean. Let me recoil from all abuse of it. Let me look upon my body as a temple, and let the service of consecration continue all day long."

WALK CLOSER TO GOD

When God required a sacrifice from his people, he asked for the cream of the crop. In the same way, God is looking today for living sacrifices that can serve him in prime condition and energetic consecration.

Are you ready to give him that? Remember, your body is the temple in which his Spirit resides (see 1 Corinthians 6:19). ✤

OVERCOMING EVIL WITH GOOD

Do not be overcome by evil, but overcome evil with good.

ROMANS 12:21

Being familiar with the book of Romans is one thing. Putting its teaching to work in your life is something else again.

Beginning with chapter 12, the book's focus is on the practical side of Christian living. Home and government, church and community—each should reflect the dynamic nature of the doctrine you believe, as John Henry Jowett describes.

WALK WITH JOHN HENRY JOWETT

"How can we cast out evil?

"The surgeon cannot cut out the disease if his instruments are defiled; while he removes one ill growth, he sows the seeds of another.

"It must be health which fights disease.

"And therefore I must cultivate a virtue if I would eradicate a vice. If there is some immoral habit in my life, the best way to destroy it would be to cultivate a good one.

"Take the mind away from the evil one. Deprive it of thought food. Give the thought to the nobler mood, and the ignoble will die.

"And this also applies to the faults and vices of my brother. I must fight them with their opposites. If he is harsh and cruel, I must be considerate and gentle. If he is grasping, I must be generous. If he is acting devilish, I must act Christlike.

"This is the warfare which tells upon the empire of sin. I can overcome evil with good."

WALK CLOSER TO GOD

As darkness is the absence of light, evil is the absence of good.

And all that is necessary for evil to prevail is for good men to do nothing, to take their light and hide it under a bushel basket, to "leave well enough alone."

Overcome. It's a word that demands an active response if what you believe is truly going to affect how you behave. ❖

june24

THE BLESSING OF CIVIL GOVERNMENT

Let everyone be subject to the governing authorities, for there is no authority except that which God has established. The authorities that exist have been established by God.

ROMANS 13:1

"Those whom God hath joined together let no man put asunder." In a traditional wedding, those words are the last ones heard before the couple is pronounced man and wife. The idea is that mere mortals do not have the right to "tear apart" an institution God established.

Just as God established marriage, he established civil government. To arbitrarily rebel against what he established is to rebel against him. On the other hand, to govern without regard to the one who established government is equally rebellious. In one brilliant stroke Paul forbids anarchy and tyranny.

What does this mean in our time? W. H. Griffith Thomas gives helpful application.

WALK WITH W. H. GRIFFITH THOMAS

"(1) *How beautifully applicable this teaching is to every form of government.* Whatever country may be ours these great principles apply. The institution of civil authority is according to the will and plan of God, but no particular type is necessarily expressive of the divine will.

"(2) *How clearly the apostle insists on the Christian's fulfillment of his duties to the state.* They are as truly an obligation as the most spiritual of our church functions. Paying taxes is just as Christian as praying at a meeting. Of course, we are not to do at the bidding of the state that which is morally wrong, but, short of this, submission, not resistance, is the Christian law.

"(3) *How entirely independent of the moral character of the civil government is this fulfillment of our duty.* Questions as to the state's precise moral character do not touch our duty, so long as the demand does not entrench on the domain of the conscience.

"(4) *How agreeable it would be to the progress and welfare of Christianity if such loyalty and submission were always practiced.* If our duties as citizens were fully realized, it would constitute a splendid witness for God."

WALK CLOSER TO GOD

Paul wrote this at a time when the civil rulers were unbelievers. Yet he still called for submission to God's institution.

In our time, we are both the governed and the government. Since we have the privilege to play a role in placing our leaders in their positions, we share responsibility for how they lead. Have you considered ways that you can be faithful in this stewardship God has providentially given you? ❖

LOVE: THE FULFILLMENT OF THE LAW

Let no debt remain outstanding, except the continuing debt to love one another ... Love does no harm to a neighbor. Therefore love is the fulfillment of the law.

ROMANS 13:8,10

Love and law.

Seemingly incompatible. Until you recall that the two greatest commands in the Bible are commands to love: "Love the Lord your God ... Love your neighbor as yourself" (Matthew 22:37,39).

How do you fulfill the law of God? Not by gritting your teeth and trying harder, but by loving God and neighbor.

Augustine provides this helpful illustration of the permeating effect of love in life's relationships.

WALK WITH AUGUSTINE

"If a man loves a certain actor and enjoys his art as a great good, he loves all those who share his love for the actor—not on their own account, but on account of him whom they love together.

"And the more fervent is his love for the actor, the more he will behave in every way possible so that the actor will be loved by many.

"Does not this pattern of behavior fit the action of us who are united in the brotherhood of the love of God?

"Thus it is that we also love our enemies. For we do not fear them, since they cannot take away that which we love. Rather, we are sorry for them.

"If they were to turn to him and love him as the source of blessedness, they would necessarily love us also as companions in a great good."

WALK CLOSER TO GOD

Augustine elsewhere summarizes the demands of the Christian life this way: "Love God, and do as you please."

That is, when your vertical relationship with God is right, then your horizontal relationships with others will be right.

When your goal is to please the Father, it's remarkable how well you will get along with your brothers and sisters in the family of God.

Try it—and see how fulfilling love can be. ❖

june26

UNDER THE SCRUTINY OF THE LORD

For this very reason, Christ died and returned to life so that he might be the Lord of both the dead and the living ... So then, each of us will give an account of ourselves to God.

ROMANS 14:9,12

Aspiring politicians dread the thought of skeletons in the closet coming to light. But even the most anonymous John or Jane Doe will one day stand before the light of God's judgment. And then no secrets will be safe.

"Everything is uncovered and laid bare before the eyes of him to whom we must give account" (Hebrews 4:13). The God who knows even the thoughts and intentions of the heart will one day judge all.

Donald Barnhouse advises the Christian how to live in the light of that knowledge.

WALK WITH DONALD BARNHOUSE
"We must understand that 'what he sows' (Galatians 6:7) must be taken in its widest meaning, and that every thought and intent of the heart will come under the scrutiny of our Lord at his coming.

"We can be sure that at the judgment seat of Christ there will be a marked difference between the Christian who has lived his life before the Lord, clearly discerning what was for the glory of God, and another Christian who was saved in a rescue mission at the tag end of a depraved and vicious life, or a nominal Christian saved on his deathbed after a life of self-pride, self-righteousness, self-love, and self-sufficiency.

"All will be in heaven, but the differences will be eternal. We may be sure that the consequences of our character will survive the grave and that we shall face those consequences at the judgment seat of Christ."

WALK CLOSER TO GOD
Although the penalty of sin is removed for the Christian, the consequences of sin continue to operate in a fallen world. Murder always means the loss of life; adultery, the destruction of a home; lying, the loss of integrity—for Christian and non-Christian alike.

This is ample reason to keep on your toes and stay on your knees in your walk with the Lord. ✤

THE GENTLE CALMNESS OF TRUE STRENGTH

Let us therefore make every effort to do what leads to peace and to mutual edification.
ROMANS 14:19

Consider the irony of freedom.

Define it as "the right to do as you please," and you will never be truly free.

Define it as "the right to do as you ought," and you will have discovered the essence of true freedom.

In Romans 14 Paul described the use—and abuse—of Christian liberty, as H. C. G. Moule explains.

WALK WITH H. C. G. MOULE

"In principle, Paul's own convictions lay with the 'strong,' those who knew that 'nothing is unclean' (Romans 14:14).

"He knew that the Lord was not grieved, but pleased, by the moderate and thankful use of his natural bounties.

"But though the strong may be right in principle concerning certain activities, this leaves untouched the still more stringent overruling principle, to 'walk in the way of love' (Ephesians 5:2); to live for the benefit of others.

"The strong are not to be ashamed of their liberty. But they are to be ashamed of one hour's unloving conduct.

"Their 'strength' in Christ is never to be ungentle. It is to be shown, first and most, by patience. It is to take the form of the calm, strong readiness to understand another's point of view."

WALK CLOSER TO GOD

When it comes to the exercise of Christian freedom, God is looking for men and women who are strong in the Lord, yet tender toward those who are weak in the faith; he is looking for believers who temper their freedom with love.

When you encounter a "gray area" in your walk with God, when you're not sure of the right course of action, when the Scriptures are silent on a particular activity—what then?

Then put Paul's principle to work: When in doubt, love! ❖

june28

THE EVER-RELEVANT WORD OF GOD

For everything that was written in the past was written to teach us, so that through the endurance taught in the Scriptures and the encouragement they provide we might have hope.

ROMANS 15:4

Thousands of years separate you from the events of Scripture. But even though life today seems very different, those inspired words remain your instruction manual from the Creator of the world.

No matter what your age—or distance from the Scripture's writing—God's truth is never out of date.

John Calvin, lifelong student of the Scriptures, has this to say about God's eternally relevant Word.

WALK WITH JOHN CALVIN

"There is no part of the Scriptures which cannot contribute to our instruction and to the forming of our life and manners.

"The Word of God contains nothing vain or unprofitable. Diligent study and reading of these records of unchanging wisdom cannot help but contribute to our holiness of life.

"Let us, therefore, labor diligently to learn the contents of the Book of God, and never forget it is the only writing in which the Creator of heaven and earth condescends to converse with mankind.

"The Scriptures are chiefly devoted to the object of forming in us patience—of strengthening and confirming our faith—of raising us to the hope of eternal life—and of keeping our meditation and contemplation fixed on that glorious kingdom of God."

WALK CLOSER TO GOD

Patience, comfort, strength—just a few of the dividends you'll receive from mastering God's Word and allowing it to master you.

Study, diligence, meditation—the investment you must make to achieve that end.

God has placed all that you need to know about him between the covers of the Bible. But only you can open its pages to discover what he is saying to you. ❖

PRAISING GOD WITH THE ANGELS

Therefore I glory in Christ Jesus in my service to God.

ROMANS 15:17

You may know the heart of the gospel—salvation in Jesus Christ. But do you have a heart for the gospel—a passion to proclaim it?

After presenting the contents of his message, Paul shared the burden he carried for communicating that message to others. Motivated by a desire to glorify God, he wanted to go where no other messenger of the gospel has gone before.

David Brainerd, another of God's choice servants, was equally compelled to reach others for God's glory. Even a few weeks before his death, he wrote of his desire to serve God.

WALK WITH DAVID BRAINERD

"I do not go to heaven to be advanced, but to give honor to God. It is no matter where I shall be stationed in heaven; to love, and please, and glorify God is all.

"Had I a thousand souls, if they were worth anything, I would give them all to God; but I have nothing to give, when all is done.

"I long to be in heaven, praising and glorifying God with all the holy angels. All my desire is to glorify God.

"There is nothing in the world worth living for but doing good and finishing God's work, doing the work that Christ did.

"I see nothing else in the world that can yield any satisfaction besides living to God, pleasing him, and doing his whole will."

WALK CLOSER TO GOD

David Brainerd. The apostle Paul. Both shared burdens for God's glory and people's souls.

They experienced the comfort of the gospel. But beyond that, they felt the compulsion of the gospel—the restless dissatisfaction of knowing that others had not yet heard.

You enjoy the same gospel of life that transformed David Brainerd and Paul. Ask God to give you the same burden that ignited their lives to his glory. ✤

DOXOLOGY FOR THE REVEALED MYSTERY

Now to him who is able to establish you in accordance with my gospel, the message I proclaim about Jesus Christ, in keeping with the revelation of the mystery ....

ROMANS 16:25

According to Paul, the Good News was a mystery for many years. But the final page fell open with the coming of Jesus Christ. And Paul's response in Romans 16—after explaining the mystery of Christ and the gospel—is praise.

Columba, one the earliest missionaries to Scotland, provides this fitting doxology of praise.

WALK WITH COLUMBA

God, Thou art the Father
   Of all that have believed:
From whom all hosts of angels
   Have life and power received.
O God, Thou art the Maker
   Of all created things,
The righteous Judge of judges,
   The almighty King of Kings.

High in the heavenly Zion
   Thou reignest God adored;
And in the coming glory
   Thou shalt be Sovereign Lord.
Beyond our view Thou shinest,
   The everlasting Light;
Ineffable in loving,
   Unthinkable in might.

Thou to the meek and lowly
   Thy secrets dost unfold;
O God, Thou doest all things,
   All things both new and old.
I walk secure and blessed
   In every clime or coast,
In name of God the Father,
   And Son, and Holy Ghost.

WALK CLOSER TO GOD

Remember, what is the Good News to you may still be a mystery to others around you—others who will gladly join in your chorus of praise once they have heard and responded. ✤

july1

I WILL GLORY IN THE LORD

Because of him ... you are in Christ Jesus ... Therefore, as it is written: "Let the one who boasts boast in the Lord".

1 Corinthians 1:30–31

Prestige and pride. They often go together. The city of Corinth provides a case in point.

A crossroads of trade and transportation, Corinth became a first-century boomtown. Gold was abundant—and with it came a kind of "fool's gold" glory based on human wisdom and material prosperity.

Jonathan Edwards comments on Paul's first letter to the Corinthians and the problem of misplaced pride.

WALK WITH JONATHAN EDWARDS

"Let us exalt God alone and ascribe to him all the glory of redemption.

"Man is naturally prone to exalt himself and depend on his own power or goodness. But this chapter should teach us to exalt God alone, not only by trust and reliance, but also by praise: 'Let the one who boasts boast in the Lord.'

"Do you have hope that you are converted, that your sins are forgiven, and that you have been received into God's favor and are his child, an heir of eternal life? Then give God the glory!

"If you excel in holiness, take no glory to yourself, but ascribe it to him whose workmanship you are."

WALK CLOSER TO GOD

From a human perspective, the Corinthians had much to brag about.

But God sent his Son to save not those who gloried in their achievements but those who willingly acknowledged they were "foolish ... weak ... lowly ... despised ... that no one may boast before him" (1 Corinthians 1:27–29).

What a glorious thought!

God saved you—"foolish" sinner that you were—that you might become a trophy of his love, a mirror of his glory.

You can reflect his glory back to him right now by giving thanks for his grace on your behalf. ❖

july2

THE SOUL TURNED TOWARD GOD IN OBEDIENT FAITH

In the same way no one knows the thoughts of God except the Spirit of God. What we have received is not the spirit of the world, but the Spirit who is from God, so that we may understand what God has freely given us.

1 CORINTHIANS 2:11–12

At birth you received five senses with which to perceive the physical world around you.

Coming to Christ, you received a "sixth sense" in the person of the Holy Spirit who opens up a world of spiritual reality.

Read carefully as F. B. Meyer examines the work of God's "sixth sense" in the lives of men and women.

WALK WITH F. B. MEYER

"When we turn toward God in obedient faith, we are lifted through faith into union with the heavenly man, the Lord Jesus Christ, and rise above the natural level.

"Then we walk in a new world; then we become aware of the unseen and eternal; then the spiritual senses are as quick to discern good and evil as our physical is to distinguish light from dark.

"The spirit is our capacity for God. When it is brought to life, we move on to new levels of experience; we touch reality.

"When a channel is formed between the Spirit of God and the spirit of man, there is an instant communication of grace and power which finds its way into every avenue of the soul, enlightening the mind and imparting a divine enthusiasm."

WALK CLOSER TO GOD

Jesus said, "When he, the Spirit of truth, comes, he will guide you into all the truth ... and he will tell you what is yet to come" (John 16:13).

The Spirit was given to help you understand the world as it really is — the world as God sees it.

Do you need guidance to choose the right path? Wisdom to correctly order your priorities?

Then look to the Spirit of God. He will guide you, through prayer and the pages of Scripture, into a realm of insight about which the world knows nothing. ❖

BEING WISE IN GOD'S EYES

If any of you think you are wise by the standards of this age, you should become "fools" so that you may become wise. For the wisdom of this world is foolishness in God's sight.

1 CORINTHIANS 3:18 – 19

Suppose a renowned scientist reported the conclusion that there is no God.

What would you conclude about his conclusion?

If you are wise, you would respond with the words of the psalmist: "The fool says in his heart, 'There is no God'" (Psalm 14:1).

John Calvin provides a helpful insight into this issue of human foolishness.

WALK WITH JOHN CALVIN

"Paul does not require that we should altogether renounce the wisdom that is implanted in us by nature but simply that we subject it to the service of God.

"The 'wisdom of this world' is that which assumes to itself authority, and does not allow itself to be regulated by the Word of God. We become a fool in this world when we give way to God and embrace with fear and reverence everything he teaches us, rather than follow what seems plausible.

"It is necessary for our wisdom to vanish in this way in order that God may have authority over us, and that we be emptied of our own understanding and be filled with the wisdom of God.

"Until an individual acknowledges that he knows nothing but what he has learned from God, he is wise in the world's account, but he is foolish in the estimation of God."

WALK CLOSER TO GOD

The Christian acknowledges that God exists. The world thinks it is wise to try to live without him.

What do you think?

The Christian knows there is a God—and is labeled a "fool" by the world for believing so. The world denies there is a God—and is labeled a "fool" by God's Word for believing so.

In the final analysis, whose "fool" would you rather be? ✤

TO MAKE KNOWN THE TREASURES OF HIS LOVE

This, then, is how you ought to regard us: as servants of Christ and as those entrusted with the mysteries God has revealed. Now it is required that those who have been given a trust must prove faithful.

1 CORINTHIANS 4:12

It may surprise you to learn that your responsibilities as a steward extend far beyond your financial resources.

You are also commanded to be a steward of God's grace (see 1 Peter 4:10), of your words (see Matthew 12:36), of your time (see Psalm 90:12)—in short, of yourself (see Romans 14:12).

Andrew Murray explains your role as a steward of money ... and much more.

WALK WITH ANDREW MURRAY

"A steward is the one to whom the master entrusts his treasures or goods, to divide among those who have a right to them.

"God in heaven is looking for men and women on earth to make known the treasures of his love by giving them to those who have need.

"A steward must be a faithful person, fully devoted to his life task. And the messenger of the gospel must be faithful in living each day in the love and fellowship of God. God's messenger must be faithful also to others, ready to recommend God's love and to share it with others.

"Child of God, seek to have a deeper insight into what it means to be a steward of the wonderful love of God to sinners."

WALK CLOSER TO GOD

Paul underscored the attitude of a steward this way: "What do you have that you did not receive?" (1 Corinthians 4:7).

Nothing! And you are responsible for everything you have received—to do with as God wills.

The 12 disciples were the first trustees of the message of life. If they had proven unfaithful in the task, where might you be today?

Now the responsibility is yours. You can give so that others might receive the gift of life.

It's a stewardship of something far more precious than money. Are you handling it that way? ✤

A TRULY UNLEAVENED LUMP

Don't you know that a little yeast leavens the whole batch of dough? Get rid of the old yeast, so that you may be a new unleavened batch—as you really are.

1 Corinthians 5:6–7

The Corinthian church was suffering from a serious condition—and didn't realize it.

Moral laxness, like yeast in a batch of dough, was threatening to permeate the entire assembly—a radical condition calling for an equally radical solution, as G. Campbell Morgan explains.

WALK WITH G. CAMPBELL MORGAN

"The whole body of Christ is affected by the sin of one member.

"The church's life is weaker if one in the fellowship continues in sin. The church's testimony to those outside is weakened by that fact.

"Thus, we have no right to refuse to exercise the discipline of love in the case of anyone who, to our knowledge, has flagrantly sinned.

"The law which the apostle states here is that the leaven [yeast] is to be purged. Leaven communicates itself, spreads its own corrupting force wherever it goes.

"A little leaven—one man sinning and permitted to remain within the fellowship of the church—will spread, first unconsciously and insidiously, but most surely throughout the whole church.

"There is no more difficult or delicate thing awaiting us in our church fellowship than the matter of discipline.

"May God give us of his Spirit that we may dare to deal with sin and refuse to give it harbor or refuge within our fellowship."

WALK CLOSER TO GOD

Surgery is never pleasant. But when the choice is between difficult, delicate discipline and a body whose strength is sapped by sin, which course would you choose?

Better yet, don't wait until surgery is called for. Deal with sin promptly, personally, Biblically (see Matthew 18:15–17). It's much less painful than surgery for all involved. ✣

july**6**

GIVING ALL, GAINING ALL

Do you not know that your bodies are temples of the Holy Spirit, who is in you, whom you have received from God? You are not your own.

1 Corinthians 6:19

"Haven't you heard?"

It's a question often asked when a piece of news—good or bad—is assumed to be common knowledge.

In chapters five and six, Paul used a similar question to jog the memories of the church members at Corinth. Seven times he challenged them by asking, "Do you not know?" (1 Corinthians 5:6; 6:2,3,9,15,16,19).

Listen as A. B. Simpson expounds on how you belong to God.

WALK WITH A. B. SIMPSON

"What a privilege that we may consecrate ourselves! What rest and comfort lie hidden in those words, 'not your own.'

"I am not responsible for my salvation, not burdened by my cares, not obliged to live for my interest, but I am altogether his. I am redeemed, owned, saved, loved, and kept in his strong, unchanging arms.

"Oh, the rest from sin and self and anxiety-producing care which true consecration brings. To be able to give him our poor weak life, with its awful possibilities and its utter helplessness. To know he will accept it, and take a joy and pride in making out of it the utmost possibilities of blessing, power, and usefulness. To give all, and find in so doing that we have gained all. To be so yielded to him in entire self-surrender that he is bound to care for us as for himself.

"We are putting ourselves in the hands of a loving Father, more solicitous for our good than we can be, and only wanting us to be fully submitted to him that he may be more free to bless us."

WALK CLOSER TO GOD

God owns you because he bought you at a staggering price. Your salvation—though a free gift to you—was no "cheap grace" from God. Rather, it cost him "the precious blood of Christ, a lamb without blemish" (1 Peter 1:19).

What—haven't you heard? ❖

TWO PLUS ONE EQUALS ONE

The husband should fulfill his marital duty to his wife, and likewise the wife to her husband.

1 CORINTHIANS 7:3

No other institution has been pushed, pulled, probed and prodded over the centuries like the institution of marriage. And yet it has never grown obsolete, because it is not merely a good idea—it is God's idea.

Martin Luther, a husband and father of six, considered marriage to be a school of character building. Listen as he extols the high calling of holy matrimony:

WALK WITH MARTIN LUTHER

"Married life is no jest or to be taken lightly, but it is an excellent thing and a matter of divine seriousness.

"For it is of the highest importance to God that people be raised who may serve the Lord and promote knowledge of him through godly living and virtue, in order to fight against wickedness and the devil.

"I have always taught that marriage should not be despised, but that it be regarded according to God's Word, by which it is adorned and sanctified.

"Therefore it is not a peculiar estate [condition], but the most common and noblest estate, which pervades all Christendom, and even extends through all the world."

WALK CLOSER TO GOD

For two to become truly one, there must be a third: God—the one who designed marriage in the first place.

And he has authored the most successful marriage manual of all time. That "manual," of course, is the Bible. But do you know what it says in such important chapters as 1 Corinthians 7, Ephesians 5, and 1 Peter 3? If not, it's time to find out.

After all, who should know more about helping your marriage to succeed than the one who performed the first wedding—and blessed it with his benediction (see Genesis 1:28)! ❖

LORD OF ALL GRAND DESIGNS AND DAILY DETAILS

Yet for us there is but ... one Lord, Jesus Christ, through whom all things came and through whom we live.

1 CORINTHIANS 8:6

Jesus had no less than 40 names! Names such as Son of God, Alpha and Omega, Good Shepherd. Names that describe who he is, what he is like, what he does and will do.

But one word summarizes them all: Lord.

It's a designation the Corinthians had lost sight of, causing them to abuse their Christian freedom and ignore their Christian obligations.

Allow Cyril of Jerusalem to explain why "Lord" is a summary of who Jesus is.

WALK WITH CYRIL OF JERUSALEM

"It is for the good of each individual that the Savior comes in many characters.

"He stands as the Door before those who should be entering. Before those who have prayers to pray, he stands as their mediating High Priest. He is the Lamb, to those with sins upon them, to be slain for those sins.

"He 'become[s] all things to all people' (1 Corinthians 9:22), and yet never changes from his own proper nature. He adapts himself to our infirmities as the kindest of physicians or as an understanding teacher.

"He really is Lord, not because he worked at achieving it, but because he possesses by nature the dignity of being Lord. He is not called Lord out of courtesy but because he is Lord in sheer fact.

"He is the Maker of all things; thus, he is Lord of all things."

WALK CLOSER TO GOD

"In him all things were created ... He is before all things, and in him all things hold together" (Colossians 1:16–17). That means he has owner's rights to the universe. And that includes you.

He owns you because he made you. And he loved you enough to die for you. No wonder he deserves to be called Lord of your life. ✤

july9

MASTERING THE SELF, CONQUERING THE FLESH

Everyone who competes in the games goes into strict training ... I strike a blow to my body and make it my slave.

1 CORINTHIANS 9:25,27

The Corinthians had much to learn about moderation and self-control—lessons Paul was eager to teach them.

In ancient times athletes disciplined their minds and bodies just to win a fragile wreath of laurel. How much more one who "competes in the games" with eternal, indestructible rewards in view!

More than 500 years ago, Thomas à Kempis gave this counsel about the problem of self-control.

WALK WITH THOMAS À KEMPIS

"Various desires and longings often inflame you and drive you forward with vehemence. But consider whether you are not moved for your own advantage rather than for God's honor.

"Not every desire which seems good is immediately to be followed; nor again is every unpleasant desire at the first to be avoided.

"It is sometimes expedient to use restraint even in good desires and endeavors, so that they do not become annoying distractions.

"Sometimes you must use physical means to resist valiantly the desires of the senses, and disregard what the flesh wants.

"The flesh must be disciplined and forced to remain under servitude until it is prepared for everything, and until you learn to be content with little and to be pleased with plain and simple things, not murmuring against any inconvenience."

WALK CLOSER TO GOD

"Competes ... strike ... make it my slave." Those words demand a willful resolve and an active response.

How much you eat, sleep, exercise, relax—all these are part of learning self-mastery, so that you might be strong and ready for the Master's service.

Many are unwilling to pay the price and are therefore unprepared for the rigors of the "marathon race" known as the Christian life.

How will you resolve—and respond? ❖

IN DAYS OF DANGER, SEEING THE PATHS OF SAFETY

God is faithful; he will not let you be tempted beyond what you can bear. But when you are tempted, he will also provide a way out so that you can endure it.

1 CORINTHIANS 10:13

Thomas à Kempis was right when he said, "Temptations discover what we are."

Daily confrontation with temptation is part of the price of being human.

But while you have no say in the matter of whether you will be tempted (you will be!), you do have much to say about the outcome. There will always be a way out.

John Calvin highlights this important but infrequently applied truth.

WALK WITH JOHN CALVIN

"Paul exhorts us to look to the Lord, because even the slightest temptation will overcome us if we rely on our own strength.

"He speaks of the Lord as faithful and true to his promises, as though he had said, 'The Lord is the sure guardian of his people, under whose protection you are safe. For he never leaves his people destitute.'

"When you are under his protection, you have no cause to fear, provided you depend entirely upon him.

"Now God helps us in two ways so that we may not be overcome by the temptation: he supplies us with strength, and he sets limits to the temptation. He knows the measure of our power, which he has conferred. According to that he regulates our temptations."

WALK CLOSER TO GOD

Since God has promised a way out when temptation strikes, then the real issue is not, "Can I emerge victorious?" You can!

Rather, the questions are: "Lord, am I willing to look for your way out? When I find it, am I willing to use it? And once I've used it, am I willing to resist the urge to leave a forwarding address?"

Where there's a *willingness*, there's a way! ✤

july11

GOD'S PRESENCE IN TROUBLED TIMES

When we are judged in this way by the Lord, we are being disciplined so that we will not be finally condemned with the world.

1 CORINTHIANS 11:32

Joseph in the pit. Job among the ashes. Jeremiah in the dungeon. Paul in the Philippian jail.

Individuals God forgot about? Quite the contrary! Individuals in close communication with their Creator. Each learned that a child of God need never be alarmed at the presence of trouble when God is an ever-present companion.

Martin Luther underscores this truth.

WALK WITH MARTIN LUTHER

"Reason holds that if God had a watchful eye on us and loved us, he would prevent all evil and not let us suffer. But now, since all sorts of calamities come to us, we conclude: 'Either God has forgotten me, or God is hostile to me and does not want me.'

"Against such thoughts, which we harbor by nature, we must arm ourselves with God's Word. We must not judge according to our opinion but according to the Word.

"First Corinthians 11 tells us that God disciplines those whom he intends to keep and preserve for eternal life—that he cannot be hostile to them, but that they must nonetheless suffer all sorts of trouble, crosses, and temptations. We should cling to such passages in times of temptation.

"Suppose a person has a trouble from which he would gladly be relieved. If he thinks: 'See here! If I did not have this affliction, I would fall into this or that mischief; God is acting in my best interests, to keep me in his fear and drive me to the Word and prayer.' It will clearly appear that God does not discipline us because he is hostile to us, but to show us his love."

WALK CLOSER TO GOD

Father, I confess how frequently I view my problems as evidence that you have forgotten me, rather than as tokens of your constant watch and care over me.

When troubles and trials cause me to doubt your goodness, help me instead to cling to your Word. ✤

july12

THE BODY—WHERE ALL THE BITS FIT

There are different kinds of gifts, but the same Spirit.

1 CORINTHIANS 12:4

Chances are good you've never seen your stapes or sternum, your spleen or scapula. But look up those words in a medical dictionary, and you'll be glad they're on the job!

Each part of your anatomy differs from all the others, but all the parts work together harmoniously, enabling you to live, breathe, walk and talk. Each member of Christ's body depends on all the other members for life, health and growth.

This interdependence leads John Henry Jowett to remind us to concentrate on making our unique contribution to the life of the body.

WALK WITH JOHN HENRY JOWETT

"Our gifts will be manifold, and we must not allow the difference to breed a spirit of suspicion. Because my brother's gift is not mine, I must not suspect his calling. To one is given a trumpet, to another a lamp, to another a spade. All are holy gifts of grace.

"And thus the gifts are manifold in order that everyone may find his completeness in his brother. One person is like an eye—he is a seer of visions! Another is like a hand—he has the genius of practicality. He is a 'handy-man'! One is the architect, the other is the builder. And each requires the other, if either is to be perfected.

"And so, by God's gracious Spirit, the individual is only a bit, a portion, and he is intended to fit into the other bits, and so make the complete body of Christ."

WALK CLOSER TO GOD

Are you a trumpeter for the Lord? Then blow your horn!

Does your lamp brighten another's darkness? Keep it burning!

Do you have the voice of an angel? Then let your tongue sing God's praises!

Someone else in the body needs your ministry. Only you can perform a particular act of service. Don't neglect that responsibility, for God counts on *your* response to *his* ability! ✤

july13

THE LAST WORD ON LOVE

And now these three remain: faith, hope and love. But the greatest of these is love.

1 CORINTHIANS 13:13

Love means giving yourself. It is patterned on the example of God himself.

God gave his only Son to individuals deserving far less. In words of beauty and depth, Paul calls on grateful believers to love in return.

Jonathan Edwards probes the Bible's greatest chapter on love.

WALK WITH JONATHAN EDWARDS

"A true respect for either God or man consists in love. If a man sincerely loves God, it will lead him to show all proper respect to him; and men need no other motivation to show each other all the respect that is due than the motivation of love.

"Love for God will lead a man to honor him, worship and adore him, and heartily acknowledge his greatness, glory, and dominion.

"And so it will lead to acts of obedience to God; for the servant that loves his master—like the citizen that loves his ruler—will be inclined to proper subjection.

"Love will lead us to praise God for the mercies we receive from him. Love will incline our hearts to submit to the will of God, for we are more willing that the will of those we love should be done than the will of others.

"True affection for God will lead us to acknowledge God's right and worthiness to govern.

"The true Christian is willing to admit that God is worthy of this, and it is with delight that he casts himself before the Most High, because of his sincere love for him."

WALK CLOSER TO GOD

Today "I love" often means "I want" or "I desire." A fallen world has twisted the meaning of love 180 degrees.

As both Jonathan Edwards and Paul suggest, love is what you give, not what you get.

Loving God means giving yourself to God.

When was the last time you told your heavenly Father, "I love you"? ❖

SPIRIT OF WORSHIP, SPIRIT OF GOD

I will pray with my spirit, but I will also pray with my understanding; I will sing with my spirit, but I will also sing with my understanding.

1 CORINTHIANS 14:15

In one church, the piano is out of tune, the sound system buzzes, the hymnals are dog-eared, and few in the congregation can sing on key. In another church, the building is a historic treasure, the choir is resplendently robed, singing is accompanied by organ and orchestra, and the service moves with flawless precision.

Question: In which church is worship taking place?

Answer: Either or neither or both. It all depends on who is leading the service. Confused?

Listen as Johann Peter Lange helps to unravel the mystery.

WALK WITH JOHANN PETER LANGE

"In all true worship that is honorable to God and beneficial to his children, the Holy Spirit is the reason that it is so.

"It is only so far as he helps our infirmities and teaches us how to pray, only so far as he gives us an insight and understanding into divine truth, only so far as he inspires our songs and praises, that our worship is truly spiritual and edifying.

"So what is most needed in preparation for worship is to seek his presence and aid.

"No amount of learning, natural gifts, acquired skills, or refinements of art can compensate for that anointing of the Holy One which is promised to the believer to teach him all things."

WALK CLOSER TO GOD

With the Holy Spirit, you can worship in spirit and truth, regardless of any "technical problems."

Without the Holy Spirit, you can create an elaborate production that pleases people—without worshiping God.

You needn't wait till Sunday to worship the Lord. Even now, the Spirit can lead you to declare his greatness and goodness in adoring praise.

Whether you're on key or off, the Spirit can tune your worship to please God. ❖

PEACE: A PRIORITY FOR WORSHIP

For God is not a God of disorder but of peace.

1 CORINTHIANS 14:33

The pastor was leading a group of young children from his church in a spelling bee. "All right," he turned to the next child, "your word to spell is *worship*."

"Warship. W-A-R-S-H-I-P. Am I right?" the child asked. With a deep sigh, the pastor replied, "Yes, unfortunately, much of the time you are!"

In the Corinthian church, confusion and strife were marking the worship services. John Calvin points to the importance of peace and order as priorities in corporate worship.

WALK WITH JOHN CALVIN

"We do not serve God unless we are in any case lovers of peace and are eager to promote it. Whenever there is a disposition to quarrel, there you can be certain God does not reign.

"Yet many people fly into a rage about nothing, or they trouble the church from a desire that they may somehow ride into view and seem to be someone.

"Let us therefore bear in mind that, as servants of Christ, this mark must be kept in view—to aim at peace and concord, conduct ourselves peaceably, and avoid contentions to the utmost of our power.

"For if we are called to contend against wicked doctrines, we must persevere in the contest. We must make it our aim that the truth of God may maintain its ground without contention."

WALK CLOSER TO GOD

Interruptions and distractions, disorder and discord—not a pretty scene under any circumstances but particularly inappropriate in the church of Jesus Christ.

Why? Because God has called his people to worship him in a way that draws attention to the object of worship, not to the worshipers themselves. Worship that is in spirit, in truth, in peace, in order.

As John Calvin has commented, "How easy it is to *say* this!" But what will you do about it? ❖

july16

SILVER THREAD OF THE RESURRECTION

And if Christ has not been raised, your faith is futile; you are still in your sins ... But Christ has indeed been raised from the dead, the firstfruits of those who have fallen asleep.

1 CORINTHIANS 15:17,20

Resurrection, the grand theme of 1 Corinthians 15, is the heart of the Christian faith. Expose it as a fraud, and all else becomes meaningless.

Yet the resurrection is no mere illusion. It is a fact of history, confirmed by hundreds of eyewitnesses and abundant evidence.

Charles Spurgeon expands these thoughts.

WALK WITH CHARLES SPURGEON

"Christianity rests upon the fact that 'He [Christ] has risen from the dead' (Matthew 28:7). The deity of Christ finds its surest proof in his resurrection, since he was 'appointed the Son of God in power by his resurrection from the dead' (Romans 1:4). It would be reasonable to doubt his deity if he had not risen.

"Moreover, Christ's sovereignty depends upon his resurrection, 'for this very reason, Christ died and returned to life so that he might be Lord of both the dead and the living' (Romans 14:9).

"Our justification is linked with Christ's triumphant victory over death and the grave; for he 'was delivered over to death for our sins and was raised to life for our justification' (Romans 4:25).

"And most certainly our ultimate resurrection rests here; for 'he who raised up Christ from the dead will also give life to your mortal bodies because of his Spirit who lives in you' (Romans 8:11).

"The silver thread of resurrection runs through all the believer's blessings, from his regeneration to his eternal glory, binding them together."

WALK CLOSER TO GOD

Many have scoffed at the resurrection, only to find themselves later bowing in submission to the risen Christ. The Athenians responded with mocking and ridicule (see Acts 17:32); the Bereans, with careful investigation and belief (see Acts 17:11–12).

And you? What will you do with the compelling evidence for the resurrection — evidence only a scoffer would ignore? ✣

THE BELIEVER'S SURE VICTORY — IN JESUS

"Where, O death, is your victory? Where, O death, is your sting?" . . . But thanks be to God! He gives us the victory through our Lord Jesus Christ.

1 CORINTHIANS 15:55,57

An eternity with God and away from the presence of corruption and sin — for the Christian, that's the glory that lies beyond the doorway of death.

That's a thought that prompts Paul to break forth in thanks and praise.

Matthew Henry adds his own postscript of praise — a word written not long before his death.

WALK WITH MATTHEW HENRY

"What can be more joyous in itself than the saints' triumph over death, when they shall rise again?

"Those who remain under the power of death can have no heart to praise. But such triumphs tune the tongues of the saints to thankfulness and praise for the victory and for the means by which it is obtained.

"That victory is not obtained by our power, but by God's power; not given because we are worthy, but because Christ is worthy.

"How many springs of joy to the saints and thanksgiving to God are opened by the death and resurrection, the suffering and conquest, of our Redeemer! With what acclamations will saints rising from the dead applaud him! How the heavens will resound with his praises forever!

"'Thanks be to God' will be the theme of their song, and angels will join the chorus and declare their consent with a loud 'Amen. Hallelujah!'"

WALK CLOSER TO GOD

Those without Christ face a hopeless end; those with Christ look forward to an endless hope.

Those under the power of death can have no heart to praise. But you have a message of life to share with those living in the fear of death.

What grander chorus of praise could you sing to God — or share with others — than that of victory in Jesus! You'll never tire of singing it eternally. ✣

july**18**

THE TEST OF OUR LOVE

If anyone does not love the Lord, let that person be cursed! Come, Lord!.

1 CORINTHIANS 16:22

The last chapter of 1 Corinthians poses the "final examination question" on which all others hinge: Do you love the Lord Jesus Christ?

No matter how impressive your record of service, how extensive the credentials or expertise you bring to the Lord or offer to his people, you must honestly answer that basic question. If you love the Lord with the same kind of love that a child shows a parent, you will pass life's final exam — and all the others in between — as Charles Hodge explains.

WALK WITH CHARLES HODGE

"If we love Christ, we shall be zealous for his glory. Any neglect or irreverence shown the Savior will wound our hearts. Any honor rendered him will give us delight.

"We will love those who love and honor him, and avoid those who neglect and abuse him.

"The son who loves his father desires to please him, to do his will, obey his command, observe his counsel, always and in all places. So those who love Christ keep his commandments. This is the test of love for Christ: not emotion, not excited feelings, but obedience.

"What say you? Do you love the Lord Jesus Christ? On this question depends eternity.

"Here on earth those who love and those who do not love form distinct classes, though intermingled. Hereafter they will be separated. Do you desire to love? It is love only if it leads to a constant endeavor to do his will and to associate with his people."

WALK CLOSER TO GOD

Jesus lovingly came to bring God's love to earth. He lovingly served all who acknowledged their need. He lovingly sacrificed his life that sins might be forgiven.

Now he waits for you to return that love in simple gratitude, in loving obedience to him, in loving service to others, in loving fellowship with those who call him Lord. ♣

TROUBLE: SIGN OF AN ACTIVE SOUL

For just as we share abundantly in the sufferings of Christ, so also our comfort abounds through Christ.

2 CORINTHIANS 1:5

When Christ gives peace, he says, "I have told you these things, so that in me you may have peace. In this world you will have trouble. But take heart! I have overcome the world" (John 16:33).

He is a peace that conquers and comforts.

The opening words of the second letter to the Corinthians speak of the comfort of Christ. But as John Henry Jowett points out, peace comes to aid us in the struggle, not help us avoid it.

WALK WITH JOHN HENRY JOWETT

"It is possible to evade a multitude of sorrows by the cultivation of an insignificant life.

"Indeed, if a man's ambition is to avoid the troubles of life, the recipe is simple: Shed your ambitions in every direction, cut the wings of every soaring purpose, and seek a little life with the fewest contacts and relations.

"If you want to get through the world with the smallest trouble, you must reduce yourself to the smallest compass. Tiny souls can dodge through life; bigger souls are blocked on every side.

"As soon as a man begins to enlarge his life, his resistances are multiplied. Let a man remove his petty selfish purposes and enthrone Christ, and his sufferings will be increased on every side.

"So it was with the Savior. His all-absorbing, redemptive purpose was bound to introduce him to endless suffering."

WALK CLOSER TO GOD

Who is better qualified to work for peace than those who have experienced God's peace firsthand?

You have been comforted by Christ—not to make you comfortable but to make you a comforter, a dispenser of peace.

But it begins with a life at peace with God—forgiven, cleansed, comforted.

Is that you?

It can be if you make 2 Corinthians 1:3–5 the prayer of your heart ... right now. ❖

A LETTER TO THE WORLD

You yourselves are our letter, written on our hearts, known and read by everyone ... written not with ink but with the Spirit of the living God.

2 CORINTHIANS 3:2–3

In this passage, Paul likened the Christian to a literary production ("letter") of Christ—a letter others can read.

It's as if he were asking the reader: "Would the message of your life demonstrate the personality and character of Christ ... or something else?"

H. A. Ironside itemizes what some of those markings of Christ in your life might be.

WALK WITH H. A. IRONSIDE

"Do people see something of the patience of Christ, the meekness of Christ, the purity of Christ, the love of Christ, and the tender compassion of Christ in me?

"As I mingle with others in my daily employment, those with whom I have the most to do should see a difference.

"Do they say, 'Well, so-and-so may be a Christian; if he is, I do not think much of Christianity'?

"Or are we so living Christ that others looking upon us say, 'Well, if that is Christianity, I wish I knew something of it in my own life'?

"Long for someone to say to you: 'I cannot help but believe in the reality of the message you preach because of the effect it has on the people I have seen who believe it.'

"This is what Paul means when he says that we are the letter of Christ."

WALK CLOSER TO GOD

When you are truly a letter of Christ, no one will be able to deny the fact.

The markings will be there: "love, joy, peace, forbearance, kindness, goodness, faithfulness, gentleness and self-control"—in essence, all the fruit of the Spirit (Galatians 5:22–23).

Your life can be an open book for all to see the life of Christ in you—a love letter to a lost world.

The "letter" of one life is worth a thousand words. But only you can determine the content of that letter and what it will reveal to those who take the time to read it. ✣

FOCUSING ON THE FUTURE IS
A GLORIOUS WAY TO LIVE

For our light and momentary troubles are achieving for us an eternal glory that far out-weighs them all.

2 CORINTHIANS 4:17

Anticipation is the delight of looking forward to not-yet-experienced events: graduation, Christmas, birthdays, reunions, vacations.

And for the Christian, life after death and a home in heaven.

When the present is unpleasant, take the advice of Charles Spurgeon and try focusing instead on the future.

WALK WITH CHARLES SPURGEON

"In our Christian pilgrimage, it is good to be looking forward.

"Whether it be for hope or joy, for consolation or for the inspiring of our love, the future must, after all, be the grand object of the eye of faith.

"Looking into the future, we see sin cast out, the body of sin and death destroyed, the soul made perfect and fit to be a partaker of the saints in light.

"Looking further yet, the believer's enlightened eye can see death's river passed and the celestial city standing ahead.

"He sees himself enter the gates, hailed as more than conqueror, embraced in the arms of Jesus, glorified, and made to sit together with him.

"The thought of this future may well relieve the darkness of the past and the gloom of the present.

"The joys of heaven will surely compensate for the sorrows of earth."

WALK CLOSER TO GOD

Struggles with sin. Pressures at work. Relationships that have soured.

The "light and momentary troubles" Paul spoke about certainly weren't reserved for only first-century believers!

But when the outlook is bleak, try the uplook.

You have an eternity with the Father to look forward to. Dwelling on the past may cause you to groan. But focusing on the future is a glorious way to live! ❖

july22

BRINGING DELIGHT TO THE HEART OF GOD

For we must all appear before the judgment seat of Christ, so that each one of us may receive what is due us for the things done while in the body, whether good or bad.

2 CORINTHIANS 5:10

People want approval and acceptance and will do any number of things to achieve it.

It is one thing to seek the fleeting approval of a parent, spouse or employer. It is something infinitely more significant to seek—and experience—the approval of almighty God, as C. S. Lewis explains.

WALK WITH C. S. LEWIS

"How God thinks of us is infinitely more important than how we think of God. Indeed, how we think of him is only of importance in so far as it is related to how he thinks of us.

"In the end that face which is the delight or the terror of the universe must be turned upon each of us either with one expression or the other, either conferring glory inexpressible or inflicting shame that can never be cured or disguised.

"It is written that we shall 'stand before' him (Romans 14:10), shall appear, shall be inspected. The promise of glory is the promise—only possible by the work of Christ—that some of us shall find approval with God.

"To please God, to be a real ingredient in the divine happiness, to be loved by God, not merely pitied, but delighted in as an artist delights in his work or a father in his son—it seems impossible, a weight or burden of glory which our thoughts can hardly sustain. But so it is."

WALK CLOSER TO GOD

Perhaps without knowing it, you have been bringing delight to the heart of God. The satisfaction of an artist gazing at his masterpiece, the joy of a Father well pleased with his child.

Put the two together, and they spell "approval"—approval that will one day be expressed and rewarded at the judgment seat of Christ.

It's an "eternal glory" (2 Corinthians 4:17) that can lift your thoughts in praise to the one who made it possible. ❖

OUR ARBITRATOR, COUNSELOR, AND MEDIATOR

All this is from God, who reconciled us to himself through Christ and gave us the ministry of reconciliation.

2 CORINTHIANS 5:18

Two companies working on a contract experience irreconcilable differences. Two teams during a game disagree on the interpretation of a particular rule. A husband and wife have problems that threaten to break up their marriage.

In each case the need is the same: an arbitrator, umpire, counselor, mediator—someone to reconcile the alienated parties. In a similar way sin has caused a breach in our relationship with God. But it is not an "irreconcilable difference." Matthew Henry explains.

WALK WITH MATTHEW HENRY

"Sin has broken the friendship between God and humanity. The heart of the sinner is filled with enmity against God, and God is justly offended by the sinner. Yet there may be a reconciliation; the offended Majesty of heaven is willing to be reconciled. He has appointed the Mediator of reconciliation, Jesus Christ.

"As God is willing to be reconciled to us, we ought to be reconciled to God. And it is the great end and design of the gospel, the word of reconciliation, to prevail upon sinners to lay aside their enmity against God.

"Wonderful condescension! God can be no loser by the quarrel, nor gainer by the peace. Yet by his ministers he beseeches sinners to lay aside their enmity and accept the terms he offers, that they would be reconciled to him, to believe in the Mediator, to accept the atonement, and comply with his gospel."

WALK CLOSER TO GOD

Ambassadors represent their native lands in foreign countries. They provide the crucial link between homeland and host land.

Your privilege as a Christian on planet Earth is similar: to represent the Mediator and his "native land." To be involved in the "ministry of reconciliation" by sharing the word of reconciliation with sinners alienated from God. ❖

A DWELLING IN WHICH GOD LIVES

We are the temple of the living God. As God has said: "I will live with them and walk among them, and I will be their God, and they will be my people".

2 CORINTHIANS 6:16

Temples don't mean much to twenty-first-century Christians. Most of us worship God in places that have little in common with the temples of antiquity.

To understand more fully what Paul's temple metaphor means, we need to be "time travelers"—we need to put ourselves in the historical context of Paul and his audience.

Travel back in time with Alfred Edersheim as he shows us how one old temple ceremony perfectly pictured the new temple made up of Christ and those on whom he has poured living water.

WALK WITH ALFRED EDERSHEIM

"When the water was being poured out, the temple music began. When the choir sang 'Hosanna, Lord,' all the worshipers shook their palms towards the altar. One year, on the last day of the feast (after the priest had poured out the water and the interest of the worshipers had been raised to its highest pitch), a voice resounded through the temple from amidst the mass of people chanting and shaking a forest of leafy branches. It was Jesus, who stood and cried, 'Let anyone who is thirsty come to me and drink ... Rivers of living water will flow from within them' (John 7:37–38). The effect was instantaneous. Suddenly roused by being face to face with him in whom every type and prophecy is fulfilled, many said, 'Surely this man is the Prophet' (John 7:40).

"When the crowd from Jerusalem took palm branches and went out to meet him shouting, 'Hosanna to the Son of David!' (Matthew 21:9), they applied to Christ one of the chief ceremonies of the feast. They were praying that God through the Son of David would now send the salvation which was symbolized by the pouring out of water."

WALK CLOSER TO GOD

In the Old Testament, the glory of the Lord filled the temple through the cloud. In the New Testament, God the Son fills the church—the new temple—through God the Holy Spirit. Paul expected that to energize the Corinthians to greater holiness. Wouldn't he expect it to do the same for us? ❖

HIS ALL-SUFFICIENT STRENGTH

When we came into Macedonia, we had no rest, but we were harassed at every turn — conflicts on the outside, fears within.

2 CORINTHIANS 7:5

Burnout — a term that refers to the point at which a missile's fuel is completely expended — is often used today to describe the symptoms of extreme stress. Paul's words in 2 Corinthians 7:5 — "conflicts on the outside, fears within" — capture the feelings of a person who is emotionally and physically spent ... burned out.

A. B. Simpson comments on why God would allow pressure like that to attack us.

WALK WITH A. B. SIMPSON

"Why should God have to lead us thus, and allow the pressure to be so hard and constant? In the first place, it shows his all-sufficient strength and grace much better than if we were exempt from pressure and trial.

"It makes us more conscious of our dependence upon him. God is constantly trying to teach us our dependence, and to hold us absolutely in his hand and hanging upon his care. This was the place where Jesus himself stood and where he wants us to stand, not with a self-constituted strength, but with a hand ever leaning upon his, and a trust that dares not take one step alone. It teaches us trust. There is no way of learning faith except by trial. It is God's school of faith, and it is far better for us to learn to trust God than to enjoy life.

"The lesson of faith, once learned, is an everlasting acquisition and an eternal fortune made; and without trust even riches will leave us poor."

WALK CLOSER TO GOD

God may want to use you — as a minister of encouragement, a bringer of refreshment — in the life of a burned-out fellow Christian today. And that means you can't afford to be burned out yourself.

Ministering strength to others demands that you be experiencing strength yourself — strength that comes from depending on God.

"Fuel" for thought, wouldn't you agree? ✤

LITTLE IS MUCH WHEN GOD IS IN IT!

For you know the grace of our Lord Jesus Christ, that though he was rich, yet for your sake he became poor, so that you through his poverty might become rich.

2 CORINTHIANS 8:9

Have you ever wondered what you would do with a million dollars? Here is one way to know: Look at what you're doing with the money you have already.

The Macedonian believers could scarcely be called rich. And yet they gave generously to their sister churches that were suffering from famine.

George Müller, a model for selfless giving, draws this insight from their godly example.

WALK WITH GEORGE MÜLLER

"Believers should seek more and more to enter into the grace and love of God in giving his only begotten Son, and into the grace and love of the Lord Jesus Christ in giving himself in our place.

"This is so that, constrained by love and gratitude, they may increasingly surrender their bodily and mental strength, their time, gifts, talents, property, position in life, rank, and all they have and are to the Lord.

"By this I do not mean that they should give up their profession and become preachers. Nor do I mean that they should take all their money and give it to the first beggar who asks for it.

"But they should hold all that they have and are for the Lord, not as owners but as stewards, and be willing to use for him part or all that they have."

WALK CLOSER TO GOD

God doesn't expect you to carry the needs of the world on your shoulders. That's his job.

But he has given you treasure to share with others—at his bidding.

As Mr. Müller suggests, that treasure includes your "bodily and mental strength, [your] time, gifts, talents … and all [you] have and are."

You may not think that's much. But don't forget what God did with a little boy's lunch (see John 6) and a widow's two small copper coins (see Luke 21).

Little is much when God is in it! ✤

july27

GIVING THAT SHOWS GRATITUDE

And God is able to bless you abundantly, so that in all things at all times, having all that you need, you will abound in every good work.

2 CORINTHIANS 9:8

The truth of Paul's message is clear: God gives, so that you in turn might give. God causes your life to overflow, so that other lives might be touched by his love as well.

We love ... because he first loved us. We give ... because God first gave the gift of his Son.

Albert Barnes explains that such a response is as appropriate — and desperately needed — as ever.

WALK WITH ALBERT BARNES

"There is no less occasion for Christian liberality now than there was in the time of Paul. There are still multitudes of poor who need the kind and efficient aid of Christians.

"Happy are they who are influenced by the gospel to do good to all people!

"Let us remember that it was because Jesus Christ came that there is any possibility of benefiting a dying world; and that all who profess to love him are bound to imitate his example and show their sense of obligation to God for giving a Savior.

"How poor and worthless are all our gifts compared with the great gift of God; how slight our expressions of compassion for others, compared with the compassion which he has shown for us!

"When God has given his Son to die for us, what should we not be willing to give that we may show our gratitude!"

WALK CLOSER TO GOD

The gift of Christ is "the gift that keeps on giving" — through you!

It can happen each day as you share the gospel, share your possessions, share your life.

No doubt you thank God often for what you receive. But when was the last time you thanked him for what he has privileged you to give?

After all, when a world is dying around you, that's not the time to hoard the gift of eternal life. ❖

GREATNESS THAT COMES THROUGH TOTAL SURRENDER

For it is not the one who commends himself who is approved, but the one whom the Lord commends.

2 CORINTHIANS 10:18

When it came to credentials, the apostle Paul didn't have to apologize. He had traveled thousands of miles, preached countless sermons, faced criticism and persecution, all for the sake of the gospel. Yet some people accused Paul of selfish motives and self-serving methods. Paul's defense was to boast—not about his accomplishments, but about his Lord.

As G. Campbell Morgan points out, letting the Lord work through him made Paul great.

WALK WITH G. CAMPBELL MORGAN

"The apostle's greatness was created in the first place by the absoluteness of his surrender to Jesus. On the way to Damascus—surprised, startled, and stricken to the earth by the revelation of the living Christ—he in one brief and simple question handed over his whole life to Jesus. 'What shall I do, Lord?' (Acts 22:10).

"The greatness of Paul as an apostle is further to be accounted for by his attitude toward all the things of his former life. 'But whatever were gains to me I now consider loss for the sake of Christ' (Philippians 3:7).

"Finally, his greatness is to be accounted for by the resulting experience which he crystallized into one brief sentence, 'To me, to live is Christ' (Philippians 1:21).

"Truly this was the great apostle, the great pattern for all time for those who would desire to be messengers of the cross of Christ."

WALK CLOSER TO GOD

Paul served Christ. Paul sacrificed for Christ. Paul lived for Christ.

Once you have met a truly great man like Paul—a Christlike man who could not care less for money or fame—you will know how poor you really are … until you respond as he did. By seeking the commendation of God, not man. By counting all things as loss for the sake of your Lord. By living only for his glory. ❖

STANDING FIRM AGAINST SATAN'S SCHEMES

And no wonder, for Satan himself masquerades as an angel of light.

2 CORINTHIANS 11:14

If you had the task of devising clever schemes to deceive people about the person and program of God, what dirty tricks would you suggest?

Perhaps you would start a "God Can't Be Trusted" campaign or you'd encourage people to procrastinate with their souls or you'd spread the lie that Christians don't enjoy life. Sadly, all of these schemes—and countless others—have been used by Satan, the "father of lies" (John 8:44), and his demons.

The need has never been greater for Christians who can stand tall against Satan's deceitful attacks, as Martin Luther points out.

WALK WITH MARTIN LUTHER

"The person who takes to heart the lesson that Christ hurts when the heart of a Christian is sad or frightened has won half the battle. For when I get to know the enemy who wants to frighten and depress me, I already have solid ground on which I can stand against him.

"The devil disguises himself as an angel of light. But this is a sign by which we may recognize him: He creates a timid, frightened, troubled conscience.

"False teachers cannot comfort or make happy a timid conscience; they only make hearts confused, sad, and melancholy so that people are gloomy and act sad. This, however, is nothing but the deception of the devil, who delights to make hearts fearful, cowardly, and timid.

"To be sure, a Christian leads a life that has much suffering and many temptations on the outside. Nevertheless, he can have a confident, happy heart toward God and can expect the best from him."

WALK CLOSER TO GOD

For the first half of his life, Luther lived like the very people he describes: afraid of God, dismayed by life. But once he understood the grace of God, Luther's fears gave way to a contagious exuberance that God would use to transform a continent.

Don't be deceived by an angel of light. Instead, fall at the feet of the light of the world, and discover anew that life is worth living. ✣

NEVER A BURDEN THAT HE CANNOT BEAR

Three times I pleaded with the Lord to take it away from me. But he said to me, "My grace is sufficient for you, for my power is made perfect in weakness".

2 CORINTHIANS 12:8−9

Few verses on prayer are quoted as frequently as James 4:2: "You do not have because you do not ask God." And few are quoted as rarely as James 4:3: "When you ask, you do not receive, because you ask with wrong motives."

For the Christian, there is no such thing as an unanswered prayer. God's answer may be "no" or "not yet." But the requests of his children never go unheeded—even the misguided ones.

J. Hudson Taylor has this to say about God's wise answers to his children's prayers.

WALK WITH J. HUDSON TAYLOR

"Paul was distressed by a burden which he had not strength to bear, and asked that the burden might be removed.

"God answered the prayer not by taking it away, but by showing him the power and grace to bear it joyfully.

"Thus, that which had been the cause of sorrow and regret became the occasion of rejoicing and triumph.

"And wasn't this really a better answer to Paul's prayer than the mere removing of the thorn?

"The latter course would have left him open to the same trouble when the next distress came; but God's method at once delivered him from all the oppression of the present and of all future similar trials.

"God's answer to Paul is a lesson to all. Let none fear to step out in glad obedience to the Master's command."

WALK CLOSER TO GOD

God may have sent you something quite different—like more problems!

Don't be hesitant to pray. But don't be surprised if God answers in ways you never expected in order to show you—as he did Paul—that his grace is sufficient. ❖

DELIBERATE LOVE THAT PLAYS FOR KEEPS

So I will very gladly spend for you everything I have and expend myself as well. If I love you more, will you love me less?

2 CORINTHIANS 12:15

Paul didn't know when to quit loving people. They might stop loving him, but he would never stop loving them.

The Corinthians found this out. Paul loved them enough to reprimand them and set them straight. And when they protested by criticizing him, he didn't turn away. After all, they didn't ask him to love them; God did!

God's love is like that—seeking even those who spurn it, as Oswald Chambers describes.

WALK WITH OSWALD CHAMBERS

"When the Spirit of God has shed abroad the love of God in our hearts, we begin deliberately to identify ourselves with Jesus Christ's interests in other people—and Jesus Christ is interested in every kind of person there is.

"We have no right in Christian work to be guided by our affinities; this is one of the biggest tests in your relationship to Jesus Christ.

"The delight of sacrifice is that I lay down my life for my Friend—not fling it away, but deliberately lay my life out for him and his interests in other people, not for a cause.

"Paul spent himself for one purpose only—that he might win people to Jesus Christ.

"Paul attracted others to Jesus all the time, never to himself. 'I have made myself a slave to everyone, to win as many as possible' (1 Corinthians 9:19)."

WALK CLOSER TO GOD

You may not like the people you are called to love. But you have someone to fall back on when you find it difficult to respond with smiles and warm feelings.

Paul was willing to spend everything he had for the Corinthians, though his love was seldom returned.

After reading his two inspired letters this month, do you think it was a wise investment?

Who are you investing your life in—a day at a time? ✣

august1

FINDING THE PATH FROM PRISON TO PEACE

The Lord Jesus Christ ... gave himself for our sins to rescue us from the present evil age.
GALATIANS 1:3–4

Nearly 500 years ago, a young monk wrestled with the question of his relationship to God. He had done all he knew to do but still had found no peace in his soul. It seemed that everything he tried fell short of heaven's demands.

Though at times he despaired of ever getting right with God, he one day found the forgiveness he had sought "through Jesus Christ our Lord" (Romans 7:25).

What acts of piety alone could not give, Martin Luther experienced in Christ—and you can too!

WALK WITH MARTIN LUTHER

"Say with confidence: 'Christ, the Son of God, was given not for the righteous, but for sinners!' (see Matthew 9:13). If I had no sin I should not need Christ.

"My sins are not imaginary transgressions, but sins against God: unbelief, doubt, despair, contempt, hatred, ingratitude, ignorance of God, misuse of his name, neglect of his Word; and sins against others: dishonor of parents, disobedience of government, coveting another's possessions.

"Even if I have not committed murder, adultery, theft, or similar sins in deed, nevertheless I have committed them in the heart, and therefore I am a transgressor of all the commandments of God.

"Because my transgressions are multiplied and my own efforts at self-justification more a hindrance than a furtherance, therefore Christ the Son of God gave himself unto death for my sins.

"To believe this is to have eternal life."

WALK CLOSER TO GOD

Luther staggered under a load of sin and guilt that no amount of penance could fit. Finally, leaving that burden at the cross, he experienced the peace that only God can give.

Have you, like Luther, been trying to live the Christian life without knowing the giver of life?

The first step is to receive gratefully the gift of God's Son. Only then can you rise up in joyful service for your Lord and Savior. ❖

august2

BECOMING LIKE HIM IN DEATH — AND IN LIFE

I have been crucified with Christ and I no longer live, but Christ lives in me.

GALATIANS 2:20

To the Roman mind, the cross marked a place of execution, not a haven for life.

And yet that cruelest of deaths would one day become a mark of distinction. Paul would later rejoice to proclaim, "I have been crucified with Christ."

Confused? Listen as Andrew Murray probes the significance of the cross in Jesus' day ... and in yours.

WALK WITH ANDREW MURRAY

"All his life Christ bore his cross — the death sentence that he should die for the world.

"And each Christian must bear his cross, acknowledging that he is worthy of death, and believing that he is crucified with Christ, and that the Crucified One lives in him.

"When we have accepted the life of the cross, we will be able to say with Paul: 'May I never boast except in the cross of our Lord Jesus Christ' (Galatians 6:14).

"Let the disposition of Christ on the cross, his humility, his sacrifice of all worldly honor, his spirit of self-denial, take possession of you.

"The power of his death will work in you, and you will become like him in his death; you will know him and the power of his resurrection."

WALK CLOSER TO GOD

Christ died an ignoble death that he might rise to glorious life. Now he invites you to "live by faith in the Son of God" (Galatians 2:20). You are crucified with Christ that you might experience the life of Christ.

Let the words of Isaac Watts lift your heart in praise for the life-bringing cross of Christ:

> Alas! and did my Savior bleed?
> And did my Sov'reign die?
> Would He devote that sacred head
> For such a worm as I?
> But drops of grief can ne'er repay
> The debt of love I owe:
> Here, Lord, I give myself away,
> 'Tis all that I can do! ✤

august3

OPEN YOUR HANDS TO RECEIVE
WHAT CHRIST GIVES

Understand, then, that those who have faith are children of Abraham.

GALATIANS 3:7

Abraham lived long before camera crews could follow his every step. But Abraham's name is enshrined in Scripture as one of the great examples of a person who took God at his word.

"Abraham believed God, and it was credited to him as righteousness" (Romans 4:3). Faith was the sole basis of Abraham's right standing with God.

Does that seem hard to believe? It did to the Galatians! So Paul reminded them in Galatians 3 of the sufficiency of faith—the same truth underscored by F. B. Meyer in this insight.

WALK WITH F. B. MEYER

"The strong tendency of the Galatian Christians to depend on ceremonies or legal obedience in addition to their faith in Christ, brings about in this chapter a magnificent demonstration of the sufficiency of faith alone.

"Faith had marked the beginning of the [Galatians'] Christian lives. They had found peace with God through faith.

"Faith had been the means, too, of Abraham's acceptance with God. Long before he had become a Jew by the initial rite of Judaism, he had been a humble believer in God's promise, on the basis of which he was reckoned righteous.

"Simple faith was the only condition that he had fulfilled. Surely what was sufficient for the father of the faithful is good enough for his children!

"Let each reader see to it that he does not merely believe about Christ, but believes in him."

WALK CLOSER TO GOD

Abraham was "fully persuaded that God had power to do what he had promised" (Romans 4:21).

Abraham did not earn salvation (see Galatians 3:6) nor did he deserve it (see Galatians 3:22). His responsibility was simply to receive it by believing what he heard (see Galatians 3:2,5).

Incredible? Unbelievable? Too good to be true? You'll never know until you open your empty hands to receive what Christ alone can give. ✤

august4

LIVING BY FAITH IN THE SON

So the law was our guardian until Christ came that we might be justified by faith.

GALATIANS 3:24

Although the Galatians had graduated from "law school," they were living like undergraduates. But the law's work as their schoolmaster was finished. Since they had received salvation through faith in Christ, they didn't need to return to their "alma mater." Paul reminded them that the law's chief purpose was to point men and women to faith in Christ.

As Christians, the Galatians were guilty of making the law's demands their path to perfection. As John Calvin relates, the Christian life is walking in the light of God's revealed Word.

WALK WITH JOHN CALVIN

"Faith denotes the full revelation of those things which, during the darkness of the shadows of the law, were dimly seen; for Paul does not intend to say that the fathers, who lived under the law, did not possess faith. Those who were under the law were partakers of the same faith as New Testament believers.

"The Old Testament might be said to foreshadow Christ, but to us he is represented as actually being present. They had only the mirror; we have the substance.

"Whatever might be the amount of darkness under the law, the fathers were not ignorant of the road in which they ought to walk. Though the dawn is not equal to the splendor of noon, yet, as far as a trip is concerned, travelers do not wait till the sun is fully risen. Their portion of light resembled the dawn, which was enough to preserve them from all error and guide them to everlasting blessedness."

WALK CLOSER TO GOD

If the Old Testament people of God possessed light that resembled the dawn, you enjoy the full blaze of the noontime sun.

If they were able to live by faith with only a glimpse of the coming Savior, you can surely live by faith, thanks to the full portrait of his appearing, which you possess in the Word of God. ✤

august**5**

GRACE — THE GREAT EXPENSE

You are all children of God through faith.

GALATIANS 3:26

Paul knew both the agonies and the ecstasies of spiritual parenthood. He was like a mother, nurse, tutor, father and friend. He longed for each of the Galatians to reach maturity in Christ. He reminded them that every Christian is a member of God's own family, a son or daughter of the Lord.

Martin Luther discusses Paul's writings in relation to the costly grace of God. You are a child of God, Luther observes, because God was willing to pay the terrible price to redeem you.

WALK WITH MARTIN LUTHER

"Above all things, Christ must be kept in this matter of salvation.

"It certainly is truth that, as David says (Psalm 32:2) and Paul writes (Romans 4:8): 'Blessed is the one whose sin the Lord will never count against them.' Paul shows that this divine imputation comes only to him who believes in Christ and not because of good works.

"Although out of pure grace God does not impute our sins to us, he nonetheless did not want to do this until complete and ample satisfaction of his law and his righteousness had been made. Since this was impossible for us, God ordained for us, in our place, one who took upon himself all the punishment we deserve.

"He fulfilled the law for us. He averted the judgment of God from us and appeased God's wrath. Grace, therefore, costs us nothing, but it cost Another much to get it for us. Grace was purchased with an incalculable, infinite treasure, the Son of God himself."

WALK CLOSER TO GOD

Because both Paul and Luther studied the Scriptures intently, they were able to proclaim clearly the necessity of faith in Christ. Both men remind Christ's forgetful followers of the high price of God's grace.

Think of it as the family secret of the faithful—a secret God never intended for you to keep to yourself! ❖

august**6**

THE OBJECT OF OUR HOPE

For through the Spirit we eagerly await by faith the righteousness for which we hope.

GALATIANS 5:5

Waiting room. The very words conjure up images of unpleasant times in the doctor's or dentist's office. For the Christian, waiting on God is a way of life.

Paul spent much of his early Christian life alone in the desert—learning to wait. In Galatians 5:5, he shared one of the keys he had discovered about waiting on God: waiting by faith.

Matthew Henry explains why waiting is an essential discipline.

WALK WITH MATTHEW HENRY

"Here we observe what Christians are waiting for—the hope of righteousness, the happiness of the other world. This is called the hope of Christians, the great object of their hope, which they desire and pursue above everything else.

"Though a life of righteousness leads to this happiness, yet it is the righteousness of Christ alone which has procured it for us.

"We also learn how Christians hope to obtain this happiness by faith in Jesus Christ, not by the works of the law, or anything they can do to deserve it, but only by faith, receiving and relying on him as the Lord, our righteousness. We also see how Christians are waiting for the hope of righteousness—through the Spirit.

"They act under the direction and influence of the Holy Spirit. Under his conduct and by his assistance, they are both persuaded and enabled to believe on Christ, and to look for the hope of righteousness through him."

WALK CLOSER TO GOD

A long wait is often helped by having someone to wait with you. You have been given such a companion—the Holy Spirit. His presence can help you view disappointments as divine appointments.

Commit your waiting moments to him. Ask for insight in knowing how to use each postponement and delay for eternal purposes. And while you wait, meditate on the hope of righteousness—eternal life with Jesus Christ. ✤

august7

A CONFLICT OF INTERESTS

Those who belong to Christ Jesus have crucified the flesh with its passions and desires.

GALATIANS 5:24

Two wrestlers grapple in the ring, each striving to master the other. Their names: "Flesh" (that is, your sinful nature) and "Spirit." The ring in which they struggle is the arena of your life.

The "Flesh" keeps trying to lure you away from the things of God. The "Spirit" continues to woo you with the love of Christ. And the one to whom you yield your life will dominate your life, as Johann Peter Lange explains.

WALK WITH JOHANN PETER LANGE

"Paul's meaning is not that the flesh, with its affections and lusts, is no longer present at all with those that have become Christians, but that a walk in the flesh should not any longer exist in the case of Christians. A walk in the Spirit might be rightly expected of believers. This is only possible for those who have crucified the flesh. The word is not slain, but crucified. It is a task of the Christian to be accomplished only by continual effort (see Colossians 3:5).

"In 'crucified,' however, the simple slaying is not the main idea, but the condemning, giving sentence, surrendering to infamous death. This has necessarily taken place in becoming Christ's. Fellowship with Christ involves a crucifixion of the flesh for the very reason that it is fellowship with Christ's death on the cross.

"Christ indeed has only suffered what people have deserved on account of their sinful flesh. Whoever appropriates to himself Christ's death upon the cross regards the flesh in himself no longer. For him, in Christ's death, the flesh has been crucified."

WALK CLOSER TO GOD

Have you identified the forces wrestling for control in your life? Paul contrasts the works of the flesh with the works of the Spirit. He reminds you of your twofold responsibility: to crucify the flesh and to cultivate the fruit of the Spirit. Flesh or Spirit. Which one will you yield to right now? ✣

august8

LEAVING A LEGACY THAT WILL NOT BE FORGOTTEN

Therefore, as we have opportunity, let us do good to all people, especially to those who belong to the family of believers.

GALATIANS 6:10

Doing good was never an "extra-curricular activity" with Jesus; it was a Spirit-empowered way of life.

As Jesus went about doing good, that goodness marked the lives of those he touched. According to Thomas Chalmers, there's no better way to leave a lasting legacy.

WALK WITH THOMAS CHALMERS

"Thousands of Christians breathe, move and live, pass off the stage of life, and are heard no more—why?

"They did not partake of good, and none in the world were blessed by them. None could point to them as the guide to their redemption. They wrote nothing, and nothing they said could be recalled. And so they passed on, remembered no more than insects of yesterday.

"Will you live and die this way, O man immortal? Live for something. Do good, and leave behind a monument of virtue. Write your name in kindness, love, and mercy on the hearts of all you come in contact with; you will never be forgotten.

"No, your name, your deeds will be as legible on the hearts you leave behind as the stars on the brow of evening. Good deeds will shine as the stars of heaven."

WALK CLOSER TO GOD

The *good* life. For some, it's defined as *getting* all you can *out of* life. For the Christian, it's *giving* all you can *to* life.

Jesus put it this way: "Let your light shine before others, that they may see your good deeds and glorify your Father in heaven" (Matthew 5:16).

The possibilities are endless: brightening someone's day with a kindness; returning good for evil in the office, the classroom or on the highway; sharing someone's grief.

The person you help may never know your name. But God will never forget the good you did in his name. ❖

august**9**

SPIRITUAL TREASURES ALL BELIEVERS POSSESS

Praise be to the God and Father of our Lord Jesus Christ, who has blessed us in the heavenly realms with every spiritual blessing in Christ.

EPHESIANS 1:3

Words cascade when something excites the heart.

In the original Greek text, Ephesians 1:3–14 is one continuous sentence of praise to God for benefits and blessings that are all "connected" in the person of Christ.

Don't be surprised if you find Paul's attitude contagious as you read A. W. Tozer's description of these riches in Christ—past, present and future.

WALK WITH A. W. TOZER

"The spiritual blessings which are ours in Christ may be divided into three types:

"The first are those which come to us immediately upon our believing unto salvation, such as forgiveness, justification, sonship in the family of God. In Christ we possess these even before we know they are ours!

"The second are those riches which we cannot enjoy in actuality until our Lord returns. These include ultimate mental and moral perfection, the glorification of our bodies, and the maturing of the divine image in our redeemed personalities. These treasures are as surely ours as if we possessed them now!

"The third consists of spiritual treasures which only come as we make a determined effort to possess them. These include deliverance from the sins of the flesh, victory over self, fruitfulness in service, awareness of God's presence, growth in grace, and an unbroken spirit of worship. These come as our faith and courage mount."

WALK CLOSER TO GOD

As you read that catalog of blessings, perhaps you found yourself getting excited.

Excited about what God has already done—in Christ. Confident about what he has promised to do—in Christ. Committed to claim his resources for today—in Christ.

Past. Present. Future. His blessings encompass your entire life—in Christ. ✤

august**10**

TAKING TIME FOR PRAYER

For this reason, ever since I heard about your faith in the Lord Jesus and your love for all God's people, I have not stopped giving thanks for you, remembering you in my prayers.
EPHESIANS 1:15 – 16

"I can't believe it. I absolutely promised myself (more important, I promised God!) that I would pray for at least 30 minutes this morning. Instead, I pushed the snooze button on the alarm so many times that I didn't have time to pray at all. The worst of it is that I haven't had a decent quiet time now for four days in a row! What in the world is wrong with me?"

Sound familiar? Many of us have feeble prayer lives. In contrast, Paul prayed constantly and instructed us to do the same. Our world is a busy world, and God understands that. But it remains true that a prayerless Christian is unheard of in Scripture—but not unheard of in our day.

Alexander Whyte encourages us to work at prayer (rather than just pray at work).

WALK WITH ALEXANDER WHYTE

"I am certain that the secret of much mischief to our own souls and to the souls of others lies in the way that we starve our prayers by hurrying over them. Prayer that God will call true prayer takes far more time than one-in-a-thousand thinks. After all that the Holy Spirit has done to make true prayer independent of times, and of places, and of all kinds of instruments and assistances—as long as we remain in this unspiritual and undevotional world—we shall not succeed in prayer without such times, and places, and other assistances.

"Take good care lest you take your salvation far too cheaply. If you find your life of prayer to be always so short, and so easy, and so spiritual, as to be without strain and sweat to you, you may depend upon it, you have not yet begun to pray. As sure as you sit there, it is just in this matter of *time* in prayer that so many of us are making shipwrecks of our souls and of the souls of others."

WALK CLOSER TO GOD

"The Spirit helps us in our weakness. We do not know what we ought to pray for, but the Spirit himself intercedes for us through wordless groans" (Romans 8:26). Keep that in mind and you will struggle *in* prayer rather than *with* prayer. ✣

ADDING UP THE FACTS ABOUT FAITH

For it is by grace you have been saved, through faith—and this not from yourselves, it is the gift of God—not by works, so that no one can boast.

EPHESIANS 2:8–9

In Romans 1:21 Paul spoke of people who, "although they knew God, they neither glorified him as God nor gave thanks to him." Though the fact of God's existence was before them, they closed their eyes to the truth of it.

Faith that saves is more than acquired facts about Christianity.

Philip Melanchthon helps set the facts straight about faith. Read his words slowly and prayerfully.

WALK WITH PHILIP MELANCHTHON

"That faith which justifies is not merely an acknowledgment of facts, but it is a recognition of the promise of God in which, for Christ's sake, the remission of sins and justification are freely offered.

"It is regarding with my whole heart the promises of God as certain and true, through which there are offered me, without my merit, the forgiveness of sins, grace, and salvation through Christ the Mediator.

"Faith means that my whole heart takes to itself this treasure. It is not my doing, not my presenting or giving, not my work of preparation.

"Rather, my heart comforts itself, and is perfectly confident with respect to this, namely, that God sheds upon me as a gift every treasure of grace in Christ."

WALK CLOSER TO GOD

Fact: Christ died for sins.

Fact: Christ was buried.

Fact: Christ rose the third day.

Fact: Christ is the only way to God.

The evidence is ample to confirm these facts (see 1 Corinthians 15:1–8; John 14:6). And you may agree with all that has been said so far. But, according to Paul, true faith is something more. It is recognizing that these facts apply to you.

Fact: Eternal life can be yours—right now.

That's a fact everyone needs to take to heart by reaching out by faith to receive Jesus as Savior. ❖

august12

PEACE WITH GOD AND WITH OTHERS

For he himself [Jesus Christ] is our peace, who has made the two groups [Jews and Gentiles] one and has destroyed the barrier, the dividing wall of hostility.

EPHESIANS 2:14

Class struggle, generation gap, racial tension—none of these problems is unique to our century.

Consider the Jews and Gentiles of Paul's day. Their prejudice ran so deep that it was not uncommon for a Jew to pray, "I thank you, God, that you have not seen fit to make me a Gentile."

Yet healed relationships can result when both sides see their need for the same Savior. Only Jesus Christ can bring peace that overcomes prejudice, as Albert Barnes relates.

WALK WITH ALBERT BARNES

"Formerly Jews and Gentiles were alienated and separate. The Jews regarded the Gentiles with hatred; the Gentiles regarded the Jews with scorn.

"Now, says the apostle, they are at peace. They worship the same God. They have the same Savior.

"They depend upon the same atonement. Reconciliation has not only taken place with God, but with each other.

"The best way to produce peace between alienated minds is to bring them to the same Savior. The love of Christ is so absorbing, and the dependence on his blood so entire, they will lay aside these alienations and cease their contentions.

"The work of the atonement is thus designed not only to produce peace with God, but peace between alienated and belligerent minds."

WALK CLOSER TO GOD

In the last 3,500 years of recorded history, less than 300 have been warless. In that same period of time, more than 8,000 treaties have been made—and broken.

Why? Because parties alienated from God cannot help but be alienated from one another.

Christ came to provide peace with God (see Romans 5:1) and peace with others (see Ephesians 2:14)—permanently.

Where else but in Jesus Christ could that kind of peace be found? ❖

august13

EXALTING THE SAVIOR WORTHY OF PRAISE

I pray ... that Christ may dwell in your hearts through faith. And I pray that you, being rooted and established in love, may ... know this love that surpasses knowledge.

EPHESIANS 3:16–19

Awe is an appropriate response to glorious sights of nature: the Grand Canyon, Niagara Falls, the Milky Way. But how do you respond to the wonder of salvation?

After nearly three chapters of explanation regarding life in Christ, Paul broke forth in spontaneous exaltation of the praiseworthy Christ.

A few centuries later Bernard of Clairvaux captured his emotions at the thought of his Lord this way.

WALK WITH BERNARD OF CLAIRVAUX

Jesus, the very thought of thee
　　With sweetness fills my breast;
But sweeter far thy face to see,
　　And in thy presence rest.

O Hope of every contrite heart,
　　O Joy of all the meek,
To those who fall, how kind thou art!
　　How good to those who seek!

But what to those who find? Ah, this
　　Nor tongue nor pen can show,
The love of Jesus, what it is
　　None but his loved ones know.

Jesus, our only joy be thou,
　　As thou our prize wilt be;
Jesus, be thou our glory now,
　　And through eternity.

WALK CLOSER TO GOD

Paul challenged the Ephesians to comprehend "how wide and long and high and deep is the love of Christ" (Ephesians 3:18). He ended by saying, "To him be glory in the church and in Christ Jesus throughout all generations, for ever and ever! Amen" (Ephesians 3:21).

Reread Paul's prayer in chapter three. Then voice your own praises to the one who enabled you to become his "loved one" eternally. ✤

THE BEST WAY TO PROMOTE UNITY

Live a life worthy of the calling you have received ... Make every effort to keep the unity of the Spirit through the bond of peace.

EPHESIANS 4:1,3

Paul's concern in chapter four was for one body—the body of Christ—and the unity needed to encourage its healthy growth.

To do this, Paul emphasized the "ones" of the faith—one body, one Spirit, one hope, one Lord, one faith, one baptism, one God—and the responsibilities of the body's members one to another.

Charles Spurgeon adds these thoughts on promoting soundness and oneness in the body of Christ.

WALK WITH CHARLES SPURGEON

"Let us cultivate everything that would tend to unity. Are any sick? Let us care for them. Are any suffering? Let us weep with them. Do we perceive faults in a brother? Let us admonish him in love and affection.

"Let us remember that we cannot keep the unity of the Spirit unless we all believe the truth of God.

"Let us search our Bibles, therefore, and conform our views to the teaching of God's Word.

"Let us live near to Christ, for this is the best way of promoting unity. Divisions in churches never begin with those full of love for the Savior. Cold hearts, unholy lives, inconsistent actions—these are the seeds which sow schisms in the body.

"But he who lives near to Jesus, wears his likeness and copies his example, will be, wherever he goes, a holy link to bind the church more closely than ever together."

WALK CLOSER TO GOD

Paul exhorted his readers to unity in Christ; Jesus spent his last evening before the crucifixion praying for the same thing: "I in them and you in me—so that they may be brought to complete unity. Then the world will know that you sent me" (John 17:23).

The nearer you draw to the Lord Jesus Christ, the stronger your love will grow for others in his body—and the closer you will move to the oneness of heart and purpose for which Christ prayed. ✤

august15

THE MIND IS A TOOL IN THE HAND OF GOD

You must no longer live as the Gentiles do, in the futility of their thinking. They are darkened in their understanding ... because of the ignorance that is in them due to the hardening of their hearts.

EPHESIANS 4:17–18

You may not understand how one death 2,000 years ago can bring forgiveness of sins today, but you still believe it.

And building on that belief, your understanding begins to grow as you learn to lean on God rather than on your own understanding.

Reliance on human wisdom can keep you from God. But once enlightened by faith, your mind can also become a keen tool for God. Martin Luther describes the wise use of human wisdom.

WALK WITH MARTIN LUTHER

"The natural wisdom of a human creature in matters of faith, until he is born anew, is altogether darkness. But in a person who is regenerated by the Holy Spirit through the Word, the mind is a glorious instrument and work of God: for all God's gifts are wholesome to the good and godly.

"The understanding, through faith, receives life from faith; that which was dead is made alive again.

"Just as our bodies in broad daylight are likely to rise, move, and walk more readily and safely than they would in the dead of night, so it is with dark reason, which, when enlightened, does not strive against faith but rather advances it."

WALK CLOSER TO GOD

Without faith it is impossible to please God (see Hebrews 11:6). Without faith, a person is in the dark concerning the things of God (see Romans 1:21).

Wisdom to understand God's ways must come from a heavenly source. Therefore, "if any of you lacks wisdom, you should ask God" (James 1:5).

If you wait until you understand all about God before you come to him, you will wait for eternity.

On the other hand, if you come to him today to learn from him, you'll discover that you can both know and do his will. ✣

THE CONCRETE FORM OF GOODNESS

Live as children of light ... find out what pleases the Lord ... "and Christ will shine on you".
Ephesians 5:8,10,14

The question of how to live like Jesus Christ is easy to ask but hard to answer—and even harder to achieve.

And yet Christlikeness is a theme that dominates the writings of Paul (see Romans 8:29), Peter (see 2 Peter 1:4) and John (see 1 John 3:2).

Alexander Maclaren offers this helpful explanation of what Christlikeness is and how God expects us to achieve it.

WALK WITH ALEXANDER MACLAREN

"What is it that pleases Jesus Christ? His own likeness.

"Jesus Christ desires most that we be like him. That we are to bear his image is a comprehensive and at the same time specific way of defining Christian duty.

"And what is the likeness of Jesus Christ which is thus our supreme obligation to bear? We can put it all into two thoughts: suppression of the self-will and continual consciousness of obedience to the divine will.

"The life of Jesus Christ is the great example of these two qualities. His life contains within its narrow compass adequate direction for human life.

"The man or woman who has in his heart these thoughts—that the definition of virtue is pleasing Jesus Christ, that the concrete form of goodness is likeness to him in denying self and obeying God—needs no other goal to fill his life."

WALK CLOSER TO GOD

Is it really possible to live a godly life in an ungodly world?

Absolutely!

Jesus modeled it for his disciples, then commanded, "Do as I have done" (John 13:15).

Paul modeled it for his churches, then exhorted, "Live as children of light" (Ephesians 5:8).

Let your steps be guided today by the prayer that Jesus prayed in the Garden of Gethsemane: "Not as I will, but as you will" (Matthew 26:39). ❖

august17

UNITY AND DIVERSITY IN THE BODY

For we are members of his body.

EPHESIANS 5:30

Every cell in the human body is alike in some ways to every other. But different cells perform different functions in the body—an analogy C. S. Lewis draws on and applies to your role in the body of Christ.

WALK WITH C. S. LEWIS

"The society into which the Christian is called is not a collective but a body. It is in fact that body of which the family unit is an image on the natural level.

"If anyone came to it with the misconception that the church was a massing together of persons as if they were pennies or chips, he would be corrected at the threshold by the discovery that the Head of this body is utterly unlike its inferior members—they share no divinity with him except by analogy.

"We are summoned at the outset to combine as creatures with our Creator, as mortals with immortal, as redeemed sinners with sinless Redeemer.

"His presence, the interaction between him and us, must always be the overwhelmingly dominant factor in the life we are to lead within the body; and any conception of Christian fellowship which does not mean primarily fellowship with him is out of order."*

WALK CLOSER TO GOD

You are a cell in the body of Christ—like millions of other Christians.

But are you a

> nerve cell (to feel)?
> blood cell (to nourish)?
> brain cell (to direct)?
> muscle cell (to strengthen)?
> bone cell (to support)?

Cells are alike, yet each is different. And each is crucial to the effective functioning of the body. The nucleus of all these cells is Christ himself. Without the nucleus, the cell dies. Unity is found only in Christ; diversity of function is vital in his body. ❖

*From *Transposition and Other Addresses*; used by permission of William Collins Sons and Co., Ltd.

august**18**

FAMILY LIFE AT ITS FINEST

Children, obey your parents in the Lord, for this is right. "Honor your father and moth-er"—which is the first commandment with a promise.

EPHESIANS 6:1–2

Paul quoted the words of Moses to show that things "go well" for obedient children and they "enjoy long life on the earth" (Ephesians 6:3). And obedient children develop best when rooted "in the training and instruction of the Lord" (Ephesians 6:4).

John and Charles Wesley, great eighteenth-century revival leaders in England, were taught to obey as Jesus did. Their mother, Susannah Wesley, gave this description of their upbringing.

WALK WITH SUSANNAH WESLEY

"I insisted on conquering a child's will, for when this is thoroughly done a child can be governed by the reason and piety of his parents until its own understanding comes into maturity, and the principles of religion have taken root in its mind.

"Self-will is the root of all sin and misery. Whatever promotes this in children ensures their wretchedness; whatever checks it increases their future happiness. The parent who indulges the child's self-will does the devil's work: makes religion impracticable, salvation unattainable, and is working to damn his child's soul forever.

"Without renouncing the world no one can follow my method. Very few would devote more than twenty years of their life to save the souls of their children which they think may be saved without so much ado. Yet that was my intention, however unskillfully and unsuccessfully managed."

WALK CLOSER TO GOD

Young person, if God's own Son willingly submitted to earthly parents, is he asking too much for you to do the same? Parents, if your child sees you as standing in the place of God, what needs to change in order for the picture to be accurate and consistent?

Obedient children ... honored parents ... God-honoring lives. That's family life at its finest—in the family of God! ♣

august19

BETTER A CONQUEROR THAN A CASUALTY

Therefore put on the full armor of God, so that ... you may be able to stand your ground, and after you have done everything, to stand.

EPHESIANS 6:13

As a Christian you are confronted daily with an all-too-familiar struggle—the struggle against the world, the flesh and the devil.

And without proper protection, you would quickly find yourself a casualty rather than a conqueror.

In Ephesians 6:10–18, Paul provided a checklist of spiritual armor. Check to see that yours is in place as H. C. G. Moule itemizes each piece.

WALK WITH H. C. G. MOULE

"The soldier of faith appears before us made strong for a victory which is impossible, except by his relation to his Lord.

"He is safe because he is spiritually right with Christ in God-given truth and righteousness; because he is sure of Christ beneath his feet as the equipment of the gospel of peace for his own soul; because he finds Christ the mighty shield against the fiery volley when he follows him in faith; because he covers his head in the day of battle with Christ as his salvation; because Christ speaks through the Word of God, and so makes himself his servant's sword to cut the accuser down; because prayer in the Spirit grasps him and holds him fast.

"Yes, here, to the last hour of our conflict and our siege—and here only—lies our victory.

"It is Christ himself, not the armor alone. It is the all-sufficient Lord whom the believer stands safely behind."

WALK CLOSER TO GOD

It's dangerous to be ineffective because of faulty or missing equipment. Now would be a good time for an inspection of your spiritual armor.

Have you put on the full armor of God? Is every piece in place? Are you covered from head to toe?

If not, consult your omnipotent supplier and general. He has everything you need for spiritual victory.

In fact, he is everything you need! ✤

august20

SUFFERING: AN HONOR CONFERRED RATHER THAN A BURDEN ENDURED

Now I want you to know, brothers and sisters, that what has happened to me has actually served to advance the gospel.

PHILIPPIANS 1:12

Chains could not chill Paul's zeal for the gospel. On the contrary, he saw his imprisonment as an opportunity for the gospel to penetrate where no preacher had gone before.

If Christ could be magnified more from a dungeon than from a pulpit, so be it!

G. Campbell Morgan explains how Paul considered his calling to be of greater concern than his circumstances.

WALK WITH G. CAMPBELL MORGAN

"Paul's situation is an example of how life in fellowship with Christ triumphs over all adverse circumstances. It is a recognition of the fact that all apparently adverse conditions are made allies in victory under the Lord's dominion.

"'What has happened to me has actually served to advance the gospel,' exclaimed the apostle. His very bonds opened the door of opportunity throughout the Praetorian guard.

"Suffering on behalf of Christ is referred to as an honor conferred, rather than a burden endured. It is something granted to the Christian as a privilege, the very granting of which is a gift of grace. To this concept all will agree who have ever really known what it is to suffer on behalf of Christ.

"They are not callous; the suffering is very real, very acute. But it brings a sense of joy which finds no equal in human experience."

WALK CLOSER TO GOD

A man dives into an icy river to save a drowning child and later comments that he never felt the cold. His mind was on something more important.

For Paul, being in prison didn't matter when there was preaching to be done; he considered himself privileged to be there.

What do you focus on—the circumstances that confront you or your calling that surmounts any circumstance? ✣

august21

WHAT TRIFLING SACRIFICES HE ASKS OF US

Christ Jesus ... being in very nature God ... made himself nothing by taking the very nature of a servant, being made in human likeness.

PHILIPPIANS 2:5 – 7

At your annual job review, your employer praises you for your outstanding work — but instead of the promotion you had hoped for, he demotes you so that others might receive promotions. How do you react?

Jesus, seated at the right hand of the Father, willingly "demoted" himself to take a servant's role. God condescended to become a man so that sinners might be "promoted" to heaven.

With J. Hudson Taylor, consider the humility of Christ.

WALK WITH J. HUDSON TAYLOR

"Let us reflect on what he gave up on leaving heaven's throne to be cradled in a manger.

"Having filled all things and wielded omnipotence, he became a feeble infant and was wrapped in swaddling clothes. Being the Loved One of the Father, never unappreciated, never misunderstood, and always receiving the ceaseless adoration of the hierarchies of heaven, he became a despised Nazarene, misunderstood even by his followers, suspected by those whom he came to bless, rejected by those who owed him their very being, and whose salvation he had come to seek.

"Finally, he was mocked and spit upon, crucified and slain, with thieves and outlaws.

"Will any brother or sister in Christ reflect on this, and yet hesitate to make the trifling sacrifices he asks us to make?"

WALK CLOSER TO GOD

Being like Christ means thinking like Christ (see Philippians 2:5). And when he came from heaven, he wasn't thinking of himself; he was thinking of others. Loss of privilege and setting aside of power meant little, if by that he might save the objects of his love.

Would you be willing to volunteer for a similar demotion?

Think carefully before you respond; he may take you at your word. ❖

august22

AN ACCURATE REFLECTION OF THE LIGHT WITHIN

Become blameless and pure, children of God without fault in a warped and crooked generation. Then you will shine among them like stars in the sky.

PHILIPPIANS 2:15

Reflections in a dirty mirror aren't very flattering, are they? Nor is it flattering when Christ is reflected in the mirror of an unclean life.

Paul described Christlikeness as reflecting the glory of the Lord (see 2 Corinthians 3:18). You reflect Christ to a world in darkness.

Here's how Albert Barnes describes the radiant Christian life.

WALK WITH ALBERT BARNES

"Christians should let their light shine. God has called them into his kingdom so that they may illustrate in their lives the nature of the gospel and show its value in purifying the soul and in sustaining it in the time of trial.

"The world is dependent upon Christians for a correct view of religion, and every day that a Christian lives he either honors or dishonors the gospel.

"Every word that is spoken, every expression of the eye, every cloud or beam of sunshine on his brow, will have some effect in doing this.

"A believer cannot live without making some impression upon the world around him, either favorable or unfavorable to the cause of his Redeemer."

WALK CLOSER TO GOD

Take a bright light, reflect it off a surface, and what do you see? If the surface is dirty, the reflection will be dull. If the surface is uneven, the reflection will be fuzzy. And therein lies a parable of the Christian life.

You are called to be a light for the world, providing an accurate reflection of the light that is within you. Light that is clean (see 1 John 1:9), consistent (see Ephesians 5:8), inviting (see Luke 8:16).

You cannot live a day without making an impression—either a positive one or a negative one—on those around you. What needs to change for your life to become a clear reflection of the Savior you serve? ✤

august23

GOD'S WILL, YOUR WILLINGNESS

For everyone looks out for their own interests, not those of Jesus Christ.

PHILIPPIANS 2:21

WANTED: Understudy for well-traveled, soon-to-retire missionary. Must be able to suffer hardship; to teach and be taught; to evangelize, organize and perform a variety of vital church functions. Low pay, long hours, intense opposition. Interested applicants contact Paul the apostle.

That ad is fictitious, but the position was real. It was filled by a young man named Timothy.

Timothy was like a spiritual son to Paul, so when Paul needed someone to check on the Philippians' spiritual growth, he knew he could count on Timothy. Albert Barnes discusses Timothy's commitment to Paul and to the ministry of Christ at Philippi.

WALK WITH ALBERT BARNES

"How many professing Christians in our cities and towns are there now who would be willing to leave their comfortable homes and go on embassy duty to Philippi as Timothy did?

"How many are there who would not seek some excuse, and thus show that they 'look[ed] out for their own interests' rather than the things which pertained to the kingdom of Jesus Christ?

"Paul implies here that it is the duty of those who profess faith to seek the things which pertain to the kingdom of the Redeemer, to make that the great and leading object of their lives.

"There are few Christians who deny themselves much to promote the kingdom of the Redeemer. People live for their own ease, for their families, for their businesses—as if a Christian could have anything which he has a right to pursue, and without regard to God's will and glory."

WALK CLOSER TO GOD

The foremost qualification for the job of disciple was, and still is, willingness— willingness to learn, to obey, to serve. Timothy demonstrated this willingness to do God's will at the sacrifice of his own will. You can do the same today.

So what will you do? ✤

THE CHOICE THAT SHAPES YOUR DESTINY

I consider everything a loss because of the surpassing worth of knowing Christ Jesus my Lord, for whose sake I have lost all things.

PHILIPPIANS 3:8

When Jesus Christ confronts an individual, choices are inevitable. The rich man in Mark 10:17–23 chose to keep his possessions rather than follow Jesus. Centuries later, another rich man made a far different choice. Francis of Assisi set aside the inheritance that awaited him to spend his life serving Christ.

The rich man of Jesus' day was never heard from again. Francis of Assisi is still remembered for his devotion to Christ. The choice of each man helped shape his destiny. Let this old Irish hymn guide you into the choice of a lifetime.

WALK WITH AN IRISH HYMN WRITER

Be Thou my Vision,
　　O Lord of my heart;
Nought be all else to me,
　　Save that Thou art—
Thou my best thought,
　　By day or by night,
Waking or sleeping,
　　Thy presence my light.

Be Thou my Wisdom,
　　And Thou my true Word;
I ever with Thee
　　And Thou with me, Lord;
Thou my great Father,
　　I Thy true son;
Thou in me dwelling,
　　And I with Thee one.

Riches I heed not,
　　Nor man's empty praise,
Thou mine inheritance,
　　Now and always:
Thou and Thou only,
　　First in my heart,
High King of heaven,
　　My treasure Thou art.

High King of heaven,
　　My victory won,
May I reach heaven's joys,
　　O bright heaven's Sun!
Heart of my own heart,
　　Whatever befall,
Still be my Vision,
　　O Ruler of all.

WALK CLOSER TO GOD

Two rich men wrestled with life-changing decisions. One concluded, "I will follow my gold"; the other, "I will follow my God." One thought he had gained the world, yet lost his own soul; the other knew he had lost much from the world's perspective, yet had gained far more.

What will be the end result of your decision? ✣

PUTTING THE PAST BEHIND

One thing I do: Forgetting what is behind and straining toward what is ahead.

PHILIPPIANS 3:13

Paul's past as a persecutor of the faith could have paralyzed him as an apostle of the faith. But knowing the power of God's grace to forgive and forget, Paul was able to put away his sordid past and reach for "what is ahead."

F. B. Meyer shows how you can make the same freeing discovery.

WALK WITH F. B. MEYER

"We ought not to dwell upon our past sins as though they were ever present to the eye of God, so we will not be incapacitated for high and holy service.

"What would Peter have done on the day of Pentecost if he had persisted in pensively dwelling on the scenes of the denial, and had not dared to believe that all was forgiven and forgotten?

"What would have been the effect on the apostle Paul if he had allowed the memory of his share in the harrying of the saints to overcast his spirit when summoned to found churches, write epistles, and traverse continents?

"When once we confess it, sin is immediately put away. God will never mention it again. It need not be a barrier on our service; it should not hinder us from aspiring to and enjoying the most intimate fellowship which is within the reach of mortals."

WALK CLOSER TO GOD

The choice is yours: Either brood over your past or "press on toward the goal to win the prize for which God has called [you] heavenward in Christ Jesus" (Philippians 3:14).

Nothing compares with the excellency of knowing and serving Jesus Christ. So don't allow the haunting reminder of past sin to deflect you from pursuing your present goal. Concentrate instead on developing your relationship with Jesus, and your mind and heart will be filled with dreams, goals, projects and prayers for the days ahead.

Press toward the goal of knowing Jesus and of making him known. It's the best way to move toward the mark in your Christian life. ❖

august26

LEARNING THE SECRET OF CONTENTMENT

I am not saying this because I am in need, for I have learned to be content whatever the circumstances.

PHILIPPIANS 4:11

Contentment. It's rare in a world in which people are searching for more money, more power, more status.

But God has a different perspective: "Better a little with the fear of the LORD than great wealth with turmoil" (Proverbs 15:16).

It's a viewpoint shared by Paul in Philippians 4. And as A. W. Pink observes, once you know God, you have more than the world could ever offer.

WALK WITH A. W. PINK

"Contentment is the product of a heart resting in God. It is the soul's enjoyment of the peace that passes all understanding.

"Contentment is the outcome of my will being brought into subjection to the divine will. It is the blessed assurance that God does all things well and is even now making all things work together for my ultimate good.

"Contentment is only possible as we maintain the attitude of accepting everything that enters our lives as coming from the hand of him who is too wise to err and too loving to cause one of his children a needless tear.

"Our final word is this: Real contentment is only possible by being in the presence of the Lord Jesus. Only by cultivating intimacy with the One who was never discontent, only by daily fellowship with him who always delighted in the Father's will, will we learn the secret of contentment."

WALK CLOSER TO GOD

Paul had ample reason to complain about his circumstances: hostile audiences, misunderstood motives, physical abuse.

Instead, he chose to "rejoice greatly in the Lord" (Philippians 4:10). His life radiated the very words he wrote to the Philippians: "Whatever is true ... noble ... right ... pure ... lovely ... admirable ... excellent or praiseworthy—think about such things" (Philippians 4:8).

Like Paul, don't be content to settle for less than God's best. And that "best" includes contentment found only in him! ✤

august27

THE WORDS YOUR FATHER LOVES TO HEAR

Giving joyful thanks to the Father, who has qualified you to share in the inheritance of his holy people in the kingdom of light.

COLOSSIANS 1:12

In the opening lines of his letter to the Colossians, Paul echoed the psalmist's thought that "it is fitting for the upright to praise [the LORD]" (Psalm 33:1).

Listen as R. A. Torrey explains that prayer is more than bringing a "grocery list" of needs and wants to God. It is an opportunity to express gratitude for God's good gifts to us.

WALK WITH R. A. TORREY

"If any one of us would stop and think how many of the prayers we have offered to God have been answered, and how seldom we have thanked God for the answers thus given, I am sure we would be overwhelmed with conviction.

"We should be just as definite in returning thanks as we are in prayer. We come to God with specific petitions, but when we return thanks to him our thanksgiving is vague.

"Doubtless one reason why so many of our prayers lack power is because we have neglected to return thanks for blessings already received. If anyone were constantly to come to us asking help from us, and should never say 'thank you' for the help thus given, we would soon tire of helping one so ungrateful.

"Doubtless our heavenly Father, out of a wise regard for our highest welfare, oftentimes refuses to answer petitions that we send up to him in order that we may be brought to a sense of our ingratitude and be taught to be thankful."

WALK CLOSER TO GOD

No doubt you are learning to be specific in your requests to God. But have you learned yet to be specific in your thanks as well?

After all, if you aren't thankful for what you have as a "share in the inheritance," you aren't likely to be thankful for what God holds in store for you!

"Father, thank you." Those are words any father loves to hear—even your heavenly one. ✤

JOINED TO THE FATHER THROUGH THE SON

For God was pleased to have all his fullness dwell in him [the Son].

COLOSSIANS 1:19

Mention the name Jesus Christ, and many images come to mind: a babe in a manger, a rugged carpenter, an authoritative teacher, a crucified Savior.

But in speaking of Christ in Colossians 1, Paul mentioned none of these. Instead, he focused on the Christ who has existed through eternity, who is the Creator and the image of God himself.

It's a big picture of Christ, a full picture. John Calvin speaks of the significance of this larger-than-life Christ for the Christian.

WALK WITH JOHN CALVIN

"Whatever God has, he has conferred upon his Son, that he may be glorified in him.

"He shows us that we must draw from the fullness of Christ everything good that we desire for our salvation, because God will not communicate himself or his gifts to people, except by his Son.

"So it follows that whatever detracts from Christ, or takes away a drop from his fullness, stands in opposition to God's eternal counsel.

"It is a magnificent commendation of Christ that we cannot be joined to God except through him.

"Our happiness consists in our cleaving to God.

"Christ is the bond of our connection with God, and apart from him we are most miserable because we are shut out from God.

"What God ascribes to Christ belongs solely to him, that no portion of this praise may be transferred to any other."

WALK CLOSER TO GOD

What is the most important question confronting the human race today?

Is it the threat of nuclear war, the economy, respect for human life, poverty, race relations?

They're important issues, to be sure. But the most important question is: What do you think about the Christ?

It's a question thinking people cannot avoid. What do *you* think? ❖

august**29**

GOD'S PERSPECTIVE ON LIFE'S PRIORITIES

Do not let anyone judge you ... with regard to a religious festival, a New Moon celebration or a Sabbath day. These are a shadow of the things that were to come; the reality, however, is found in Christ.

COLOSSIANS 2:16–17

Is Christianity a segment of your schedule or the focus of your existence?

If God asks for the first day of your week, does that mean he doesn't care about the other six?

Abraham Kuyper points out God's perspective on right priorities.

WALK WITH ABRAHAM KUYPER

"In his Word God absolutely forbids every inclination and every attempt to divide your life into two parts, one part for you and the other for him.

"There must be no division. Not six days for you and Sunday for God. Not a secular life sprinkled with godliness.

"No, on this point the claim of Scripture is as inclusive as possible; and though it may sound strange to your ears, the obligation is imposed upon you that whatsoever you do, you shall do it as unto the Lord.

"He who as child of God, as servant of Christ, lives his life in this world must in everything be led and carried by his faith. He who divides and makes distinctions robs God of a part that belongs to him alone.

"If you are to love your God with all your heart, all your soul, and your mind and powers, every avenue of escape is closed against you."

WALK CLOSER TO GOD

You have only one life to live for God—and he is vitally interested in all of it.

Viewing one day as more holy—or one dollar as more heavenly—"robs God of a part that belongs to him alone."

By contrast, agreeing that you and all you have are wholly his says with your life—as well as your lips—"All that God wants is all of me, and that's all he gets!" ❖

august**30**

COMING TO LOVE THE THINGS THAT ENDURE

Since, then, you have been raised with Christ, set your hearts on things above, where Christ is, seated at the right hand of God.

COLOSSIANS 3:1

In Colossians 3 Paul introduced the subject of practical Christian living by telling his readers to look to Christ. Later in the same chapter, he summed up the Christian's earthly life this way: "Whatever you do, whether in word or deed, do it all in the name of the Lord Jesus" (Colossians 3:17).

Peter Marshall, former chaplain of the United States Senate, prayed this prayer for heavenly perspective in the midst of earthly pursuits.

WALK WITH PETER MARSHALL

"There awaits just behind the curtain a life that will never end, a life of beauty and peace and love, a life of reunion with loved ones, a life to be lived in the very presence of God.

"There will be no more pain, no more sorrow, nor tears, nor crying, nor parting, nor death after death. Age shall not weary them, nor the years erode. We shall enter into that for which we were created. It shall be the journey's end for the heart and all its hopes.

"And yet there are those among us whose actions—let us eat, drink, and be merry, for tomorrow we die—suggest that they believe in no better hereafter.

"There never was a time when the conviction of immortality was more needed than in this day when materialism has so exalted present life as to make it all-important."

WALK CLOSER TO GOD

The Christian life, as Paul described it, is an "off and on" experience (see Colossians 3:8–10).

We put off the deeds of anger, lying and idolatry—behavior unbecoming a child of God—and put on the qualities of kindness, patience and love.

Like a change of clothing, this involves exchanging the soiled conduct of the world for the holy garments of heavenly living.

Putting on Christ. It's a wardrobe that will never go out of style. ✤

august31

TOUCH THE WORLD — THROUGH PRAYER

Epaphras, who is one of you and a servant of Christ Jesus, sends greetings. He is always wrestling in prayer for you.

COLOSSIANS 4:12

Contrary to what you may have heard, a Skype call is not the next best thing to being there. Prayer is!

Epaphras was far away from those to whom he had ministered. But his absence from them made his heart grow fonder in prayer for them.

His example of zealous prayer provides F. B. Meyer with these thoughts for present-day prayer warriors.

WALK WITH F. B. MEYER

"Epaphras had come from Colossae with tidings for the apostle Paul; but amid all the crowding interests of his visit to Rome, his heart was with his friends, and he sought to help them, as we may all help dear ones far away.

"He strove for them in prayer. It was not hastily mumbled prayer that he gave; no light breathing of desire; no formal mention of their names; but it seemed as though he were a wrestler whose muscles stood out like whipcord as he agonized and labored for the prize.

"We shall never know, till we stand in heaven, how much has been done by prayer. Probably the work of which we are prone to pride ourselves is due far less to us than we suppose, and far more to unrecognized fellow workers who labor in prayer for us."

WALK CLOSER TO GOD

A close friend or relative comes to Christ. A tense conflict at work or home is resolved. A troubling deadline passes with no problem. Later you tell a Christian friend what happened, and he replies, "I prayed for you that day."

Coincidence? Or your sovereign God at work through long-distance prayer?

It isn't always possible to be with the one you love. But you can always pray.

Take a moment to call out on someone's behalf. You may be calling at just the right time! ❖

september1

A GRATEFUL SENSE OF GOD'S GOODNESS TO OTHERS

We always thank God for all of you and continually mention you in our prayers. We remember before our God and Father your work produced by faith.

1 THESSALONIANS 1:2–3

Paul's customary greeting in his letters included gratitude for God's goodness. And the Thessalonians provided plenty of reasons for thanksgiving.

For instance, they "became a model to all the believers in Macedonia and Achaia" (1 Thessalonians 1:7). Their reputation sparked the spread of the gospel and Paul's gratitude to God. Matthew Henry has this to say about Paul's thankfulness.

WALK WITH MATTHEW HENRY

"Since the apostle is about to mention the things that were a matter of joy to him and highly praiseworthy in them, he chooses to do this by way of thanksgiving to God who is the Author of all good that comes to us, or is done by us, at any time.

"God is the object of all worship by prayer and praise. And thanksgiving to God is a great duty, to be performed constantly. Even when we do not actually give thanks to God by our words, we should have a grateful sense of God's goodness on our minds.

"Thanksgiving should be repeated often; and not only should we be thankful for the favors we receive ourselves, but also for the benefits bestowed on others."

WALK CLOSER TO GOD

"Things God Has Done in My Life." Chances are good you could construct a long list in a short time on that subject. But could you make a list entitled "Things God Has Done in the Lives of My Brothers and Sisters in Christ"?

You could—if you have been mentioning them in your prayers, if their problems were your cause for intercession, if their joys were your cause for celebration.

Where your time and energy are invested, "there your heart will be also" (Luke 12:34).

Getting involved in the lives of others is something they—and you—will both be thankful for! ✣

september**2**

THE BENEFITS OF TRUTH CLOTHED IN TENDERNESS

Just as a nursing mother cares for her children, so we cared for you ... We dealt with each of you as a father deals with his own children.

1 THESSALONIANS 2:7,11

Parenting a child. Nurturing a church. It's no accident Paul uses the first to illustrate the second. And in each case, the key is love.

Love begets love. It's a principle Paul embodied in his parent-like care for the Thessalonians. Albert Barnes gleans this lesson for today.

WALK WITH ALBERT BARNES

"Those who minister the gospel should be gentle, tender, and affectionate.

"Nothing is ever gained by a sour, harsh, crabby, dissatisfied manner. Sinners are never scolded into either duty or heaven. No man is a better or more faithful preacher because he is rough in manner, coarse or harsh in his expressions, or sour in his speech. Not thus was either the Master or Paul.

"There is no crime in being polite and courteous; and there is no piety in outraging all the laws which promote happy communication.

"What is wrong we should indeed oppose—but it should be in the kindest manner towards those who do wrong. What is true and right we should maintain and defend—and we shall always do it more effectively if we do it kindly."

WALK CLOSER TO GOD

To summarize Mr. Barnes's last paragraph: Hate the sin, love the sinner. It sounds so simple—until you try it with a child ... or a Christian ... or a church exhibiting immature attitudes and actions.

C. S. Lewis struggled with the same principle. He wrote, "For a long time I used to think this a silly, straw-splitting distinction—how could you hate what a man did and not hate the man? But later it occurred to me that there was a man to whom I had been doing this all my life—namely myself."

Take that attitude, which you so naturally show toward yourself, and try it on someone else. Then discover how truth clothed in tenderness can mark the lives of those you are called to "parent." ❖

september3

THE SPIRITUAL GOLD OF A GODLY LIFE

We sent Timothy ... so that no one would be unsettled by these trials. For you know quite well that we are destined for them.

1 THESSALONIANS 3:2 – 3

Mining for gold requires a willingness to work long hours in uncomfortable surroundings. But once a strike is made, the toil and tears seem a small price to pay.

The spiritual gold of a godly life is no different. Holiness and hardship are inseparable parts of the same endeavor. F. B. Meyer examines the purpose behind God-appointed trials in the Christian life.

WALK WITH F. B. MEYER

"We all love the sunshine, but the Arabs have a proverb that 'all sunshine makes the desert.'

"And we commonly observe how the graces of Christian living are more often apparent in the case of those individuals who have passed through great tribulation.

"God desires to get as rich a crop as possible from the soil of our natures. There are certain plants of the Christian life, such as meekness, gentleness, kindness, humility, which cannot come to perfection if the sun of prosperity always shines.

"As the weights of the clock or the ballast in the vessel are necessary for their right ordering, so is trouble in the soul-life. The sweetest scents are only obtained by tremendous pressure; the fairest flowers grow amid Alpine snow-solitudes; the rarest gems have suffered longest from the cutter's wheel; the noblest statues have borne the most blows of the chisel.

"All, however, is under God's supervision. Nothing happens that has not been appointed with consummate care and foresight."

WALK CLOSER TO GOD

Just as the sculptor's chisel reveals the hidden beauty in a chunk of marble, so difficulties pare away the rough edges in your life. Even as the gardener's shears prune bushes for greater beauty and productivity, so the difficulties in your life prepare you for fruit-bearing in God's kingdom.

And when they do, you have the "consummate care and foresight" of God to thank. ❖

september4

THE DEEP ROOTS THAT YIELD DELIGHTFUL FRUIT

It is God's will that you should be sanctified.

1 THESSALONIANS 4:3

One teenage boy straightens his room every day without being asked. Another straightens his only after endless appeals from his parents. Either way, the result is a clean room. But only one is the result of a right attitude.

Abraham Kuyper points out the proper balance between a heart that wills and hands that work in the Christian life.

WALK WITH ABRAHAM KUYPER

"The difference between sanctification and good works should be well understood.

"Many confuse the two and believe that sanctification means to lead an honorable and virtuous life; and, since this is equal to good works, sanctification—without which no one shall see God—is made to consist in the diligent effort to do good works.

"Instead, sanctification is God's work in us in which he gives us a holy disposition, inwardly filling us with delight in his law and repugnance to sin. But good works are acts of mankind, which spring from this holy disposition. Hence sanctification is the source of good works.

"Sanctification is a work of God. It works internally, imparts something to the believer, and roots him like a tree. Good works are of men, are external, and are the fruit produced by a tree that is rooted. To confuse the two leads people astray."

WALK CLOSER TO GOD

It's impossible for a tree to produce fruit without first being planted and nurtured. Only then can the nourishment rise to bring forth fruit.

Sanctification and good works have a cause-effect relationship. God, in sanctifying you, gives you the capacity to bear spiritual fruit that is pleasing to him—fruit in abundance, fruit in season and out, fruit that is rooted in trusting him.

Read about it, thank God for it, then let your roots go down deep into the one who can make your life a source of fruit to his glory. ❖

THE MORTAL ENEMY ALL MUST FACE

We do not want you to be uninformed about those who sleep in death, so that you do not grieve like the rest of mankind, who have no hope.

1 THESSALONIANS 4:13

Death. It's a reality every mortal must face. Some view it with horror; others see it as a homecoming.

What is it that can transform a funeral into a praise gathering? Listen as Elizabeth Rowe presents the ringing note of hope that can—and should—accompany the death of a child of God.

WALK WITH ELIZABETH ROWE

"What unutterable ecstasies I shall feel when I meet those smiles which enlighten heaven and exhilarate all the celestial regions ... when I shall view his glory without one interposing cloud ... when I shall drink my fill at the fountain of joy that flows from his right hand forever.

"How dazzling is your prospect, O city of God, of whom such glorious things are spoken. There holy souls keep perpetual sabbaths; there newly-arrived saints are crowned with wreaths of light, while ivory harps and silver trumpets sound; there flaming seraphs sacred hymns begin, and cherubs loud responses sing."

WALK CLOSER TO GOD

For the Christian, the loss of a loved one in the Lord is only for a time. Death is rest, not regret, for reunion is certain.

As Paul proclaims, "'Where, O death, is your victory? Where, O death, is your sting?' ... But thanks be to God! He gives us the victory through our Lord Jesus Christ" (1 Corinthians 15:55,57).

Many refrains have been written capturing the essence of that victory. Here is one to reflect on:

> Brief life is here our portion,
> Brief life, short-lived care.
> The life that knows no ending,
> The tearless life, is there.
> O happy retribution!
> Short toil, eternal rest;
> For mortals and for sinners
> A mansion with the blest! ❖

september6

WHEN HIS LIFE LIGHTS MY LIFE

You are all children of the light and children of the day. We do not belong to the night or to the darkness.

1 THESSALONIANS 5:5

For the Christian, light and darkness represent the conflict between the ways of God and the ways of the world.

As John described it in his Gospel: "In him [Christ] was life, and that life was the light of all mankind. The light shines in the darkness, and the darkness has not overcome it" (John 1:4–5). You will learn more about living in the light by reading Charles Hodge's helpful description.

WALK WITH CHARLES HODGE

"Christians should live as children of the light. Light stands for knowledge, holiness, and happiness. Darkness stands for ignorance, sin, and misery.

"The exhortation therefore is, in its negative form, not to sink back into the world, which belongs to the kingdom of darkness. That is, not to give yourself up to the opinions and practice of the world, and thus inevitably involve yourself in the ruin in which the kingdom of darkness must ultimately issue.

"It is an exhortation to act as becomes those who are members of the kingdom of Christ. An exhortation to exhibit the knowledge and holiness, especially in faith, hope, and charity, which characterize those who belong to that kingdom.

"The motive by which this exhortation is enforced is that we are destined not to wrath but to salvation (see 1 Thessalonians 5:9). And this salvation is secured by Christ who died, that whether we live or die, we should live together with him."

WALK CLOSER TO GOD

As a Christian, you no longer live in the darkness. Christ has become your light. And because of that light, you can see where you are going, you can avoid life's pitfalls, you can follow the paths of holiness.

Jesus said it best: "I am the light of the world. Whoever follows me will never walk in darkness, but will have the light of life" (John 8:12). Invite him to do what light does best in your life ... right now. ❖

september7

DEVELOPING A HEART OF CEASELESS PRAYER

Pray continually.

1 Thessalonians 5:17

Continual prayer in a nonstop world—that's your assignment. It's hard enough to "pray continually" while kneeling! But how do you "pray continually" while driving? Eating?

Paul was concerned with more than the posture of prayer. He knew as well that the attitude of prayer was all-important. And there's plenty of challenge in developing a heart for continual prayer, as Alexander Maclaren explains.

WALK WITH ALEXANDER MACLAREN

"Can I pray continually? Not if prayer means only words of supplication and petition. But if prayer also means a mental attitude of devotion and a subconscious reference to God in all that we do, unceasing prayer is possible.

"Do not let us blunt the edge of this commandment by discussing whether the ideal of unbroken communion with God is possible in this life. At all events it is possible for us to approximate that ideal more closely than we have ever done.

"If we are trying to keep our hearts in contact with God in the midst of daily duty, and if during the press of our work we cast a thought towards him and a prayer, then joy and hope and patience will come to us in a degree that we do not know much about yet, but might have known all about long, long ago."

WALK CLOSER TO GOD

The effectiveness of prayer does not rest on the volume of words spoken or the time spent. Consider these examples of to-the-point prayers:

Peter: "Lord, save me!" (Matthew 14:30).

The tax collector: "God, have mercy on me, a sinner" (Luke 18:13).

Nehemiah: "Then I prayed to the God of heaven, and I answered the king …" (Nehemiah 2:4–5).

Short. To the point. Fervent. Offered with the attitude of going to God in every situation, of keeping the lines of communication open, of having fellowship with the one who is your very life. Such is the privilege to excite the heart of every believer! ❧

september8

THE FRAGRANT FLOWER OF A RENEWED HEART

We ought always to thank God for you ... because your faith is growing more and more.
2 THESSALONIANS 1:3

A farmer plows, enriches the soil with fertilizer, and then waters throughout the dry months. And come harvest time, what does he have to show for his labors? Nothing—unless he has also planted the seed, for no amount of cultivation can make up for a lack of life.

Until you have the life of Christ within, there can be no Christ-honoring fruit without—a principle Charles Spurgeon probes from the example of the Thessalonians.

WALK WITH CHARLES SPURGEON

"The holiness which will honor Christ at last is a holiness based on faith in him, a holiness of which this was the root—that the Thessalonians trusted in Christ, and then, being saved, they loved their Lord and obeyed him. Holiness is an inner as well as an outer purity, arising out of the living and operative principle of faith.

"If any think they can achieve holiness apart from faith in Christ, they are as much mistaken as one who would hope to reap a harvest without casting seed into the furrows. Faith is the bulb, and holiness is the fragrant flower that comes of it when planted in the soil of a renewed heart.

"Beware of any pretense to a holiness arising out of yourselves and maintained by the energy of your own unaided will. True holiness must spring from confidence in the Savior of sinners."

WALK CLOSER TO GOD

Faith in Christ. Without it, holiness is all labor and no fruit. But once the seed of new life in Christ has been planted in your life, barrenness gives way to growing faith (see 2 Thessalonians 1:3), growing perseverance (see 2 Thessalonians 1:4), growing glory to God (see 2 Thessalonians 1:10).

Are you trying to cultivate a godly walk without first having received the "word planted in you, which can save you" (James 1:21)?

Only the seed of life in Christ can lead to a harvest that will last for eternity. ❖

september9

LIVING IN THE LIGHT OF CHRIST'S RETURN

Concerning the coming of our Lord Jesus Christ ... we ask you, brothers and sisters, not to become easily unsettled or alarmed.

2 THESSALONIANS 2:1–2

Setting dates for the events related to Christ's return is a popular pastime. Preoccupation with the when often obscures the what and why of that "blessed hope" (Titus 2:13). It's more exciting to speculate on the unknown than to live in the purifying light of what is known about Christ's return.

The thought of that future prompted poet John Milton to compose this psalm of meditation.

WALK WITH JOHN MILTON

The Lord will come and not be slow,
    His footsteps cannot err;
Before him righteousness shall go,
    His royal harbinger.
Truth from the earth, like to a flower,
    Shall bud and blossom then;
And justice, from her heavenly bower,
    Look down on mortal man.

Rise, God, judge thou the earth in might,
    This wicked earth redress;
And Thou art he who shall by right
    The nations all possess.
For great thou art, and wonders great
    By thy strong hand are done;
Thou in thy everlasting seat
    Remainest God alone.

WALK CLOSER TO GOD

You may not know when Christ is coming back, but Scripture sheds plenty of light on what will happen when he does. Milton's poem is a helpful summary: righteousness, truth, justice, judgment, retribution.

Christ will come to set things right. How should you live in light of that knowledge?

> Be prepared (see Matthew 24:44).
> Be faithful (see Luke 19:13).
> Be blameless (see 1 Thessalonians 5:23).
> Be obedient (see 1 Timothy 6:14).
> Be expectant (see Titus 2:13).

That's enough to keep you busy until he returns! ❖

september10

BECOMING INSTRUMENTS OF GOD'S PEACE

May our Lord Jesus Christ himself and God our Father ... encourage your hearts and strengthen you in every good deed and word.

2 THESSALONIANS 2:16–17

Stories abound of people who, during their final hours on earth, became the givers rather than the recipients of consolation. Even the apostle Paul, imprisoned and on trial for his life, could offer words of encouragement in his letters to the churches. His secret? The "living love of God." Charles Spurgeon explains.

WALK WITH CHARLES SPURGEON

"Union with the risen Lord is a consolation of the most abiding order: it is, in fact, everlasting. Let sickness prostrate us; have we not seen hundreds of believers as happy in the weakness of disease as they would have been in the strength of hale and blooming health? Let death's arrows pierce us to the heart; our comfort dies not, for have not our ears often heard the songs of saints as they have rejoiced because the living love of God was shed abroad in their hearts in dying moments?

"Yes, a sense of acceptance in the Beloved is an everlasting consolation. Moreover, the Christian has a conviction of this security.

"Whatever may occur in providence, whatever onslaughts there may be of inward corruption or outward temptation, he is safely bound up with the person and work of Jesus. Is not this a source of consolation, overflowing and delightful?"

WALK CLOSER TO GOD

Francis of Assisi, thirteenth-century saint, perhaps said it best:

"Lord, make me an instrument of thy peace. Where there is hatred, let me sow love; where there is injury, pardon; where there is doubt, faith; where there is despair, hope; where there is darkness, light; where there is sadness, joy.

"O divine Master, grant that I may not so much seek to be consoled as to console, to be understood as to understand, to be loved as to love; for it is in giving that we receive, it is in pardoning that we are pardoned, and it is in dying that we are born to eternal life." ♣

september**11**

GOD FEEDS THE SPARROWS, BUT HE DOESN'T THROW THE WORMS

We hear that some among you are idle ... Such people we command ... to settle down and earn the food they eat.

2 THESSALONIANS 3:11–12

Eat, drink and be merry, "for tomorrow we die." That was the misguided notion of God's people in Isaiah's day (Isaiah 22:13).

"Eat, drink and be merry, for tomorrow the Lord returns." That was the equally misguided notion of God's people in Paul's day. But Paul had a word of advice for the Thessalonians: "The one who is unwilling to work shall not eat" (2 Thessalonians 3:10). Martin Luther underscores this point.

WALK WITH MARTIN LUTHER

"To put it briefly, God wants people to work. It is true that God could support you without work, could let food and drink grow on the table for you. But he will not do this. He wants you to work and to use your reason in this matter.

"In everything God acts in such a way that he will provide, but we should work. If God did not bless, not one hair, not a solitary wisp of straw, would grow.

"At the same time God wants me to take this stand: I would have nothing whatever if I did not plow and sow. God does not want to have success come without work, and yet I am not to achieve it by my work.

"He does not want me to sit at home, to loaf and wait till a fried chicken flies into my mouth. That would be tempting God."

WALK CLOSER TO GOD

God has promised to meet your needs, but as Martin Luther points out, he never promised to deliver your meals!

His responsibility, rather, is to "meet all your needs according to the riches of his glory in Christ Jesus" (Philippians 4:19).

Your responsibility is this: "Whether you eat or drink or whatever you do, do it all for the glory of God" (1 Corinthians 10:31).

Therefore, the best place for you to be when Christ returns: somewhere hard at work! ❖

THE GRACE OF LAW

We know that the law is good if one uses it properly.

1 TIMOTHY 1:8

"Dear Paul, I have a question. In some places the Scripture says things like I have been released from the law, and that I am not under the law, but under grace. In other places it says that the perfect law gives freedom. Is this a contradiction?"

Have you ever wished you could write a similar letter to the apostle? How do we reconcile these apparently contradictory statements about God's law? R. L. Dabney explains that the word *law* has different meanings in Scripture.

WALK WITH R. L. DABNEY

"First, the law is the authoritative declaration of God's character. It is the unchanging expression of how God distinguishes right from wrong.

"Second, the law was 'our guardian until Christ came' (Galatians 3:24). By showing us our sinfulness it prepares us to submit to the Redeemer.

"Third, the believer has been chosen to be holy and blameless; he has been redeemed from all wickedness to be one of Christ's very own people, eager to do what is good. This great end, the believer's sanctification, can only be attained through a holy rule of conduct. Such a rule is the law. It is to be diligently observed as the guide to holiness.

"Fourth, its precepts restrain the aboundings of sin. They partially instruct the consciences even of the unrenewed. They guide secular laws, and thus lay a foundation for a wholesome civil society.

"And last, the publication of the law convicts God's enemies on earth in a way that foreshadows their conviction on judgment day.

"For these reasons, the preaching and expounding of the law is to be kept up diligently in every gospel church."

WALK CLOSER TO GOD

John saw God's law as the standard that distinguishes love (see 1 John 5:3) from sin (see 1 John 3:4).

James expressed the same thought when he wrote of the law as a mirror that shows us where our spiritual complexion is blemished and where it is clear (see James 1:22–25).

Paul shows us that God's law defines and restrains civil criminals (see 1 Timothy 1:8–11).

Have you been quick to use God's grace as an excuse for ignoring his commands? Meditate on Psalm 119 for a different perspective. ❧

september**13**

IMMORTAL, INVISIBLE, GOD ONLY WISE

Now to the King eternal, immortal, invisible, the only God, be honor and glory for ever and ever.

1 TIMOTHY 1:17

"Due to circumstances beyond our control ..." are usually words that generate frustration. But the apostle Paul owed his very salvation to circumstances beyond his control (see 1 Timothy 1:12–16), and he wouldn't have had it any other way!

Intercepted by Christ on the road to Damascus, Paul's plans underwent a dramatic change. The "worst" of sinners found mercy in Christ.

And the result? Patrick Fairbairn, in commenting on Paul's expression of praise, probes the motive behind Paul's spontaneous doxology (see 1 Timothy 1:17).

WALK WITH PATRICK FAIRBAIRN

"The train of reflection into which Paul had been led naturally brought the thought of God very prominently before him.

"Penetrated with a sense of the infinite greatness and overruling wisdom, power, and goodness of God, Paul winds up his personal discourse by a devout acknowledgment of God as the Lord of the universe, and glorifies him as such.

"When God is spoken of as King of the ages, he is presented to our view as supreme Lord and Director—the Sovereign Epochmaker, who arranges everything pertaining to the affairs of this world beforehand, according to the counsel of his own will, and controls whatever takes place, so as to subordinate it to his own design."

WALK CLOSER TO GOD

Meditate for a few moments on Walter Chalmers Smith's hymn:

> Immortal, invisible, God only wise,
>> In light inaccessible, hid from our eyes,
> Most blessed, most glorious, the Ancient of days,
>> Almighty, victorious, Thy great name we praise.
> To all, life Thou givest—to both great and small
>> In all life Thou livest, the true life of all.
> We blossom and flourish as leaves on the tree,
>> And wither and perish—but naught changeth Thee. ❖

september14

GUIDEBOOK FOR GODLY LIVING

And for this purpose I was appointed a herald and an apostle ... and a true and faithful teacher of the Gentiles.

1 TIMOTHY 2:7

You can find support for almost anything in the Bible:

Stealing: "Anyone who has been stealing must steal" (Ephesians 4:28).

Atheism: "There is no God" (Psalm 14:1; 53:1).

Of course, none of these verses means what it appears to say when taken out of its context.

That's why the task of a teacher and preacher is so important. They are charged with correctly handling "the word of truth" (2 Timothy 2:15).

Charles Simeon expresses his high regard for God's Word—and explains how it should be handled.

WALK WITH CHARLES SIMEON

"I love the simplicity of the Scriptures; and I wish to receive and communicate every truth precisely in the way, and to the extent, that it is set forth in the inspired volume.

"My endeavor is to bring out of Scripture what is there, and not to thrust in what I think might be there. I have a great conviction on this point; never to speak more or less than what I believe to be the mind of the Spirit in the passage I am expounding.

"It is an invariable rule with me to give to every portion of the Word of God its full and proper force. Where the inspired writers speak in unqualified terms, I think myself at liberty to do the same, judging that they need no instruction from me as to how to propagate the truth."

WALK CLOSER TO GOD

In order to be a teacher of the Scripture, you must first be a learner.

The assignment will not always be simple. Even Peter admitted Paul's letters contained some things that were weighty and "hard to understand" (2 Peter 3:16). Yet Peter never used that excuse to twist Paul's words into something more palatable—but false!

Whether you are called on to teach others or merely to teach yourself, the need is the same: to come to the Bible as God's trustworthy guidebook for your life.

It's always safe to say, "I will do nothing else." ❖

september15

THE RIGHT PERSON IN THE RIGHT JOB

Here is a trustworthy saying: Whoever aspires to be an overseer desires a noble task.

1 TIMOTHY 3:1

Prospective employers often seem more concerned with outward achievement than with inward character. In the business world, quality of life often takes a back seat to accomplishments.

Not so in the family of God! There, what you are counts for more than what you have achieved. The work of the ministry demands more than good businessmen, good civic leaders, good politicians. It demands good people.

Patrick Fairbairn discusses the importance of good character in the selection of godly leaders in the church.

WALK WITH PATRICK FAIRBAIRN

"The apostle's list of qualifications is predominantly moral and consists of attributes of character rather than gifts and endowments of mind. The latter are included only as they might be required to form clear perceptions of truth and duty, to distinguish between things that differ, and in difficult or perplexing circumstances to discern the right and know how to maintain and vindicate it.

"Yet it is the characteristics which go to constitute the living, practical Christian, the man or woman of God, that are here brought into view.

"And whatever the church finds necessary to add to the number, in order to render her leaders fit for the varied work and service to which they are called, the grand moral characteristics specified here must still be regarded as the primary and more essential elements in the qualifications of a true spiritual overseer."

WALK CLOSER TO GOD

Father, as I seek to minister to others in your name, make me conscious that serving you is more than doing the right things; it is being the right person—your Christlike child.

Build into my life those qualities that make serving you not simply a job but rather a lifestyle. In the name of him whose hands and heart were never in conflict. Amen. ✤

september16

THE MOST PROFITABLE THING IN THE WORLD

Train yourself to be godly. For ... godliness has value for all things, holding promise for both the present life and the life to come.

1 TIMOTHY 4:7–8

Godliness is often associated with individuals past the age of 65. But it may surprise you to learn that Paul talked more about godliness in his letters to two young disciples (Timothy and Titus) than in any of his other correspondence.

Johann Peter Lange comments on the practical importance of making godliness your goal.

WALK WITH JOHANN PETER LANGE

"That godliness is profitable for all things, and thus the most profitable thing in the world, cannot be too strongly enforced against an abstract idealism on one side, and an irreligious materialism on the other.

"There are many who know that godliness is good for a peaceful death but do not hold it necessary for a happy life. Many others think faith very beautiful for the poor, the weak, the suffering, and the dying, but not for real, able, practical people.

"It must always be remembered that the gospel is a power which grasps the whole person. The true Christian is not only the happiest person, but the bravest citizen, the best patriot, the greatest leader. In a word, the Christian is, in all relations, a co-worker with God and an honor to Christ."

WALK CLOSER TO GOD

"Godliness ... is great gain" (1 Timothy 6:6). It is also a great challenge—a balance between two equally ungodly extremes.

On the one hand is "abstract idealism," as characterized by Simeon Stylites, a fifth-century ascetic who lived atop a pillar most of his life in an attempt to become "saintly." On the other is "irreligious materialism" leading to a preoccupation with wealth.

Genuine godliness makes "real, able, practical" Christians—men and women who respond to God and government, family and society, as he intended—regardless of their age. ❖

september**17**

FILLING THE MIND WITH TIMELESS TRUTH

Devote yourself to the public reading of Scripture, to preaching and to teaching ... Be diligent in these matters.

1 TIMOTHY 4:13,15

"Garbage in, garbage out." It's a principle of computer programming that states that a computer can only respond to a question on the basis of information it has been supplied. If all you put in is "garbage," that's all you will get back in return.

What you feed your mind becomes the basis for the lifestyle you lead. Charles Hodge discusses the significance of good "input" in the Christian life.

WALK WITH CHARLES HODGE

"It is unreasonable to expect to be conformed to the image of God unless the truth concerning God operates continuously upon the mind.

"How can the love of Christ increase in those who hardly ever think of him or of his work? We cannot make progress in holiness unless we devote much time to reading, hearing, and meditating upon the Word of God, which is the truth whereby we are sanctified.

"The more this truth is brought before the mind—the more we commune with it, entering into its concerns, applying it to our own case, appropriating its principles, rejoicing in its promises—the more we may expect to be transformed by the renewing of our minds.

"Those distinguished for their godliness have been those accustomed to withdraw the mind from the influence of the world and to bring it under the influence of the Word of God."

WALK CLOSER TO GOD

Here is a helpful "five finger" method for getting a grasp on a passage of Scripture:

1. Read it.
2. Hear it.
3. Study it.
4. Memorize it.
5. Meditate on it.

The grasp will be weaker or stronger depending on the number of fingers you use and how often you exercise that grasp. ❖

september18

REAL NEEDS AND REAL RESPONSIBILITIES

If any woman who is a believer has widows in her care, she should continue to help them and not let the church be burdened with them, so that the church can help those widows who are really in need.

1 TIMOTHY 5:16

From its earliest days, the church has sought to meet the needs of those who need help: widows (see Acts 6:1–3), hungry first-century believers in Judea (see Acts 11:29), "anyone who had need" (Acts 4:35).

But how do you discover who is truly needy? Alfred Plummer elaborates on Paul's guidelines to Timothy.

WALK WITH ALFRED PLUMMER

"The church accepts the duty which it teaches of 'providing for its own.'

"But it ought not to be burdened with the support of any but those who are truly in need.

"The near relations of those in need must be taught to leave the church free to relieve those who have no near relations to support them.

"Paul has no intention of creating a welfare class. So long as they can, the needy must maintain themselves. When they have ceased to be able to do this, they must be supported by their family. If they have no one to support them, the church must undertake their support.

"Widows as a rule ought to be supported by their own relations. Only in exceptional cases where there are no relations who can help ought the church to have to undertake this duty."

WALK CLOSER TO GOD

Paul's guidelines to Timothy are detailed and time-consuming—both to read and to implement.

It's much easier to tell someone in need, "I'll pray for you," than to say, "I'll prepare a meal for you." It's much cheaper to rely on welfare than to be responsible for the welfare of someone you love.

Once a need has been clearly established in the life of another, God's will is clear.

Commenting on a previous generation of Christians, one pagan emperor remarked, "They feed not only their poor but ours also."

Can that be said of your generation as well? ✤

september19

HOARDING, HOLDING AND LETTING GO

For the love of money is a root of all kinds of evil.

1 TIMOTHY 6:10

First Timothy 6:10 certainly would sound more appealing if it read, "The lack of money is the root of all evil." Or "Money is the root of all evil."

But notice the correct rendering of the verse. The problem does not rest in having money but in the attitude you have toward money.

The proper use of your assets begins with the proper attitude, as G. Campbell Morgan explains.

WALK WITH G. CAMPBELL MORGAN

"Love of money. Perhaps the word which best conveys the thought is the word avarice.

"'Love of money' hoards and holds.

"It is indeed a root of all evil. It dries up the springs of compassion in the soul. It lowers the whole standard of morality. It is the inspiration of all the basest things, even covetousness; for if there may be covetousness without love of money, there is never love of money without covetousness.

"Avarice is often created by prosperity and the consequent possession of money. It is often powerfully present in the lives of those who are devoid of wealth.

"It is wholly material, the result of a wrong conception of life, due to forgetfulness of the fact that 'life does not consist in an abundance of possessions' (Luke 12:15)."

WALK CLOSER TO GOD

There is good news for those with humble means. Regardless of your net worth, God wants you to be rich.

Ah, but rich in assets that time cannot tarnish and inflation cannot destroy. Rich in the assets of "righteousness, godliness, faith, love, endurance and gentleness" (1 Timothy 6:11).

You may possess vast earthly treasures, yet live like a pauper by the one standard that counts for eternity—God's standard.

Loving God versus loving gold. There's a wealth of difference between the two. And you can't afford to make the wrong choice. ❖

september**20**

BATTLING IN THE TRENCHES OF EVERYDAY EXPERIENCE

Fight the good fight of the faith. Take hold of the eternal life to which you were called when you made your good confession in the presence of many witnesses.

1 TIMOTHY 6:12

The Christian life is not something lived out from the comfort of an overstuffed armchair. Rather, it is daily battles fought and won in the trenches of everyday experience as the Spirit triumphs over the flesh.

Charles Spurgeon draws a strategic lesson from the pages of military history and challenges today's Christians.

WALK WITH CHARLES SPURGEON

"When the Spartans marched into battle, they advanced with cheerful songs, willing to fight. But when the Persians entered the conflict, you could hear as the regiments came on the crack of whips by which the officers drove the cowards into the thick of the battle. You need not wonder that a few Spartans were more than a match for thousands of Persians, that in fact they were like lions in the midst of sheep.

"So let it be with the church; never should she need to be forced to reluctant action. Full of irrepressible life, she should long for conflict against everything which is contrary to God.

"Were we enthusiastic soldiers of the cross, we should be like lions in the midst of herds and enemies, and through God's help nothing would be able to stand against us."

WALK CLOSER TO GOD

What more appropriate response to Paul's words could there be than the "call to arms" of the hymn "Onward, Christian Soldiers"?

> Onward, Christian soldiers,
>   Marching as to war,
> With the cross of Jesus
>   Going on before:
> Christ the royal Master
>   Leads against the foe;
> Forward into battle,
>   See his banners go. ❖

september**21**

THE INVISIBLE, INVINCIBLE INSIDE HELPER

Guard the good deposit that was entrusted to you—guard it with the help of the Holy Spirit who lives in us.

2 TIMOTHY 1:14

Some decisions in life are clear choices between right and wrong. Others require discernment to know what is right and what is wrong. When confronted with the second—and more difficult—kind of choice, how do you respond? According to what you think, what you were taught, what the law says, what the public believes? Here's a fifth option you might not have considered: Ask an "insider" who knows. That "insider," of course, is the Holy Spirit.

A. B. Simpson provides this helpful description of the Spirit's ministry which helps believers discern right from wrong.

WALK WITH A. B. SIMPSON

"God gives to us a power within, which will hold our hearts in purity and victory.

"It—or rather he—is the Holy Spirit. When any thought or suggestion of evil arises in our mind, the conscience can instantly call upon the Holy Spirit to drive it out, and he will expel it at the command of faith or prayer, and keep us as pure as we are willing to be kept.

"God requires us to stand in holy vigilance, and he will do exceedingly abundantly for us as we hold fast to that which is good. He will also show us the evil and enable us to detect it, and to bring it to him for expulsion and destruction."

WALK CLOSER TO GOD

Being alert to the attacks of Satan means being sensitive to the guidance of the Spirit, for his role is crucial if you are to "take your stand against the devil's schemes" (Ephesians 6:11).

Satan's power is strong; that's why you need the "sword of the Spirit" (Ephesians 6:17). Satan's attacks are persistent; that's why you need to "pray in the Spirit on all occasions with all kinds of prayers" (Ephesians 6:18).

The Holy Spirit is within you, providing wisdom and protection against invisible forces from without. Wouldn't you agree that's a truth worth thinking about? ❖

september**22**

GREATNESS THAT BEGINS IN THE HEART

You then, my son, be strong in the grace that is in Christ Jesus.

2 TIMOTHY 2:1

There is something remarkable—and unexpected—about many who receive that cherished accolade "tower of strength." They are neither towering physically nor strong emotionally.

David Brainerd was one such individual. Though physically weak and given to periods of depression, Brainerd was greatly used by God among the American Indians.

Read carefully as Jonathan Edwards, who cared for the dying young missionary, probes the inward strength behind this quiet giant.

WALK WITH JONATHAN EDWARDS

"That Brainerd's temper or constitution inclined him to despondency is no reason to suppose that his extraordinary devotion was simply the fruit of his imagination.

"Certainly his natural disposition had some influence in his religious exercises, as it did in the lives of King David, and the apostles Peter, John, and Paul. There was undoubtedly some mixture of melancholy with true godly sorrow and real Christian humility: some mixture of the natural fire of youth with his holy zeal for God.

"In spite of these imperfections, every careful reader will readily acknowledge that what is here set before him is a remarkable instance of true piety in heart and practice, and that it is most worthy of imitation."

WALK CLOSER TO GOD

Edwards's words are from the introduction to *The Life and Diary of David Brainerd*, a remarkable account of one man's walk with God.

No matter what your age or personality, you can walk with God as David Brainerd did. You may not look like a tower of spiritual strength, but you can be one—by cultivating your relationship with God.

Your appearance may be unassuming, your manner quiet and reserved, but remember—greatness in God's sight begins in the heart. ✤

september23

YOUR LIFE: GOD'S PROJECT

Those who cleanse themselves from the latter will be instruments for special purposes, made holy, useful to the Master and prepared to do any good work.

2 TIMOTHY 2:21

"Fan into flame" (2 Timothy 1:6). "Stand firm" (1 Corinthians 16:13). "Be strong" (1 Corinthians 16:13). "Endure hardship" (2 Timothy 4:5). "Avoid" (2 Timothy 2:16). "Flee" (1 Corinthians 6:18).

At first glance the Christian life might appear to be a do-it-yourself project—until you try it and discover how inadequate your own strength is.

But God never asks of you what he has not first empowered you to do—a truth John Calvin understood.

WALK WITH JOHN CALVIN

"It is clear beyond contradiction that we are called to holiness. But the calling and duty of Christians is one thing, and it is another to have the power to make it happen.

"We do not deny that the faithful are required to purify themselves; but that this is a matter which belongs to the Lord he declares himself, when through the prophet Ezekiel he promises to send forth the Holy Spirit that we may be cleansed (see Ezekiel 36:25–26).

"Therefore, we should beseech the Lord to purge us rather than vainly attempt such a matter in our own strength without his aid."

WALK CLOSER TO GOD

It is one thing to read the Word of God; it is another to live it.

Enthusiasm is easier than obedience. But it takes more than zeal and grim determination for believers to become "instruments ... useful to the Master."

For that to happen you need strength that only the Master can supply, and strength to stay morally clean and spiritually sensitive.

The world would label such a lifestyle "narrow." God calls it "holy."

And he is calling you to it—today! ❖

september24

LOVER OF GOD OR LOVER OF GOLD?

There will be terrible times in the last days. People will be ... lovers of money.

2 TIMOTHY 3:1-2

Loving God. Loving gold. Only one letter separates the two, but the outlooks are worlds apart. And the love of one will overpower the love of the other. As Jesus said, "No one can serve two masters ... You cannot serve both God and money" (Luke 16:13).

Paul accurately described the perilous times when people will be "lovers of themselves" (2 Timothy 3:2) and "lovers of pleasure" (2 Timothy 3:4)—the result of embracing the world's system of values.

John Wesley has been described as a man who died leaving behind nothing but his Bible, his horse and the Methodist Church. Listen as he echoes Paul's admonition about the deceitfulness of riches.

WALK WITH JOHN WESLEY

"Let us but open our eyes, and we may daily see the melancholy proofs of this—those who, resolving to be rich, coveting after money, the root of all evil, have already pierced themselves through with many sorrows. The cautiousness with which the apostle here speaks is highly observable. For one may possibly be rich, without any fault of his, by an overruling Providence, preventing his own choice.

"Riches, dangerous as they are, do not always 'plunge people into ruin and destruction' (1 Timothy 6:9), but the desire for riches does. Those who calmly desire and deliberately seek to attain them, whether they do in fact gain the world or not, do invariably lose their own souls.

"These are they that sell him, who bought them with his blood, for a few pieces of gold or silver."

WALK CLOSER TO GOD

Worldly voices and values clamor for your attention every day. And given the chance, they will dictate your priorities. Paul's advice has never been more timely: Focus on "the Holy Scriptures, which are able to make you wise for salvation" (2 Timothy 3:15). God's Word is a "gold mine" for the one who loves God. ✣

september25

THE REVELATION THAT'S FOREVER RELEVANT

All Scripture is God-breathed and is useful for teaching, rebuking, correcting and training in righteousness.

2 TIMOTHY 3:16

God's Word, the Bible, has been translated into more languages, printed in more sizes, and published in more editions than any other volume in history. Yet its content has never changed or become irrelevant. Its truth is as needed today as when it was first given centuries ago.

W. Graham Scroggie offers this insight into the enduring character of God's Word.

WALK WITH W. GRAHAM SCROGGIE

"This truly is the Word of God which lives and abides forever. It does not need our apologies and our special pleading. Give it a chance, and it will demonstrate its own character and its own power.

"This is the light by which millions have found their way to the shining home among the delectable mountains. This is the star which has guided mariners on stormy seas throughout the ages.

"This is the weapon with which the Christian soldier has fought his battles to glorious victory. This is the compass which has guided men in darkness and distress. This is the Book on which many a saintly Christian has laid down his head as on a pillow in the last moments of life, whispering some psalm of Scripture.

"There need be no panic. This is the rock of all ages, and those built on it are as eternal as God."

WALK CLOSER TO GOD

Timothy's education in the Scriptures began when he was only a child (see 2 Timothy 3:15), literally at the knee of his mother and grandmother (see 2 Timothy 1:5).

What can even young children learn from such exposure? They can learn "teaching" (truth about God), "rebuking" (truth about error), "correcting" (getting back on the right track) and "training in righteousness" (continuing education in the faith).

Build your life on the Word of God, and you—like Timothy—will find an unshakable foundation for this life and the next. ✤

september**26**

FELLOWSHIP IN THE FAMILY OF GOD

Do your best to come to me quickly, for Demas, because he loved this world, has deserted me.
2 TIMOTHY 4:9–10

In the world of athletics, there are two kinds of sports: individual and team. And woe to the person who joins a team but continues to play only as an individual!

Though Paul's life was characterized by personal achievement, he rarely traveled alone; he constantly spoke of the "one another" responsibilities in the body of Christ and he established churches for mutual encouragement and fellowship.

Fellowship is not an option but an imperative in the Christian life, as William Biederwolf explains.

WALK WITH WILLIAM BIEDERWOLF

"I do not believe it is possible to be a good Christian without having godly friends.

"If I could find a man who was filled with the Spirit of Jesus, I would rather know him and get into the secret of his heart, and have the benediction and blessing that necessarily come from fellowship with him, than to have all that ever came to Demas through the decision he made when he quit the fight, quit the faith, quit the race, said 'goodbye' to Paul, and went off to Thessalonica.

"Better to have one Christian friend than anything the world might offer me. And this, in the first place, is what Demas lost.

"He lost Paul."

WALK CLOSER TO GOD

Paul knew that Christians need each other, so he gave instructions on how to treat one another: "Carry each other's burdens" (Galatians 6:2). "Be kind and compassionate to one another, forgiving each other" (Ephesians 4:32). "Love one another" (Romans 13:8).

As part of God's family, you have the Lord. But you have something more: an entire family of brothers and sisters in Christ. Trying to live for him while ignoring them is a losing proposition.

And the loser is you! ❖

september27

ACTIONS REFLECTING YOUR KNOWLEDGE OF GOD

They claim to know God, but by their actions they deny him. They are detestable, disobedient and unfit for doing anything good.

TITUS 1:16

Good works cannot save you (see Titus 3:5), but the absence of good works can effectively deny what you claim to possess (see Titus 1:16).

God saved you not *by* good works but *for* good works. John Calvin explores this as he explains why true knowledge produces correct actions.

WALK WITH JOHN CALVIN

"If we want to know how our life should be regulated, let us examine the Word of God; for we cannot be sanctified by outward show and pomp, although they are highly esteemed among men.

"We must call upon God in sincerity and put our whole trust in him; we must give up pride and presumption and turn to him with true lowliness of mind so that we will not be given to fleshly affections.

"We must hold ourselves under subjection to God, and flee from gluttony, excess, robbery, blasphemy, and other evils. Thus we see what God would have us to do, in order to have our lives well regulated.

"When people try to justify themselves by outward works, it is like covering a heap of filth with a clean linen cloth. Therefore, let us put away the filthiness that is hidden in our hearts. Thus we may see wherein consists the true knowledge of God! When we understand this correctly, it will lead us to live in obedience to his will."

WALK CLOSER TO GOD

Actions are no substitute for knowledge, as John Calvin suggests. Rather, they are a reflection of knowledge—or lack of it.

People may be fooled for a time by your profession, but God is never fooled. Without the proper knowledge of him, "all our righteous acts are like filthy rags" (Isaiah 64:6).

First things first. In the matter of becoming a Christian, it's not what you do but whom you know. Take God at his word and you won't be fooling anyone—least of all yourself. ♣

september28

TO DISPLAY THE LOVELINESS OF CHRIST

In everything set them an example by doing what is good ... so that in every way [you] will make the teaching about God our Savior attractive.

TITUS 2:7,10

A picture frame—seemingly an afterthought to the picture itself—can either help or hinder the viewer's appreciation of the picture.

The same could be said of the Christian life. The masterpiece of the gospel is breathtaking, but its beauty is either tarnished or enhanced by the Christian life that frames it.

F. B. Meyer has these thoughts on adorning the gospel with the right words and deeds.

WALK WITH F. B. MEYER

"Even the lowliest worker might 'make attractive' the gospel as jewels make attractive the brow of beauty. Holy lives can display its loveliness.

"To please one's superiors in all things, so far as our loyalty to Christ permits, is to commend Christ to our households and win his approval.

"The grace of God has ever offered salvation, but in Jesus it was brought to our doors.

"Have we sat sufficiently long in the school of grace that our gentle Teacher may instruct us how to live? It must be 'self-controlled' in regard to ourselves, 'upright[ly]' toward others, and 'godly' toward God (Titus 2:12). We cannot realize any one of these unless we resolutely deny ungodliness and worldly lusts.

"This was the aim and purpose of Jesus coming to die for us. He wanted to redeem us from all iniquity, purify us as his own, and use us in all manner of good works. It is a solemn question whether that supreme purpose has been realized in our own experience. If not, why not?"

WALK CLOSER TO GOD

A bad frame draws attention to itself; a good frame highlights that which it displays. In a similar way, certain qualities of life make the gospel attractive: "integrity, seriousness and soundness of speech" (Titus 2:7–8).

Surrounding your witness with these is one way to help others realize that "the grace of God has appeared that offers salvation to all people" (Titus 2:11). ❖

september29

ASKING THE QUESTIONS GOD DELIGHTS TO ANSWER

But avoid foolish controversies and genealogies and arguments and quarrels about the law, because these are unprofitable and useless.

TITUS 3:9

How many angels can dance on the head of a pin? Can God make a rock so big that he cannot move it? Where did Cain get his wife?

Such questions produce only endless speculation—and far more heat than light!

Paul admonished both Timothy and Titus to avoid the kind of questions that serve no useful purpose but only detract from the weightier questions and pursuits of the Christian life.

Charles Spurgeon points the way to another set of questions for the child of God to consider.

WALK WITH CHARLES SPURGEON

"Our business is neither to ask nor answer foolish questions, but to avoid them altogether. And if we observe the apostle's precept to be careful to maintain good works, we shall find ourselves far too occupied with profitable business to take interest in unworthy and needless quarrels.

"There are, however, some questions which are the reverse of foolish, which we must not avoid, but fairly and honestly meet, such as these: Do I believe in the Lord Jesus Christ? Am I renewed in the spirit of my mind? Am I walking, not after the flesh, but after the Spirit? Am I growing in grace? Am I looking for the coming of the Lord?

"Such inquiries as these urgently demand our attention; and if we have all been given to making excuses, let us now turn our attention to a service much more profitable. Let us be peacemakers and endeavor to lead others both by our precept and example, to avoid foolish questions."

WALK CLOSER TO GOD

Every Christian has a growing list of questions that yearn for answers this side of heaven. Good questions. Questions God may see fit to answer ... someday. But in the meantime, you might want to ask yourself one question: "When I meet God face to face, what will be my answers to the questions he will have for me?" ❖

september**30**

TACTFUL WORDS TO TOUCH THE HEART

I prefer to appeal to you on the basis of love ... for my son Onesimus, who became my son while I was in chains.

PHILEMON 9–10

Tact has been called the ability to organize awkward truth attractively.

The case of the runaway slave Onesimus provided Paul with a supreme test of his tactfulness, for his letter to Philemon would be the basis for the reconciliation of master and slave.

Albert Barnes highlights the tender tone of Paul's brief message.

WALK WITH ALBERT BARNES

"The address and tact of Paul here are worthy of particular observation. If Paul had simply said, 'I beseech you for Onesimus'; or 'I appeal to you for your servant Onesimus,' he would at once have reminded Philemon of his slave's former conduct, his ingratitude and disobedience.

"But the phrase 'my son' makes the way easy for the mention of his name, for Paul had already found the way to Philemon's heart before his eye lighted on the name. Who could refuse Paul—a servant of Christ—the request which he made for one he regarded as his son?

"The name Onesimus is not suggested until Paul had mentioned that Onesimus has sustained to him the relation of a 'son'—the fruit of his labors while he was a prisoner.

"Then, when the name of Onesimus is mentioned, it would occur to Philemon not primarily as the name of a disobedient servant, but as one converted by labors of his own friend in prison.

"Was ever more delicacy shown in disarming one of prejudice and carrying an appeal to the heart?"

WALK CLOSER TO GOD

Cultivating tact will help you minimize friction and maximize communication.

Let these admonitions point the way: "A gentle answer turns away wrath, but a harsh word stirs up anger" (Proverbs 15:1). "Let your conversation be always full of grace" (Colossians 4:6). ❖

october1

THE MAJESTY OF THE FATHER SHINING THROUGH HIS SON

The Son is the radiance of God's glory and the exact representation of his being ... He sat down at the right hand of the Majesty in heaven.

HEBREWS 1:3

Painters have tried. Sculptors have tried. Poets have tried. Yet all have failed, for only one picture of God has ever been accurately rendered.

Jesus Christ alone is the "exact representation of God's being." In Jesus, God became a man so that all the human race might see God.

If your picture of God is a bit fuzzy, the opening verses of Hebrews will sharpen your focus, and John Calvin's words will help you better appreciate the picture.

WALK WITH JOHN CALVIN

"The Son is said to be 'the radiance of God's glory' and the 'exact representation of his being'; these are words which borrow from created things to describe the hidden majesty of God. But the things which are evident to our senses are fitly applied to God, that we may know what is to be found in Christ and what benefits he brings to us.

"When you hear that the Son is the brightness of the Father's glory, think that the glory of the Father is invisible until it shines forth in Christ, and that he is called the 'exact representation of his being' because the Father's majesty is hidden until it shows itself impressed on the Son's image.

"The writer's purpose is to build up our faith so that we may learn that God is made known to us in no other way than in Christ. Thus it follows that we are blind to the light of God until in Christ it shines on us."

WALK CLOSER TO GOD

God is light. So is Jesus: "I am the light of the world" (John 8:12).

God is truth. So is Jesus: "I am ... the truth" (John 14:6).

God is God alone. So is Jesus: "I am" (John 8:58).

"In these last days he [God] has spoken to us by his Son" (Hebrews 1:2). Therefore, you are no longer "in the dark" about God when you have met the Savior.

And that's a thought to brighten any day! ✤

october2

THE GREATEST TREASURE EVER OFFERED TO THE WORLD

How shall we escape if we ignore so great a salvation?

HEBREWS 2:3

Jesus declared, "The kingdom of heaven is like a merchant looking for fine pearls. When he found one of great value, he went away and sold everything he had and bought it" (Matthew 13:45–46).

That man knew that salvation is worth far more than anything the world has to offer.

Being reminded of the surpassing value of "so great a salvation" gives believers the right perspective when confronted with the concerns of this world, as Martin Luther explains.

WALK WITH MARTIN LUTHER

"The supreme blessing in which one can truly know the goodness of God is not temporal possessions, but the eternal blessing that God has called us to—his holy gospel.

"In this gospel we hear that God will be gracious to us for the sake of his Son, will forgive and eternally save us, and will protect us in this life against the tyranny of the devil and the world.

"To someone who properly appreciates this blessing, everything else is a trifle. Though he is poor, sick, despised, and burdened with adversities, he sees that he keeps more than he has lost. If he has no money and goods, he knows nevertheless that he has a gracious God; if his body is sick, he knows that he is called to eternal life.

"His heart has this constant consolation: Only a short time, and everything will be better."

WALK CLOSER TO GOD

Your "great" salvation carries great benefits: eternal life (see John 3:16), forgiveness of sins (see Ephesians 1:7), deliverance (see Colossians 1:13), adoption (see Galatians 4:4–7).

Salvation is not simply good news; it's great news! So when you have seen enough of this world, do as one hymn writer has suggested:

> Turn your eyes upon Jesus,
>   Look full in his wonderful face;
> And the things of earth will grow strangely dim
>   In the light of his glory and grace. ❖

october3

LEARNING TO WALK AS JESUS WALKED

For this reason he had to be made like them, fully human in every way, in order that he might become a merciful and faithful high priest in service to God.

HEBREWS 2:17

Soon after he arrived in inland China, J. Hudson Taylor spoke Chinese, wore Chinese clothes, ate Chinese food and observed Chinese customs. As a pioneer missionary to the masses of people in the interior of China, Taylor knew the importance of identifying with those he wanted to reach.

When God became man in the person of Christ, he secured our salvation by living and dying as God incarnate, in the flesh. J. Hudson Taylor explains why identification with the lost is a powerful testimony of Christ's incarnation.

WALK WITH J. HUDSON TAYLOR

"Consider the Apostle and High Priest of our profession, Christ Jesus, who was faithful to the One who appointed him, and left us an example that we should follow.

"To save man he became Man — not merely like man, but very man. In language, in costume, in everything unsinful, he made himself one with those he sought to benefit.

"Had he been born a noble Roman rather than a Jew, he would perhaps have commanded more of a certain kind of respect; and he would assuredly have been spared much indignity. This, however, was not his aim; he emptied himself.

"Surely no follower of the meek and lowly Jesus will be likely to conclude that it is beneath the dignity of a Christian to seek identification with poor people, in the hope that he may see them washed, sanctified, and justified in the name of the Lord Jesus, and by the Spirit of our God!

"Let us be followers of him."

WALK CLOSER TO GOD

J. Hudson Taylor's strategy for reaching the teeming millions of China was simple: When in China, do as the Chinese do. Those with a genuine concern for the lost will do everything they can to "free those who all their lives were held in slavery by their fear of death" (Hebrews 2:15).

Jesus did; J. Hudson Taylor did. What about you? ✤

october4

CONSIDER JESUS AND REJOICE

Therefore, holy brothers and sisters, who share in the heavenly calling, fix your thoughts on Jesus, whom we acknowledge as our apostle and high priest.

Hebrews 3:1

Take away the heart, and the body ceases to have life. Take away Christ, and whatever you have left is not the Christian life.

Hebrews 3 calls you to "fix your thoughts on Jesus." F. B. Meyer analyzes the who, why and how of that calling.

WALK WITH F. B. MEYER

"We should emulate the saints of all ages in the gaze at Christ. We must possess the holiness without which none can see the Lord, and we must live in holy love with all those who bear the name of Christ.

"What right have we to fix our thoughts on him? Because we ... 'share in the heavenly calling.' Those who have turned from the world, from the fascinations of sin and the flesh, who are seeking the heavenly city, the new Jerusalem. Surely such have a right—given them by grace—to live in daily, personal vision of their King!

"In what aspects should they fix their thoughts on him?

"As Apostle, whom God has sent out of his bosom to mankind.

"As Priest, who was in all points tempted as we are, yet without sin, who bears our needs and sins and sorrows on his heart.

"As the Son, compared with whom Moses was but a servant.

"As Creator, by whom all things were made, and without whom not any thing was made.

"As the Head of the household of those who believe.

"As the All-faithful One, who will never resign his charge.

"Consider Jesus in each of these aspects, and rejoice in him."

WALK CLOSER TO GOD

Spend a few quiet moments reflecting on your apostle, priest, creator, all-faithful One—until his greatness overwhelms you with gratitude that he is your Savior and Lord. ✤

october5

A HEART FOCUSED ON PLEASING GOD

But encourage one another daily, as long as it is called "Today," so that none of you may be hardened by sin's deceitfulness.

HEBREWS 3:13

Each day has its own challenges, responsibilities, and problems. Each can be faced only one at a time. The author of Hebrews suggests three daily disciplines to help you remain faithful, no matter what day it is:

Today, "hear his [God's] voice" (Hebrews 3:7).

Today, "encourage one another" (Hebrews 3:13).

Today, "do not harden your hearts" (Hebrews 3:8,15).

Listening to God's voice, encouraging your brothers and sisters in Christ, and refusing to harden your heart—three essentials for enjoying daily victory in Christ.

Today, Alexander Maclaren challenges you to examine and avoid that which tempts you to be unfaithful to God.

WALK WITH ALEXANDER MACLAREN

"We may get the things which tempt our desires; and there will be no illusion at all about the reality of the pleasure. But another question must be asked.

"You have received the thing you wanted; what then? Are you much the better for it? Are you satisfied with it? Is it as good as it looked when it was not yours?

"Is it as blessed now that you have stretched your hand and made it your own as it seemed when it danced there on the other side?

"Having attained the desire, do we not find that it fails to satisfy us fully?"

WALK CLOSER TO GOD

Father, thank you for your Word, which teaches me how to avoid sin. Help me to listen carefully whenever you speak to me through its pages. Cause me to encourage my brothers and sisters in Christ and to draw strength from their example and fellowship.

Above all, Lord, grant me a soft, pliable, teachable heart, one that beats strongly for you. In the name of the one who wants to keep my heart focused on pleasing you. Amen. ✤

october**6**

HEARING THE HEARTTHROBS OF GOD

For the word of God is living and active. Sharper than any double-edged sword, it penetrates even to dividing soul and spirit, joints and marrow; it judges the thoughts and attitudes of the heart.

HEBREWS 4:12

Penetrating sirens. Penetrating screams. Penetrating stares. Penetrating words.

In each case, your body reacts with quick determination. Adrenalin sends a message to your heart. "Action needed — now!"

The same could be said of the Word of God: It penetrates the heart with truth too important to ignore.

A. T. Pierson explores the power of God's forceful and piercing Word.

WALK WITH A. T. PIERSON

"The life of God is in his Word. The Word is quick, living.

"Is it a mirror? Yes, but such a mirror as the living eye. Is it a seed? Yes, but a seed hiding the vitality of God. Is it a sword? Yes, but a sword that omnisciently discerns and pierces the human heart.

"Hold it reverently, for it is a living Book. Speak to it, and it will answer you. Bend to listen, and you will hear in it the heartthrobs of God.

"This Book we are to hold forth as the Word of life and the Light of God in the midst of a crooked and perverse generation.

"Like the birds that beat themselves senseless against the light of the Statue of Liberty in New York Harbor, the creatures of darkness will assault this Word and vainly seek to put out its base, while it still rises from its rock pedestal, immovable and serene!"

WALK CLOSER TO GOD

Perhaps you find it a bit unnerving to know there is something that can penetrate all your defenses and pierce your heart with convicting truth.

You can't change the truth — but you can allow it to change you. And that is the Word's purpose: to penetrate, divide, judge and transform your life.

Hold it reverently — and often. ❖

october7

THE PRIEST WHO PASSED THROUGH THE HEAVENS

We have a great high priest who has ascended into heaven, Jesus the Son of God.
HEBREWS 4:14

The book of Leviticus clearly shows that the priesthood lived with many restrictions—and enjoyed many privileges—that were not true of the nation of Israel as a whole. But priest and people alike shared a common problem: sin.

The writer to the Hebrews pointed to a better solution: a great high priest of heavenly origin. G. Campbell Morgan extols the virtues of this perfect go-between.

WALK WITH G. CAMPBELL MORGAN

"To the Hebrew mind the phrase *High Priest* expressed the highest form of priestly service; it was the ultimate word. The phrase is still further strengthened by the word great. Jesus is not merely a priest; he is the High Priest, and in that he is great. His priestly work and position are characterized by the utmost finality.

"He has 'ascended into heaven.' The statement is far stronger than it would be if it read 'passed unto the heavens.' It helps us to think of him as entering into the place of closest nearness to God in his priestly position.

"No lower heaven is the place of his work. He passed through all heavens to the very place and being of God himself. He passed through the heavens to come to mankind, into closest identification; and having accomplished his purposes there, he passed back through the heavens to go to God."

WALK CLOSER TO GOD

Just think: Your representative before the king of creation is none other than the king's own Son! The one with whom he is well pleased. The great high priest.

"For we do not have a high priest who is unable to empathize with our weaknesses, but we have one who has been tempted in every way, just as we are—yet he did not sin. Let us then approach God's throne of grace with confidence, so that we may receive mercy and find grace to help us in our time of need" (Hebrews 4:15–16).

What are you waiting for? Come boldly to God today, for the way has already been spanned. ❖

october8

GROWING BEYOND THE BASICS

Though by this time you ought to be teachers, you need someone to teach you the elementary truths of God's word all over again.

HEBREWS 5:12

After a certain age people are expected to master the basics of life. But the Hebrews had never gotten beyond the kindergarten stage of the Christian life. Instead of becoming teachers, they were still toddlers in the faith. Growth in grace was long overdue.

It's a phenomenon not unique to the first century AD, as Albert Barnes points out.

WALK WITH ALBERT BARNES

"It often occurs that people are true Christians, yet they are ignorant of some of the elementary principles of religion.

"This is a result of such things as a lack of early religious instruction; the faults of preachers who fail to teach their people; a lack of proper interest in the subject of religion; and a greater interest in other things than in religion.

"It is often surprising what vague and unsettled opinions Christians have on some of the most important points of Christianity, and how little qualified they are to defend their beliefs.

"To some of the elementary doctrines of Christianity—about deadness to the world, about self-denial, about prayer, about doing good, and about spirituality—they are utter strangers. So also of forgiveness, and charity, and love for a dying world.

"These are the elements of Christianity—rudiments which children in righteousness should learn."

WALK CLOSER TO GOD

Perhaps you can identify with the person who said, "My favorite grade in school was the second grade, because three of the happiest years of my life were spent there!"

The problem? Lack of visible, definable, reasonable progress in the basics of education.

Maturity is the by-product of applying what you know—putting it to good use. Then you will make progress in the school of faith.

The basics. That's the best place to start—and the worst place to stop! ❖

DOING WHAT HE SAYS HE WILL DO

Because God wanted to make the unchanging nature of his purpose very clear to the heirs of what was promised, he confirmed it with an oath.

HEBREWS 6:17

"Promises are like pie crusts—they're made to be broken." It's a thought that's too often true—at least in human circles. But don't view God's promises that way. When he speaks, a promise made is as good as a promise kept.

The Old Testament is filled with examples of God keeping his word when others broke theirs. And Hebrews 6 will reassure you of God's faithfulness to his covenants. They are as sure as the ground you walk on. Charles Spurgeon calls attention to the stability of God's promises.

WALK WITH CHARLES SPURGEON

"It is a cause of much weakness to many that they do not treat the promises of God as realities. If a friend makes a promise, they regard it as a substantial thing, and look for that which it secures; but the declarations of God are often viewed as words which mean very little.

"This is most dishonoring to the Lord and very injurious to us. Rest assured that the Lord never trifles with words. 'Does he promise and not fulfill?' (Numbers 23:19). His engagements are always kept.

"God speaks deliberately, in due order and determination, and we may depend upon it that his words are sure and will be fulfilled as certainly as they are uttered. Can an instance be found in which our God has been false to his Word? The ages cannot produce a single proof that the promise-making Jehovah has run back from that which he has spoken."

WALK CLOSER TO GOD

Let these verses, one from the Old Testament and one from the New, testify regarding how well God keeps his word: "God is not human, that he should lie" (Numbers 23:19). "For no matter how many promises God has made, they are 'Yes' in Christ. And so through him the 'Amen' is spoken by us to the glory of God" (2 Corinthians 1:20).

God's promises. They're not made to be broken, but made to be kept. ❖

october**10**

MADE NEW IN RIGHTEOUSNESS
AND TRUE HOLINESS

This Melchizedek was king of Salem and priest of God Most High.

HEBREWS 7:1

Scripture records that Melchizedek was "without father or mother, without genealogy, without beginning of days or end of life, resembling the Son of God" (Hebrews 7:3).

And resembling Melchizedek, Christ is "king of righteousness" and "king of peace" (Hebrews 7:2).

But what does all this mean for the believer? Alexander Maclaren explains Jesus' role as the righteous King.

WALK WITH ALEXANDER MACLAREN

"The very heart of the Christian doctrine is this: As soon as a person puts his trembling trust in Jesus Christ as his Savior, then he receives not merely pardon and the uninterrupted flow of the divine love in spite of his sin, but an imparting to him of that new life, which, after God, is created in righteousness and true holiness.

"Do not suppose that the great message of the gospel is merely forgiveness. Do not suppose that its blessed gift is only that one is acquitted because Christ died.

"All that is true. But there is something more. By faith in Jesus Christ, I am so knit to him that there passes into me, by his gift, a life which is created after his life, and is in fact kindred with it.

"He is first of all King of righteousness. Let that which is first in all his gifts be first in all your efforts too; and do not seek so much for comfort as for grace to know and to do your duty, and strength to 'put aside the deeds of darkness and put on the armor of light' (Romans 13:12)."

WALK CLOSER TO GOD

Because Jesus is righteous, you are forgiven and God sees you as righteous. Because Jesus is righteous, you can live a righteous life—through the power of his life in you.

Abraham gave to Melchizedek a "tenth of everything" (Genesis 14:20) as a sign of his subjection to one greater than he. Is it too much to ask that you, being made righteous by the King of righteousness, give him your life in return? ❖

THE ONE WHO IS BOTH PURCHASER AND PRICE

Therefore he is able to save completely those who come to God through him, because he always lives to intercede for them.

HEBREWS 7:25

Umpires, referees, arbitrators, judges—without them, disputes could never be settled.

But a dispute of eternal dimensions between a sinful human race and the holy God required a Mediator who could go between heaven and earth. God acted to send the only one fully qualified to represent his need for justice and our need for mercy: the God-man Jesus Christ.

Jonathan Edwards discusses God's unilateral action on behalf of humanity.

WALK WITH JONATHAN EDWARDS

"The redeemed are dependent on God for all.

"All that we have—wisdom, the pardon of sin, deliverance, acceptance in God's favor, grace, holiness, true comfort and happiness, eternal life and glory—we have from God by a mediator; and this mediator is God.

"God not only gives us the Mediator, and accepts his mediation, and of his power and grace bestows the things purchased by the Mediator, but he is the mediator.

"Our blessings are what we have by purchase; and the purchase is made of God; the blessings are purchased of him; and not only so, but God is the purchaser.

"Yes, God is both the purchaser and the price; for Christ, who is God, purchased these blessings by offering himself as the price of our salvation."

WALK CLOSER TO GOD

As God incarnate, Jesus was the perfect go-between. Paul described Jesus' unique role this way: "For there is one God and one mediator between God and mankind, the man Christ Jesus, who gave himself as a ransom for all people" (1 Timothy 2:5–6).

The price for man's rebellion was high, demanding nothing less than the death of the Mediator.

The response of the Mediator was love personified: "He offered himself" (Hebrews 7:27).

And you have God to thank that he did all that for you! ✤

october**12**

THE GRACE THAT IS SUITABLE AND SUFFICIENT

This is the covenant I will establish ... declares the Lord ... I will be their God, and they will be my people.

HEBREWS 8:10

In the case of God and mankind, once the price was paid by the perfect Mediator, the foundation was laid for a lasting reconciliation.

Salvation thus involves more than forgiveness of sins; it also brings the sinner into a privileged relationship with God.

It's a remarkable relationship all believers in Christ enjoy, as Matthew Henry explains.

WALK WITH MATTHEW HENRY

"God covenants with them [believers] to take them into a near and very honorable relation to himself. He will be to them a God: that is, he will be all to them, and do all for them, that God can be and do. Nothing more can be said in a thousand volumes than is comprehended in these few words: 'I will be their God.'

"They shall be to him a people, to love, honor, and obey him; complying with his cautions, conforming to his commands, copying his example.

"Those who have the true God for their God must and will do this, for they are bound to do so as their part of the contract. And God will enable them to do it, as an evidence that he is their God and that they are his people.

"It is God himself who first establishes the relationship, and then fills it up with grace suitable and sufficient, and helps them in their measure to fill it up with love and duty."

WALK CLOSER TO GOD

"Anyone who comes to him [God] must believe that he exists" (Hebrews 11:6). But there is more: The God who exists is *your* God—filling up your life with "grace suitable and sufficient."

In exchange God offers you the matchless privilege of being called one of his people—called to love him, honor him, obey him. Called to fill up your life with love and duty.

Put it all together, and who but a Christian could declare, "I belong to him, and he belongs to me!" ❖

october13

WHEN THAT WHICH IS PERFECT IS COME

When Christ came as high priest of the good things that are now already here, he ... entered the Most Holy Place once for all by his own blood, thus obtaining eternal redemption.
HEBREWS 9:11 – 12

Which would you prefer: seeing the shadow of the Eiffel Tower or seeing the Eiffel Tower itself, seeing a famous person's picture or meeting that celebrity in person? In each case, the former hints at what only the latter can reveal.

The Old Testament system of sacrifices was an imperfect forerunner of the perfect New Testament sacrifice to come.

B. F. Westcott probes the meaning behind both the old and new sacrifices.

WALK WITH B. F. WESTCOTT

"The levitical sacrifices expressed the ideas of atonement and fellowship resting upon the idea of a covenant.

"In vivid symbols and outward forms they showed how human beings might yet reach the destiny for which they were created.

"The self-sacrifice of Christ upon the cross fulfilled absolutely all that was thus shadowed forth. That sacrifice had a spiritual, eternal, and universal validity, where the 'shadow' had been necessarily external and confined.

"And when we look back over the facts of Christ's sacrifice brought forward in the epistle, we notice two series of blessings gained for mankind by him: the one being the restoration of man's right relation to God which has been violated by sin, and the other fulfilling the purpose of creation, which is the attainment by mankind of the divine likeness."

WALK CLOSER TO GOD

What the readers of the Old Testament could only picture imperfectly, we can appreciate and appropriate fully: the perfect sacrifice of Christ.

The picture, no longer shadowy, is perfectly clear. The way of redemption and right standing with God is possible through Jesus Christ.

The question remains: Are you perfectly clear about your standing with God? ❖

october14

NO ATONEMENT APART FROM THE BLOOD

Without the shedding of blood there is no forgiveness.

HEBREWS 9:22

Many a person with oxygen to breathe and food to consume has died nonetheless. The problem: insufficient blood to transport oxygen and nutrients to the rest of the body. In short: no blood, no life.

Do you see a spiritual analogy in that? Take away the blood of Christ, and there can be no spiritual life. For sins to be covered, blood must be spilled—and that requirement was met by Jesus on the cross.

Charles Spurgeon paints a word picture of that life-giving sacrifice.

WALK WITH CHARLES SPURGEON

"By no means can sin be pardoned without atonement. Clearly, there is no hope for me outside of Christ; for there is no other blood-shedding which is worth a thought as an atonement for sin.

"All people are on a level as to their need of him. Even if we are moral, generous, amiable, or patriotic, the rule will not be altered to make an exception for us. It will yield to nothing less potent than the blood of him whom God has set forth as a satisfaction for sin.

"Persons of merely formal religion cannot understand how we can rejoice that all our sins are forgiven for Christ's sake. Their works, prayers, and ceremonies give them very poor comfort.

"And well may they be uneasy, for they are neglecting the one great salvation, and are endeavoring to get forgiveness without blood."

WALK CLOSER TO GOD

Make these words of hymnist William Cowper the basis for your prayer of praise today:

> There is a fountain filled with blood,
>   Drawn from Immanuel's veins;
> And sinners, plunged beneath that flood,
>   Lose all their guilty stains.
> Dear dying Lamb, Thy precious blood
>   Shall never lose its power,
> Till all the ransomed church of God
>   Be saved, to sin no more. ❖

THE DAILY DELIGHT OF OBEDIENCE

"I will put my laws in their hearts, and I will write them on their minds".

HEBREWS 10:16

Which motivates you more: what you are commanded to do or what you desire to do?

Often the two are in conflict. But in Christ, God changes all that. Obeying God's commands is no longer a chore to be endured; rather, it becomes your daily delight.

Ambitions and appetites change when the king rules the human heart, as John Henry Jowett explains.

WALK WITH JOHN HENRY JOWETT

"Everything depends on where we carry the law of the Lord. If it rests only in the memory, any little care may snatch it away. A thought is never secure until it has passed from the mind into the heart, and has become a desire, an aspiration, a passion.

"When God's law is taken into the heart, it is no longer merely remembered; it is loved. The strength of the heart is wrapped about it, and no passing bother can carry it away. And this is where the Lord is willing to put his laws. He wants to put them among our loves.

"And the wonderful thing is this: When laws are put among loves, they change their form, and his statutes become our songs. Laws that are loved are no longer dreadful policemen, but compassionate friends. And so shall it be unto all of us when we love the law of the Lord."

WALK CLOSER TO GOD

Here are some words to "sweeten" your taste for God's Word:

> The law of the LORD is perfect,
>   refreshing the soul.
> The statutes of the LORD are trustworthy,
>   making wise the simple.
> The precepts of the LORD are right,
>   giving joy to the heart.
> The commands of the LORD are radiant,
>   giving light to the eyes...
> The decrees of the LORD are firm
>   and all of them are righteous...
> They are sweeter than honey,
>   than honey from the honeycomb (Psalm 19:7–10).

God's Word: It tastes good. And it is good ... for you! ❖

october16

WARNING SIGNS OF DANGER

So do not throw away your confidence; it will be richly rewarded.

HEBREWS 10:35

The altitude, unpredictable weather and rugged terrain all combine to make mountain climbing a harrowing adventure. If an unsuspecting, poorly equipped hiker gets caught by a sudden storm, he or she may be in serious danger.

In life, as in mountain climbing, signposts guide the inexperienced. And it's often the hidden, unexpected dangers that pose the greatest threat to your soul's survival. Charles Hodge points to the signs that warn you of spiritual danger.

WALK WITH CHARLES HODGE

"One great and fatal offense under the Old Testament was apostasy from the worship of Jehovah. This was punishable by death. It admitted of no repentance.

"The author strives to impress upon his readers that their danger was the same, their crime if they forsook Christ would be greater, and their punishment far more severe. It was greater, as much as Christ was greater than Moses, and his blood more sacred than that of bulls and goats.

"We still need this caution and exhortation. Our danger from within is an evil heart, not to be despised, not to be neglected, but strenuously watched. Our danger also comes from the influence of the world, its avocations, its amusements, its spirit, its opinions leading to indifference, tolerance of unbelief, and unfaithfulness."

WALK CLOSER TO GOD

Affluence, deceptive teaching, improper thought life, worldly pleasures, immorality, just plain laziness—each of these can tempt you to "throw away your confidence" by chipping away at your faith. The pathway to destruction isn't necessarily taken with giant steps. More often than not, it's taken with little shuffles.

But God delights in those who diligently guard their faith, standing firmly in the confidence of his Word and pressing on toward the goal of Christlikeness—regardless of their earthly circumstances or tribulations. ✤

FAITH: SEEING WITH THE EYES OF THE SOUL

Now faith is confidence in what we hope for and assurance about what we do not see.

HEBREWS 11:1

Contrary to popular belief, faith is not a blind leap in the dark, an attempt to believe something regardless of the evidence, or a hope and a prayer.

Faith. How could something that appears so uncertain be the basis for something the Scripture communicates as certain? Either the world is wrong or the Bible is wrong. Matthew Henry explores the Biblical definition of faith.

WALK WITH MATTHEW HENRY

"Here we have a twofold definition of faith. First, it 'is confidence in what we hope for.'

"Faith and hope go together. Faith is a firm persuasion and expectation that God will perform all that he has promised to us in Christ. And this persuasion is so strong that it gives the soul a kind of possession and present fruition of those things, gives them a subsistence in the soul by the firstfruits and foretastes of them, so that believers in the exercise of faith are filled with joy unspeakable and full of glory.

"Second, it is ... 'assurance about what we do not see.' Faith demonstrates to the eye of the mind the reality of those things that cannot be discerned by the eye of the body. It is the firm assent of the soul to the divine revelation and every part of it, and sets to its seal that God is true. It is a full approval of all that God has revealed as holy, just, and good; and so it is designed to serve the believer instead of sight, and to be to the soul all that the senses are to the body."

WALK CLOSER TO GOD

In the physical realm, one can say, "I'll believe it when I see it!" But on the spiritual level, one must turn that idea around and say, "I'll see it when I believe it!"

For example, Noah and Abraham—along with many others—are enshrined in God's "Hall of Faith" (that is, Hebrews 11). They saw God at work in their lives—when they believed.

Their spiritual vision was 20/20. How's yours? ❧

october**18**

PERSECUTION THAT REVEALS THE POWER OF GOD

They were put to death by stoning ... by the sword ... They went about ... destitute, persecuted and mistreated—the world was not worthy of them ... These were all commended for their faith.

HEBREWS 11:37–39

Through the centuries, heroes of the church have announced allegiance to Christ and have refused to be moved—even in the face of death. One such hero is Polycarp, a disciple of the apostle John and an early church leader whose life ended when he refused to betray his Lord.

Asked one last time to disavow his Christ, the old man replied: "Eighty and six years have I served him, and he has done me no wrong. How can I speak evil of my King who saved me?"

Here is his martyr's prayer, as recorded by the historian Eusebius.

WALK WITH POLYCARP

"Father of your beloved and blessed Son Jesus Christ, through whom we have received the knowledge of you, I bless you that you have counted me worthy of this day and hour, that I might be in the number of the martyrs.

"Among these may I be received before you today in a rich and acceptable sacrifice, as you have beforehand prepared and revealed.

"Wherefore I also praise you also for everything; I bless you; I glorify you, through the eternal High Priest Jesus Christ, your beloved Son, through whom, with him, in the Holy Spirit, be glory unto you both now and for the ages to come. Amen."

[Eusebius adds:] "When he had offered up his amen and had finished his prayer, the firemen lighted the fire."

WALK CLOSER TO GOD

Killing believers has never been an effective way to kill the church. Instead, others see that a faith worth dying for must also be a faith worth having. Persecution merely reveals salvation at work, causing heroes of the faith to rise to the occasion.

Faith in God may not give you a long life—on this earth. But it will give you a powerful life, a persuasive life, a heroic life—in a day when heroes are in short supply. ✤

GOD'S OPINION IS THE ONLY ONE THAT REALLY MATTERS

In your struggle against sin, you have not yet resisted to the point of shedding your blood.
HEBREWS 12:4

You are in an unfamiliar city, far from home, friends and family, when suddenly you're tempted to do something wrong. Is your first thought, "What would others think?" Or is it, "What would God think?"

God's opinion is the one that really matters, and it's never right to do wrong. But have you ever considered why you do what you do when faced with temptation?

It may not be for the best of reasons, as Abraham Kuyper makes painfully clear.

WALK WITH ABRAHAM KUYPER

"Not every resistance against sin can be called 'struggle against sin.' Everything here hinges upon what it is that moves you to oppose this or that sin.

"One person will avoid a sin from concern for his health. Another is on his guard lest, if his sin became known, it would injure his good name. A third resists a temptation because yielding to it would ruin him financially. A fourth puts a mark against a particular sin because in his narrow circle of life it is sharply condemned.

"And in this way and by all sorts of persons this or that sin is put under the ban for reasons that have nothing to do with real striving against sin.

"With not a few there is even no mention of a conscious motive, and all their opposition to this or that sin springs from a certain moral instinct, from the judgment of public opinion, or from a certain impulse to be decent.

"A certain sin may decrease, but far more because it is now looked upon as coarse and impolite than from fear of the Holy God!"

WALK CLOSER TO GOD

Fear of people may keep you from certain sins, but fear of God will make you wary of all sin.

The fear of God is more than an emotional response. It is an attitude of life that seeks to please God in every action, both public and private—which is only fitting when you consider your calling: "Be holy, because I am holy" (1 Peter 1:16). ❖

october20

SEEING SIN FROM GOD'S PERSPECTIVE

Worship God ... with reverence and awe, for our "God is a consuming fire".
HEBREWS 12:28 – 29

Sinful humans usually get angry for all the wrong reasons. The holy God is angry for all the right reasons.

"The wrath of God is being revealed from heaven against all the godlessness and wickedness of people" (Romans 1:18).

God hates sin and is intolerant of anyone or anything that would compete for the glory that rightly belongs to him. A. W. Pink offers these reasons why remembering God's righteous wrath will aid you in your own struggle against sin.

WALK WITH A. W. PINK

"The wrath of God is a perfection of the divine character on which we need to meditate frequently.

"First, that our hearts may be impressed by God's hatred of sin. We are ever prone to regard sin lightly, to gloss over its hideousness, to make excuses for it. But the more we study and ponder God's abhorrence of sin and his frightful vengeance upon it, the more likely we are to realize its heinousness.

"Second, to beget a true fear in our souls for God. We cannot serve him acceptably unless there is deep reverence for his majesty and godly fear of his righteous anger. These are best promoted by frequently calling to mind that our God is a consuming fire.

"Third, to draw out our soul in fervent praise to Jesus Christ for having delivered us from the wrath to come. In truth, our readiness or our reluctance to meditate upon the wrath of God becomes a test of how our hearts stand toward him."

WALK CLOSER TO GOD

Father, I confess that I often fail to remember your consuming hatred of sin and too often forget the one on whom your wrath was poured.

Teach me to be angry at the things that anger you. Then I will sense the burning light of your holiness and the true depth of your love for me. Amen. ❖

october**21**

THE SHEPHERD WHO HAS PROMISED TO SEE US THROUGH

Our Lord Jesus [is the] great Shepherd of the sheep.

HEBREWS 13:20

Sheep have never been noted for their ability to fend for themselves. They are prone to wander, defenseless in the face of danger, easily "fleeced." What the sheep lack, their shepherd must supply. This is no less true when the sheep are Christians.

The image of Christ as Shepherd is a consistent—and comforting—picture from the pages of Scripture: Psalm 23, John 10, Ezekiel 34.

H. A. Ironside offers these encouraging reminders about Jesus, your great Shepherd.

WALK WITH H. A. IRONSIDE

"The shepherd character of our Lord Jesus suggests loving care for his own. He has given us many pictures of his Shepherd-service.

"As the *Good Shepherd* he died for us. As the *Great Shepherd* he is ever watching over us. As the *Chief Shepherd* he will gather us all about himself when he comes again.

"His promises are sufficient for every difficulty. Yet in times of stress we forget them all, and worry and fret as though we had to meet all our problems ourselves, instead of trusting in his love and wisdom to undertake for us. He has promised to see us through.

"The One to whom we have committed our souls is more than a match for all that may rise against us. He is the *unfailing shepherd*, having our best interests in view. His glory and our blessing are indissolubly linked together."

WALK CLOSER TO GOD

In Ezekiel 34 God harshly rebuked Israel's shepherds for failing to do their job, and he gave his own description of the Good Shepherd: "I will tend them in a good pasture ... I myself will tend my sheep and have them lie down ... I will search for the lost and bring back the strays. I will bind up the injured and strengthen the weak" (Ezekiel 34:14–16).

That's good news for sheep who are prone to wander! ✤

october22

LEARNING IN THE CRUCIBLE OF LIFE

Consider it pure joy, my brothers and sisters, whenever you face trials of many kinds, because you know that the testing of your faith develops perseverance.

JAMES 1:2–3

Character qualities such as perseverance develop with use and are learned not in the classroom but in the crucible of life. As Paul said, "We also glory in our sufferings, because we know that suffering produces perseverance" (Romans 5:3).

God knows the best way to build character, and he has his reasons for letting experience be the best teacher, as H. A. Ironside makes clear.

WALK WITH H. A. IRONSIDE

"It is no evidence of God's displeasure when his people are called upon to pass through great trials.

"If someone professes to have faith in the Lord, that person can be sure that his or her profession will be put to the test sooner or later.

"Alas, that we so frequently lose courage and become despondent in the hour of temptation, instead of realizing that it is the very time when we should look up into the Father's face with confidence, knowing that he is working out some purpose in us which could not be accomplished in any other way.

"We are called to consider it pure joy when we face trials. The trials of many kinds do not refer to our being tempted to sin, but rather as when God tempted Abraham, to the testing of our faith.

"The man or woman who learns to be submissive to whatever God permits glorifies him who orders all things according to the counsel of his own will."

WALK CLOSER TO GOD

Gold subjected to high temperatures emerges much the same—yet different. It is still gold, but it is a gold of a brighter, purer character.

Faith in the furnace is like gold in the fire. The heat only serves to refine it, purify it, strengthen it, deepen it. It emerges with a brighter, purer quality.

As the fire grows hotter, thank God that he values your faith in him and that this test will "result in praise, glory and honor"—to him! (1 Peter 1:7). ❖

october**23**

THE BLESSING THAT COMES ON
THE PATH OF OBEDIENCE

Do not merely listen to the word, and so deceive yourselves. Do what it says.

JAMES 1:22

The casual reader of *The Adventures of Tom Sawyer* might conclude that the boy had a severe hearing problem, for if he had heard Aunt Polly calling, surely he would have responded … wouldn't he?

But the problem is that Tom did hear and respond—though not in the way his Aunt Polly wanted!

John Henry Jowett explores James's teaching that to *hear* and not to *do* is simply not to *hear*.

WALK WITH JOHN HENRY JOWETT

"When we hear the Word but do not do it, there has been a defect in our hearing. We may listen to the Word for mere entertainment. Or we may attach a virtue to the mere act of listening to the Word. We may assume that some magical power belongs to the mere reading of the Word. All this is perverse and delusive, for no listening is healthy which is not mentally referred to obedience.

"We are to listen with a view to obedience, with our eyes upon the very road where the obedient feet will travel. That is to say, we are to listen with purpose, as though we were ambassadors receiving instructions from the king concerning some momentous mission.

"'Doing' makes a new thing of 'hearing.' The statute obeyed becomes a song. The commandment is found to be a beatitude. The decree discloses riches of grace. The hidden things of God are not discovered until we are treading the path of obedience."

WALK CLOSER TO GOD

Many excuses are offered for hearing but not obeying the King's command: "I didn't pay attention to it." "I heard it, but I didn't believe it." "I forgot."

In each case, these excuses reveal that a person has lost sight of their marching orders: to represent the King by responding to his commands. Will you tune your ears—and actions—to the one who speaks words of life? ✤

october24

CHECKING GOOD INTENTIONS AGAINST GOD'S INTENTION

For whoever keeps the whole law and yet stumbles at just one point is guilty of breaking all of it.

JAMES 2:10

Obedience to God's will is not always convenient (see Genesis 6:13–22). Nor is it always logical (see Judges 6:1–5; 7:2). But the consequences of twisting one of God's commandments into something more appealing can be deadly.

For example, Saul responded in a way that some might describe as logical or prudent: He and his fighting men "spared ... everything that was good. These they were unwilling to destroy completely ... They spared the best of the sheep and cattle to sacrifice to the LORD" (1 Samuel 15:9,15).

Good intentions. But not God's intentions. John Calvin explores this perspective on obedience.

WALK WITH JOHN CALVIN

"God will not be honored with exceptions, nor will he allow us to cut off from his law what is less pleasing to us. It is no obedience to God when obedience is rendered according to personal preference rather than all the time. Let there be, therefore, a consistency if we desire rightly to obey God.

"We then understand with James that if we cut off from God's law what is less agreeable to us, though in other parts we may be obedient, yet we become guilty of all, because in one particular thing we violate the whole law.

"It is a general principle: God has prescribed to us a rule of life, which it is not lawful for us to mutilate."

WALK CLOSER TO GOD

Sheep in the closet are always a sign that you've substituted what is convenient for what is obedient.

Saul's presumption came to light with Samuel's probing question: "What then is this bleating of sheep in my ears?" (1 Samuel 15:14).

Regardless of whether you can explain it fully, God's will is always "good, pleasing and perfect" (Romans 12:2).

And before you conclude that you have a better idea than obeying God's commandments, let Samuel's words burn their way deeply into your heart: "To obey is better than sacrifice" (1 Samuel 15:22). ❖

TRANSLATING THE PROMISES OF GOD
INTO POWERFUL DEEDS FOR GOD

In the same way, faith by itself, if it is not accompanied by action, is dead.

JAMES 2:17

No one can live for long by inhaling but never exhaling. No one can stay healthy for long by eating but never exercising.

All input and no output makes for a Dead Sea—and a dead faith. In the Christian life, the outlet of faith is good works.

Charles Hodge discusses the important balance needed to maintain a healthy walk with God.

WALK WITH CHARLES HODGE

"Although religion does not consist in outward acts, it always produces them.

"The love of God can no more fail to produce obedience to his commands than a mother's love can fail to produce watchfulness and care for her infant. A person's religion, therefore, is vain which expends itself in exercises that relate exclusively to his own salvation.

"And doubtless many Christians go limping all their days because they confine their attention too much to themselves.

"True religion as we find it in the Bible is a permanent, spontaneous, and progressive principle of spiritual life, influencing the whole man and producing all the fruits of righteousness. It is the root and spring of all right feelings and actions, manifesting itself in love and obedience toward God, in justice and benevolence toward others, and in the proper government of ourselves."

WALK CLOSER TO GOD

You needn't wonder if a tree is alive. Its fruitful—or fruitless—condition will tell you all you need to know. In the same way, a living faith produces the evidences of faith: good works.

Hebrews 11 describes people who had faith that "conquered kingdoms, administered justice, and gained what was promised; who shut the mouths of lions,... escaped the edge of the sword; ... became powerful in battle and routed foreign armies" (Hebrews 11:33–34).

Do you have a faith like that? Does your faith translate the promises of God into powerful deeds for God? ❖

october26

ENGAGING THE MIND BEFORE STARTING THE TONGUE

Anyone who is never at fault in what they say is perfect, able to keep their whole body in check.

JAMES 3:2

Be careful when you open your mouth. According to James, the unleashed tongue is an untamable beast. But don't give up, for with God's help you can "be quick to listen, slow to speak and slow to become angry" (James 1:19). Those are wise words for people who are convinced it is impossible to speak and not sin.

As F. B. Meyer points out, James's words provide insight by which you can examine your own speech patterns and the various ways the tongue can trip you up.

WALK WITH F. B. MEYER

"The tongue boasts great things. We are all apt to be vain, boastful, exaggerated. We contrive to focus attention on our own words and deeds; even in delivering God's message we manage to let it be seen that we have a clearer insight into truth or a closer familiarity with God than our fellows.

"We break the law of courtesy, and become harsh, insolent, and uncivil; or the law of purity, and repeat stories that leave a stain; or the law of truth, and practice insincerity; or the law of kindness, and are harsh toward those who are beneath us in station. Or in our desire to stand well with others we are guilty of flattery or servility.

"We disparage other workers; compliment them to their faces and disparage them behind their backs. Alas for us! How greatly we need to offer the prayer of the psalmist: 'Set a guard over my mouth, LORD' (Psalm 141:3)."

WALK CLOSER TO GOD

The antidote for misguided speech is carefully guarded silence. The Scriptures are filled with examples of periods of silence that refreshed God's people. Silence for worship, silence for thought, silence for prayer. "Be still, and know that I am God" (Psalm 46:10).

"Silence," one teacher has observed, "first makes us pilgrims. Secondly, silence guards the fire within. Thirdly, silence teaches us how to speak."

Do you want to speak well? Learn first to speak not at all as you listen to the voice of your Lord. ✛

TRUTH IS TO BE LIVED, NOT DEBATED

Who is wise and understanding among you? Let them show it by their good life, by deeds done in the humility that comes from wisdom.

JAMES 3:13

The clamor of raised voices turns the heads of everyone in the room. Two men in the corner are arguing over the merits of respective candidates in a political campaign.

Arguments tend to bring out the worst in people. Sooner or later, accusations are made that go beyond the search for right and wrong. Anger and bitterness result.

How do you react when confronted with a volatile situation? Conventional wisdom says, "Win at all cost"; godly wisdom suggests otherwise, as the helpful nineteenth-century commentary *An Exposition on the Bible* describes.

WALK WITH *AN EXPOSITION ON THE BIBLE*

"This test is a very practical one, and we can apply it to ourselves as well as to others.

"How do we bear ourselves in argument and in controversy? Are we serene about the result, in full confidence that truth and right should prevail? Are we desirous that truth should prevail, even if that should involve our being proved to be in the wrong? Are we meek and gentle toward those who differ from us? Or are we apt to lose our tempers and become heated against our opponents?

"If the last is the case, we have reason to doubt whether our wisdom is of the best sort. He who loses his temper in an argument has begun to care more about himself, and less about the truth.

"He has become like the many would-be teachers rebuked by James: slow to hear, swift to speak; unwilling to learn, eager to dogmatize; less ready to know the truth than to be able to say something, whether true or false."

WALK CLOSER TO GOD

When Christ admitted to his accusers that he was the Son of God, they violently disagreed. In order to silence the truth, they crucified him. But notice that Christ did not argue; he didn't need to. After all, truth was on his side—indeed, he was the very embodiment of truth. His enemies may have seemingly won the battle, but he triumphed in the end.

Truth has not been entrusted to you just to be debated. Indeed, the whole world waits for a convincing demonstration of the life-changing power of God's truth.

As Christ showed, the application of truth to life is the most powerful argument of all. ✤

october28

WHY WAVE THE WHITE FLAG?

Resist the devil, and he will flee from you.

JAMES 4:7

The enemy advances against overwhelming odds. He is outnumbered and outmanned—a clearly beaten foe. But suddenly the "victors" jump up and run away! The war is lost without the enemy even being engaged.

That's often how Christians respond to Satan's onslaughts. Instead of standing in the strength that God supplies, they turn and run. No wonder Satan—the defeated adversary—rules nonetheless in so many hearts and homes.

But it doesn't have to be that way! Listen to A. B. Simpson's encouraging commentary on one of James's sentence sermons.

WALK WITH A. B. SIMPSON

"'Resist the devil, and he will flee from you.' This is a promise and God will keep it. If we resist our adversary, God will compel him to flee and will give us the victory. We can, at all times, fearlessly stand up in resistance to the enemy, and claim the protection of our heavenly King, just as a citizen would claim the protection of the government against a violent man.

"At the same time, we are not to stand on the adversary's ground anywhere by any attitude of disobedience, or we give him a terrific power over us, which, while God will restrain in great mercy and kindness, he will not fully remove until we get fully on holy ground.

"Therefore, we must be armed with the breastplate of righteousness, as well as the shield of faith, if we would successfully resist the prince of darkness and the principalities in heavenly places."

WALK CLOSER TO GOD

Christian, stand your ground! When Satan attacks you today, don't run. Resist. Claim the promise of James 4:7 to put him on the run. Exercise both humility and courage in your fight against Satan. With those ingredients, plus the assurance of God's assistance to help you win the battle, victory is inevitable!

After all, why lose a single battle to Satan when Christ has already won the war? ✤

DOING GOOD BY GETTING INVOLVED

If anyone, then, knows the good they ought to do and doesn't do it, it is sin for them.

JAMES 4:17

A pedestrian is mugged in broad daylight while a dozen spectators look on in detached curiosity. When questioned, the onlookers justify their behavior by claiming, "I didn't do anything wrong." And they are right.

But not doing a right action is as wrong as doing a wrong one—a truth James declares and one that Albert Barnes explains.

WALK WITH ALBERT BARNES

"It is universally true that if a person knows what is right and does not do it, he is guilty of sin.

"If he understands what his duty is; if he has the means of doing good to others; if by his name, his influence, or his wealth, he can promote a good cause; if he can, consistently with other duties, relieve the distressed, the poor, the prisoner, and the oppressed; if he can send the gospel to other lands, or can wipe away the tear of the mourner; and if, by indolence, or avarice, or selfishness, he does not do it, he is guilty of sin before God.

"No man can be released from the obligation to do good in his world to the extent of his ability. No one should desire to be so released.

"The highest privilege conferred on a mortal—besides that of securing salvation—is doing good to others: alleviating sorrow, instructing ignorance, raising up the bowed down, comforting those that mourn, delivering the wronged and oppressed, supplying the wants of the needy, guiding inquirers into the way of truth, and sending liberty, knowledge, and salvation around the world."

WALK CLOSER TO GOD

Meeting needs is costly and inconvenient. It takes time and energy. It may earn no thanks or appreciation. But it is simply the right thing to do.

Aren't you thankful that when the Father asked his Son to bear the burden of humanity's sin, Jesus didn't say, "No—I don't want to get involved"?

What answer will you give God when he asks you to follow in his footsteps today? ✤

october**30**

KEEPING YOUR WORD SETS YOUR LIGHT ON A HILL

All you need to say is a simple "Yes" or "No." Otherwise you will be condemned.

JAMES 5:12

A mortgage is a promise to pay. Break it, and you may lose a house.

A treaty is a promise to protect. Break it, and you may lose an ally.

A wedding vow is a promise to "love, honor and cherish till death do us part." Break it, and you may lose a partner.

But something else is often lost when promises are broken: the reputation of the promise-maker.

George Müller laments the fact that even Christians are not immune to broken promises and the damage that accompanies them.

WALK WITH GEORGE MÜLLER

"It has often been mentioned to me in various places that fellow believers in business do not attend to the keeping of promises.

"I cannot but entreat all who love our Lord Jesus, and who are engaged in a trade or business, to seek for his sake not to make any promises except those which they absolutely believe they will be able to fulfill.

"They should carefully weigh all the circumstances before making any engagement, for it is even in these little ordinary affairs of life that we may either bring much honor or dishonor to the Lord. And these are the things which every unbeliever takes notice of.

"Surely it ought not to be true that we, who have power with God to obtain by prayer and faith all needful grace, wisdom, and skill, should be bad servants, bad tradesmen, bad masters."

WALK CLOSER TO GOD

In the pursuit of Christlikeness, don't overlook the importance of letting your word be your honor.

"The LORD is trustworthy in all he promises and faithful in all he does" (Psalm 145:13). "Jesus Christ is the same yesterday and today and forever" (Hebrews 13:8). "No matter how many promises God has made, they are 'Yes' in Christ" (2 Corinthians 1:20).

Remember, you may have trouble remembering the promises you made. But others will have little trouble remembering the promises you broke. ❖

october31

PRAYER AND PRAISE: LEGS FOR A BALANCED WALK

Is anyone among you in trouble? Let them pray. Is anyone happy? Let them sing songs of praise.

JAMES 5:13

James was a man of prayer. He even received the nickname "Camel Knees" because of his hard, calloused knees—the result of long hours in prayer.

According to James, the Christian should pray, whatever his needs, whatever his circumstances, both privately and publicly. Pray for wisdom (see James 1:5); pray for those who are afflicted or sick (see James 5:14–15). Why? Because "the prayer of a righteous person is powerful and effective" (James 5:16).

Real prayer penetrates every sphere of life and invokes God to answer on your behalf, as Alfred Plummer observes.

WALK WITH ALFRED PLUMMER

"It is hard enough to win converts from heathenism; but it is still harder to teach the newly converted that worshiping God has any bearing on their conduct. This idea is utterly alien to their whole mode of thought.

"They have been accustomed to regard worship as a series of acts which must be religiously performed. It has never occurred to them that they must live in accordance with their worship, or that the one has any connection with the other.

"From this it follows that when the idolater has been induced to substitute the worship of God for the worship of idols, there still remains an immense amount to be done. Prayer and praise must go hand in hand with work and life."

WALK CLOSER TO GOD

Prayer and praise—two equally important legs for a balanced walk with God. You pray, God answers, you praise.

How will you link these essentials for a harmonious walk with God? Are you discouraged, sick, struggling financially or being tested in some situation? Pray! Has God answered your prayers by blessing you with joy, health, extra money or guidance? Praise!

You'll discover how much can be accomplished as you walk with God on the sturdy legs of prayer and praise. ✤

november1

REGARDING GOD WITH TOTAL ESTEEM AND COMPLETE ADMIRATION

Praise be to the God and Father of our Lord Jesus Christ!.

1 PETER 1:3

The "worshiper" attends faithfully every Sunday, concentrating intently on the object of his worship. All week he has prepared for this day, his thoughts turning frequently to the object of his adoration. When he leaves hours later, his gratitude is profound. His team won, 14–10.

Football fans often reflect a truer attitude of worship than the average Christian. A. W. Tozer diagnoses this problem and suggests a helpful remedy.

WALK WITH A. W. TOZER

"The quality of our worship is enhanced as we move away from the thought of what God has done for us, and move nearer the thought of the excellence of his holy nature.

"This leads us to admire God. The dictionary defines admire as 'to regard with wondering esteem, accompanied by pleasure and delight; to look at or upon with an elevated feeling of pleasure.'

"According to this definition, God has few admirers among Christians today. Many are simply grateful for his goodness in providing salvation, or answering their prayer in troublesome situations. But the simple truth is that worship is still in infancy until it begins to take on the quality of admiration.

"Just as long as the worshiper is engrossed with himself and his own concerns, he is a babe. We begin to grow up when our worship passes from thanksgiving to admiration."

WALK CLOSER TO GOD

One quality that binds a fan to his favorite team is his admiration for the players' abilities. To consider the attributes of God should cause no less wonder.

He is good. Just. Merciful. Loving. Omniscient. Omnipotent. Majestic. Infinite. Perfect.

Before your next visit to a house of worship, stop to recall who made it all possible. Then "ascribe to the LORD the glory due his name" (1 Chronicles 16:29). ♣

november2

DESIGNED AND DESTINED FOR HOLINESS

But just as he who called you is holy, so be holy in all you do; for it is written: "Be holy, because I am holy".

1 PETER 1:15–16

A child complains because he received clothes for Christmas instead of toys. A teenager is disappointed because he received a savings bond rather than the car he had requested. In each case, the gifts were wise, while the requests were shortsighted.

Even in the Christian life desires often get in the way of deeper joys. Holiness may not be high on your list of "most wanted gifts," but it does bring joy to God and to his children because it fulfills the purpose for which God created you.

Oswald Chambers challenges you to remember your calling.

WALK WITH OSWALD CHAMBERS

"Continually restate to yourself what the purpose of your life is. The destined end of an individual is not happiness, not health, but *holiness.*

"The one thing that matters most is whether a person will accept the God who will make him holy. At all costs one must be rightly related to God.

"Do I believe I need to be holy? Do I believe God can come into me and make me holy?

"God has one destined end for humans—holiness. He is not an eternal 'blessing machine' for people. He did not come to save people out of pity; he came to save people because he had created them to be holy."

WALK CLOSER TO GOD

Those who attain power, fame or wealth are applauded and emulated by the world.

But God says you were created for a different purpose altogether. He made you to be like him, "conformed to the image of his Son" (Romans 8:29), fitted to enjoy all the blessings and privileges that come with being a "saint"—a holy one of God.

Holiness deserves to become the priority of your life because it is God's purpose for your life.

Fulfill that purpose and you will experience a joy that will last forever! ❖

november3

CHRIST IS MADE THE SURE FOUNDATION

In Scripture it says: "See, I lay a stone in Zion, a chosen and precious cornerstone, and the one who trusts in him will never be put to shame".

1 Peter 2:6

Houses without foundations are unstable, are susceptible to weakening at the worst possible moment, and never stand up to storms. As Jesus said in his Sermon on the Mount, a house built to stand must be built on something solid.

The imagery of Jesus as the chief cornerstone is captured in this anonymous seventh-century hymn.

WALK WITH A SEVENTH-CENTURY POET

Christ is made the sure foundation,
  Christ the Head and Cornerstone,
Chosen of the Lord and precious,
  Binding all the church in one;
Holy Zion's help forever,
  And her confidence alone.

To this temple, where we call Thee,
  Come, O Lord of hosts, today;
With accustomed loving-kindness
  Hear Thy people as they pray,
And Thy fullest benediction
  Shed within its walls alway.

Here vouchsafe to all Thy servants
  What they ask of Thee to gain,
What they gain from Thee forever
  With the blessed to retain,
And hereafter in Thy glory
  Evermore with Thee to reign.

WALK CLOSER TO GOD

Steady. Indestructible. Immovable. Jesus was all these. And now he calls you to be the same: Steady when the winds of false doctrine swirl around you, indestructible when temptations seek to weaken you, immovable when Satan tries to overwhelm you.

Peter—whose name means "rock"—lived up to his name with God's help. Today, you can build on that same foundation, "so that when the day of evil comes, you may be able to stand your ground, and after you have done everything, to stand" (Ephesians 6:13). ❖

SEEING THE RAINBOW THROUGH THE RAIN

But if you suffer for doing good and you endure it, this is commendable before God. To this you were called.

1 PETER 2:20–21

Anyone can attend a concert and enjoy a violinist's skill. But only another violinist can fully understand a violinist's suffering: the years of practice, self-denial and financial hardship it takes to achieve the expertise that others will travel miles to enjoy. Through the musician's suffering, others are richly blessed.

Peter and the early Christians understood that suffering has a place in life, and J. Hudson Taylor will help you do the same.

WALK WITH J. HUDSON TAYLOR

"It is possible to receive salvation through Christ but still have an imperfect appreciation of the nature and responsibilities of our calling.

"To what are we called? To do good, to suffer for it, and to take it patiently.

"Now none of the proceedings of God are arbitrary: All the acts and all the requirements of perfect wisdom and perfect goodness must of necessity be wise and good.

"We are called when we so suffer to take it patiently, thankfully, and joyfully because—seen from a right point of view—there is neither ground nor excuse for impatience. On the contrary, there is abundant cause for overflowing thanks and joy.

"To make the message intelligible, it must be lived. Be glad that you have the opportunity to make the grace of God intelligible to unbelievers. The greater the persecutions are, the greater the power of your testimony."

WALK CLOSER TO GOD

As J. Hudson Taylor makes clear, there is a purpose to a Christian's suffering—even if no one else understands what it is. That purpose is God's glory.

Your calling is to trust and obey, in order that the overflow of your suffering might be sweet music to God. It may be just the melody a fellow sufferer needs to hear! ❖

LOOKING YOUR BEST FOR YOUR
HEAVENLY BRIDEGROOM

Your beauty should not come from outward adornment ... Rather, it should be that of your inner self, the unfading beauty of a gentle and quiet spirit, which is of great worth in God's sight.
1 PETER 3:3–4

God could have created a very functional, very bland, black-and-white world. Instead, he made a universe abounding in luxuriant variety, rich colors and amazing textures. He created a world for all his creatures to enjoy.

The adorning of creation provides a lesson on which Peter draws in 1 Peter 3, and which poet Anne Bradstreet underscores in this insight.

WALK WITH ANNE BRADSTREET

If so much excellence abides below,
    How excellent is He that dwells on high,
Whose power and beauty by His works we know?
    Sure He is goodness, wisdom, glory, light,
That hath this under world so richly dight*...

My great Creator I would magnify,
That nature had thus decked liberally:
    But ah, and ah, again, my imbecility!
O Time, the fatal wrack of mortal things,
    That draws oblivion's curtains over kings,
Their sumptuous monuments, men know not,
    Their names without a record are forgot,
Their parts, their ports, their pomp's all laid in th' dust,
    Nor wit, nor gold, nor buildings 'scape time's rust;
But He whose name is graved in the white stone
    Shall last and shine when all of these are gone.

* Obsolete word meaning "adorned" or "arrayed."

WALK CLOSER TO GOD

Outward adornment is nice—but not necessary. By contrast, inward adornment is more than a good idea; it is a command!

God has called his bride to develop a beautiful inner life—a life adorned with the fruit of his Spirit, a life colored by the character of Christ.

And, as Peter suggests, a meek and quiet spirit is a good place to start "looking your best" for God. ❖

november6

FREEDOM FROM EVERYTHING THAT IS UNLIKE JESUS

But in your hearts revere Christ as Lord.

1 PETER 3:15

Sanctification is a term that summarizes a profound transaction: becoming like Jesus Christ. The Bible often speaks of sanctification in terms of putting off and putting on (see Ephesians 4:22–24).

Oswald Chambers shares these thoughts about the truth behind the term.

WALK WITH OSWALD CHAMBERS

"Sanctification means intense concentration on God's point of view. It means every power of body, soul, and spirit is chained and kept for God's purpose only. It will cause an intense narrowing of all our interests on earth, and an immense broadening of all our interests in God.

"Are we prepared for God to do all in us that he separated us for? The reason some of us have not entered into the experience of sanctification is that we have not realized its meaning from God's standpoint. Sanctification means being made one with Jesus so that the disposition that ruled him will rule us.

"Jesus has prayed that we might be one with him as he is one with the Father. The one and only characteristic of the Holy Spirit in a person is a strong family likeness to Jesus Christ and freedom from everything that is unlike him."

WALK CLOSER TO GOD

Do you want to be like Christ? The question may sound too basic, but before you set it aside, make sure you consider its implications:

Are you prepared for what sanctification will cost? Are you prepared for God to do in you all that is necessary to bring about transformation? Are you prepared to let God shape your life so that you bear a strong likeness to his Son?

From God's point of view, there's no higher purpose in life. But the extent that this purpose is realized in your life depends on your point of view. ❖

november7

REIGNING WITH CHRIST REQUIRES SUBMISSION TO HIS CROSS

Therefore, since Christ suffered in his body, arm yourselves also with the same attitude, because whoever suffers in the body is done with sin.

1 PETER 4:1

When one criminal testifies against another criminal, he is sometimes given a fresh start in exchange for his help—a new name, a new home, a new life. No one knows of the past, and he can either become a model citizen or revert to his old ways.

The Christian has a new life given him by God. In God's eyes, the old life of sin is done away with. The statute of limitations has run out.

F. B. Meyer suggests the following course of action for Christians in their "new life."

WALK WITH F. B. MEYER

"The apostle Peter urges the disciples to make a clean break with sin.

"As our Lord's grave lay between him and his earlier life, so should there be a clean break between our life as believers and our earthbound life which was dominated by lawless passions.

"Sometimes God employs the acid of persecution or suffering to eat away the bonds that bind us to our past. Let us accept these with a willing mind. The one condition of reigning with Christ is to submit to his cross.

"Of course, we must die to the allure of the world, and to the temptations of the evil one, but it is quite as important to die to our self-life.

"Let us cultivate the unchanging habit of looking up from our service, of whatever kind, to claim the ability to do it for the glory of God."

WALK CLOSER TO GOD

Leaving behind a life of crime, most respond with gratitude to the offer of a fresh start: offenses forgiven, new opportunities provided. The one requirement: Keep out of trouble! It's a tough assignment—especially if you keep going back and trying to mix the old with the new.

Looking back won't help you make progress in your Christian life either. Rather, look up to draw from the source of strength that God has given you to live the new life God has set before you. ✤

VIEWING OUR PAIN FROM HIS PERSPECTIVE

Dear friends, do not be surprised at the fiery ordeal that has come on you to test you ... But rejoice inasmuch as you participate in the sufferings of Christ.

1 PETER 4:12 – 13

"Misery loves company." That maxim is often invoked but seldom enjoyed. Yet when the "company" happens to be Jesus Christ, your suffering need not be burdensome. His own suffering and death will help you put your pain in perspective.

Peter's original audience had already learned this firsthand. John Calvin tells us how to prepare for similar times of trouble today. Read his words slowly, aloud, looking for the focus that provides hope in the midst of fiery ordeals.

WALK WITH JOHN CALVIN

"In order that we may be prepared when we encounter persecutions, we should accustom ourselves to such situations by meditating continually on the cross.

"Peter proves to us that the cross is useful to us by two arguments: that God thus tries our faith, and that we become thus partakers with Christ.

"In the first place, let us remember that the trial of our faith is most necessary, and that we ought thus to obey God willingly who provides for our salvation.

"However, the chief consolation is to be derived from a fellowship with Christ.

"It is a twofold joy, one part which we now enjoy in hope, and the other being the full fruition of which the coming of Christ shall bring to us. The first is mingled with grief and sorrow; the second is connected with exultation."

WALK CLOSER TO GOD

In difficult times, the cross of Christ becomes a haven of consolation. Why?

Because there you realize your own suffering is small by comparison, there you discover joy to come when the troubles are over, there you find that the glory of heaven will one day replace the gloom of earth.

So take heart! "Do not be surprised ... but rejoice"! The best is yet to come. ❖

november9

A HUMBLE WORK OUTLASTING THE STARS

Be shepherds of God's flock that is under your care, watching over them — not because you must, but because you are willing.

1 PETER 5:2

The similarities between a shepherd of sheep and a shepherd of the flock of God are many: Both provide a healthy diet for the sheep. Both protect the flock from predators. Both lead the sheep in paths that are safe. Both have a thankless job!

Charles E. Jefferson, a pastor at the turn of the century, provides this portrait of a pastor and shepherd.

WALK WITH CHARLES E. JEFFERSON

"The shepherd's work must be done in obscurity. The things which he does do not make interesting copy.

"It is a form of service which eats up a man's life. It makes a man old before his time. Every good shepherd lays down his life for the sheep.

"The finest things a minister does are done out of sight and never get reported. His joy is not that his success is being talked about on earth, but that his name is written in heaven.

"The shepherd in Bible lands had no crowd to admire him. He lived alone with the sheep and the stars.

"The messengers of Christ must not expect brass bands to attend them on their way. Theirs is humble, unpretentious, and oftentimes unnoticed labor. But if it builds souls in righteousness, it is more lasting than the stars."

WALK CLOSER TO GOD

In the pages of this devotional guide you have met many renowned shepherds of the flock of God—men and women whose ministries have continued long after their deaths.

But there are countless other such shepherds who have labored—and are now laboring—to nourish the flocks entrusted to them.

How about your own spiritual leaders? Does their labor go unnoticed by their own flock?

Thank God that you have a shepherd—and a Shepherd—who cares for you! ✤

november**10**

FARSIGHTED VISION THAT LOOKS TO HEAVEN

But whoever does not have them [these qualities] is nearsighted and blind, forgetting that they have been cleansed from their past sins.

2 PETER 1:9

Try to focus on two different objects at the same time, and you'll succeed in seeing neither clearly. It's like having one eye nearsighted and the other farsighted.

The result? Frustration and double vision—the same diagnosis given to the "person [who] is double-minded and unstable in all they do" (James 1:8).

The only cure is single-minded focus—picking one path and sticking to it. Dwight L. Moody explains the pitfalls of trying to follow both forks in a road.

WALK WITH DWIGHT L. MOODY

"The church is full of people who want one eye for the world and the other for the kingdom of God. Therefore, everything is blurred; one eye is long and the other is short; all is confusion.

"Abraham was longsighted; he had glimpses of the celestial city.

"Stephen was longsighted; he looked clear into heaven. The world had no temptation for him. He had put the world under his feet.

"Paul also had longsighted vision; he had been caught up and had seen things unlawful for him to utter, things grand and glorious.

"When the Spirit of God is on us, the world looks very empty; the world has a very small hold on us, and we begin to let go our hold of it and lay hold of things eternal.

"This is the church's need today. Oh, that the Spirit might come in mighty power and consume all the vile dross there is in us."

WALK CLOSER TO GOD

Abraham, Stephen, Paul and others saw better things ahead than the things of this world. The Spirit of God controlled the focus of their lives.

How's your spiritual vision? Are you—like Abraham—looking "forward to the city ... whose architect and builder is God" (Hebrews 11:10)?

That's the only path worth focusing on and following eternally. ❖

november11

A CONSCIENCE CAPTIVE TO THE WORD OF GOD

No prophecy of Scripture came about by the prophet's own interpretation of things. For prophecy never had its origin in the human will, but prophets, though human, spoke from God as they were carried along by the Holy Spirit.

2 PETER 1:20–21

Times have changed. But one book hasn't. With no additions or deletions, the Bible remains a foundation of truth for the Christian.

More than the product of God speaking *to* men, the Bible is the result of God speaking *through* men—moving them by the Spirit to pen "the very words of God" (Romans 3:2).

And what God has said with authority remains a source of comfort and guidance today, as Martin Luther proclaims.

WALK WITH MARTIN LUTHER

"Oh! How great and glorious a thing it is to have before one the Word of God!

"With that we may at all times feel joyous and secure; we need never be in want of consolation, for we see before us, in all its brightness, the pure and right way.

"He who loses sight of the Word of God falls into despair; he follows only the disorderly tendency of his heart and of the world's vanity, which lead him on to destruction.

"A fiery shield is God's Word; of more substance and purer than gold which, tried in the fire, loses none of its substance, but resists and overcomes all the fury of the fiery heat. Even so, he that believes God's Word overcomes all.

"The Holy Scripture is certain and true: God grant me grace to catch hold of its just use."

WALK CLOSER TO GOD

When challenged by people to renounce the teaching of Scripture, Luther replied, "Unless I am convicted by Scripture and plain reason ... my conscience is captive to the Word of God."

The Word of God comforted him, strengthened him and guided him. Truth transformed Martin Luther and, through him, his world. The same can happen to you when you "catch hold of its just use" in your life and, like Luther, obey that Word unquestioningly. ✤

november**12**

KNOWING AND LOVING THE TRUTH

But these people blaspheme in matters they do not understand.

2 PETER 2:12

Contrary to the popular notion, ignorance isn't bliss. Ignoring what you know to be true is dangerous; ridiculing what you choose to ignore can be deadly.

Peter speaks of the consequences for those who ignore the truth about God. And Thomas Manton examines some of the reasons men "blaspheme in matters they do not understand."

WALK WITH THOMAS MANTON

"I observe that truth is usually slandered out of ignorance.

"In the apostles' days, the doctrine of the cross was thought to be foolish by those who knew the least about it. Later, the Christian religion was condemned without having been heard.

"It is the devil's cunning to keep us at a distance from truth, and burden it with prejudices, so that we may suspect rather than search, and condemn out of ignorance what upon knowledge we can only love.

"When we speak out against things, we should speak out of advised knowledge, not rash zeal.

"It is a vain thing to begin with the emotions, and to hate before we know. Rash prejudices engage men in opposition, and they will not admit the truth when presented to them.

"Having hated it without knowledge, they hate it against knowledge, and so are hardened against the ways of God."

WALK CLOSER TO GOD

Ignoring the facts will never change the facts. But it will change the way the facts impact your life.

When confronted with the Word of God, many have staked their lives on it; others have ridiculed it. The former have found everlasting life; the latter stand "condemned already" (John 3:18).

When confronted with God's truth, do you respond, "I don't know," "I don't understand," "I don't care," or "I don't dare say no"?

That's a question you cannot ignore. ❖

november13

STARTLING SITUATIONS AND STRANGE REBUKES

They have left the straight way and wandered off to follow the way of Balaam ... who loved the wages of wickedness. But he was rebuked for his wrongdoing by a donkey.

2 PETER 2:15–16

Listening to a talking animal may seem very curious. But in Balaam's case, God used the donkey to show how Balaam's rebelliousness had blinded his eyes and stopped his ears to the angel of the Lord.

But though talking animals are seldom encountered, the reason for Balaam's rebellion is as common now as it was then, as Matthew Henry's insight reveals.

WALK WITH MATTHEW HENRY

"The inordinate love of this world turns people out of the way which leads to the unspeakably better things of another life. The love of riches and honor turned Balaam away from duty, although he knew the way that he took displeased the Lord.

"Hardened sinners sometimes meet with rebukes for their iniquity. God stops them in their way and opens the mouth of conscience, or by some startling circumstance confronts them.

"Though some extraordinary rebuke may for a little while cool men's courage and hinder their violent progress in the way of sin, it will not make them forsake the way of iniquity and go over into the way of holiness.

"Those who will not yield to usual methods of reproof will be but little influenced by miraculous appearances to turn from their sinful course."

WALK CLOSER TO GOD

If you're not listening to God's Word, don't be surprised if his "gentle whisper" (1 Kings 19:12) becomes loud and painfully clear through some out-of-the-ordinary circumstance. But even then, there's no guarantee you'll get the message.

As Abraham warned the rich man in Luke 16:31, "They will not be convinced even if someone rises from the dead."

It's dangerous to grow "hard of hearing" toward the things of God. What does it take for you to hear—and heed—God's Word? ✤

november**14**

MINUTES IN THE MIND OF GOD

But do not forget this one thing, dear friends: With the Lord a day is like a thousand years, and a thousand years are like a day.

2 PETER 3:8

For God, it is never too early or too late. He controls time. When the need arises, he can even stop a day in its tracks (see Joshua 10:12 – 14)!

God's timing is always perfect, a lesson his children need to learn repeatedly. When circumstances appear overwhelming and time seems to have run out, God is right on schedule, as F. B. Meyer explains.

WALK WITH F. B. MEYER

"There is no succession of time with God; no past, no future. He dwells in the eternal present, as I AM. One day is as a thousand years. He could do in a single day, if he chose, what he has at other times taken a thousand years to accomplish.

"Do not say that he must have as long to make the second heaven and earth as the first.

"All this could be changed in a moment, in the twinkling of an eye; and between sunrise and sunset God could accomplish the work of a thousand ordinary years. Periods that seem so long to our finite minds are not so to God. A thousand years in our reckoning is but a day in his.

"You say it is nearly two thousand years ago since Jesus died, or at least that we are in the evening of the second thousand. But in God's reckoning, the cross, the grave, the resurrection, took place in the morning of yesterday.

"Take wider views of God's horizon; believe in his mighty march throughout the centuries. And the centuries are the beats of the minutehand to God."

WALK CLOSER TO GOD

Time is too important to squander. Take a look at your daily schedule. How do you spend your time? How do you waste time? How can you better use the time given you?

You cannot learn too early who is best able to manage your schedule. Following him a day ... an hour ... a minute at a time is one sure way of redeeming the time. ❖

november15

NESTLING NEARER TO THE HEART OF GOD

But grow in the grace and knowledge of our Lord and Savior Jesus Christ.

2 PETER 3:18

Making marks on a door frame is one way to measure the physical growth of a child. But how do you measure the spiritual growth of a child of God?

Maturity in the faith cannot be tallied in inches or pounds. Instead, growth in the Christian life takes place in the inner person—"in the grace and knowledge of our Lord and Savior Jesus Christ."

Alexander Maclaren provides several "yardsticks" for Christian growth.

WALK WITH ALEXANDER MACLAREN

"If you are a Christian, you ought to be realizing continually a deeper consciousness of Christ's love and favor as yours. You ought to be nestling every day nearer to his heart, and getting more and more sure of his mercy and love for you.

"And you ought not only to be realizing the fact of his love with increasing certitude, but you ought to be drinking in the consequences of that love and every day deriving more and more of the spiritual gifts of which his hands are full. In him is an inexhaustible store of abundance for each of us.

"There is nothing mystical or removed from the experience of daily life in this exhortation: 'Grow in ... grace.' It is not growth in some strange experience, but a very plain, practical thing—a daily transformation, with growing completeness, into the likeness of Jesus Christ."

WALK CLOSER TO GOD

A young boy looks in the mirror and knows he is growing up. He is growing taller, stronger, wiser. He is developing a striking family resemblance to the one who calls him "son."

As Jesus grew up, he "grew in wisdom and stature, and in favor with God and man" (Luke 2:52).

There are four essential areas of growth: mental, physical, spiritual and social. Every day as you look intently into the mirror of God's Word, ask yourself what you can do to promote healthy growth in each of those areas of your life. ❖

november**16**

I KNOW THAT MY REDEEMER LIVES

That which was from the beginning, which we have heard, which we have seen with our eyes, which we have looked at and our hands have touched—this we proclaim concerning the Word of life.

1 JOHN 1:1

John's proclamation is a triumphant statement of faith.

Some Christians were stumbling over the Gnostic teaching that Jesus did not really have a body. This heresy borrowed much from contemporary philosophy but contradicted the gospel. Gnosticism had weakened the faith of some, so John wrote to remind the church of the truth of the incarnation.

How like John's audience we are! The foolish philosophies of this world easily take us captive. Robert Murray McCheyne urges us to fix our eyes on Jesus and throw doubt to the wind.

WALK WITH ROBERT MURRAY MCCHEYNE

"Oh, brethren, could you and I pass this day through these heavens and see what is now going on in the sanctuary above—could you see what the child of God now sees who died last night—could you see the Lamb with the scars of his five deep wounds sitting in the very midst of the throne—could you see the thousands, all singing, 'Worthy is the Lamb, who was slain' (Revelation 5:12)—and were one of these angels to tell you, 'This is he that undertook the cause of lost sinners; there he is upon the throne of heaven; consider him; look long and earnestly upon his wounds and glory'—could you see all these things, do you think it would be safe to trust him?

"'Yes, yes,' every soul exclaims. 'Lord, it is enough! Let me ever stand and gaze upon the almighty, all-worthy, all-divine Savior! Yes, though the sins of all the world were on my wicked head, still I could not doubt that his work is complete, and that I am quite safe when I believe in him.'"

WALK CLOSER TO GOD

John had enough faith to publicly proclaim his Christianity at a time when it brought imprisonment or death. Do you have enough faith to "salt" your conversation with Christ at a time when it might bring scorn?

If you're like most of us, you answered, "Well, maybe." Fortunately, we have a Savior who hears us when we cry, "I do believe; help me overcome my unbelief!" (Mark 9:24). Be encouraged. That is a prayer he will answer. ❧

november**17**

SINS REMOVED FOR TIME AND ETERNITY

If we confess our sins, he is faithful and just and will forgive us our sins and purify us from all unrighteousness.

1 JOHN 1:9

What happens when you incur a debt so large that you can never repay it? Then it is up to someone else to forgive you ... or else!

That's precisely what happened when you became a Christian. Your insurmountable debt of sin was forgiven by the payment of an infinite price: the blood of Jesus Christ.

Dwight L. Moody offers this illustration to help you comprehend the magnitude of forgiveness.

WALK WITH DWIGHT L. MOODY

"We greatly dishonor God by bringing up our sins after he has forgiven them. Hundreds of Christians are doing this all the time.

"Suppose my little child has disobeyed me, and comes to me and says, 'Papa, I did what you told me not to do; I want to be forgiven.' She has deep and genuine repentance. I kiss away her tears and forgive her.

"She then comes to me the next day and wants to talk about it. 'No,' I say, 'it is all forgiven.'

"The next day she says, 'Papa, won't you forgive me for that sin I did two days ago?' I think that would grieve me! Suppose she came to me every morning for six months: Would it not grieve and dishonor me?

"God has not only forgiven our sins, but has removed them for time and eternity. Ought one to grieve and dishonor him by bringing them up before him every day?"

WALK CLOSER TO GOD

God's forgiveness is like a canceled promissory note—torn apart and burned, never to be shown to you again.

Let the words of this simple chorus reflect your response to God for his forgiveness to you:

He paid a debt he did not owe,
  I owed a debt I could not pay,
I needed someone to wash my sins away.
  And now I sing a brand new song—
Amazing grace—
  Christ Jesus paid a debt that I could never pay. ✣

november**18**

WORK OUT YOUR SALVATION

We know that we have come to know him if we obey his commands. Whoever says, "I know him," but does not do what he commands is a liar, and the truth is not in that person.

1 JOHN 2:3–4

Just mention the word *commands* in our society and watch what happens. Some people bristle and the rest squirm. Sadly, that attitude permeates not only the world but also the church. But the apostle John regards obedience to God's commands as a good way to judge whether we know Christ.

John wrote this letter to refute the Gnostic heresy that matter was evil and thus Jesus could not have come in the flesh. John also wrote to correct another Gnostic error: licentiousness. Their reasoning went like this: If evil is in matter, rather than in breaking God's law, then breaking God's law is not evil. You can imagine what kind of wickedness followed.

Shouldn't the Christian want to obey God? Listen to Bishop Ryle.

WALK WITH J. C. RYLE

"Believers are eminently and peculiarly under a special obligation to live holy lives. They are not dead, blind and unrenewed; they are alive unto God, enlightened, and have a new principle within them. Whose fault is it if they are not holy? On whom can they throw the blame if they are not sanctified? God, who has given them a new heart and a new nature, has deprived them of all excuse if they do not live for his praise.

"This is a point which is far too much forgotten. A man who professes to sanctification (if indeed any at all), and coolly tells you he 'can do nothing,' is a very pitiable sight and a very ignorant man. Against this delusion let us be on our guard. If the Savior of sinners gives us renewing grace, and calls us by his Spirit, we may be sure that he expects us not to go to sleep."

WALK CLOSER TO GOD

John says God's commands distinguish love from sin and are not burdensome (see 1 John 3:4; 5:3). The world says God's commands are chains to be broken and shackles to be thrown off (see Psalm 2:3). Which attitude characterizes you? ❖

november19

LOVE AND LOYALTY IN A DANGEROUS WORLD

*Do not love the world... For everything in the world—the lust of the flesh, the lust of his
eyes and the pride of life—comes not from the Father but from the world.*

I JOHN 2:15–16

It's easier to worship what is seen than what is unseen—which helps explain why
many love the creation and neglect the Creator.

But as Paul points out in Romans 1, love for the world, when set above love for
its maker, opens the door for a downward spiral of degradation—a theme John
explores in chapter two of his letter, and Andrew Murray probes in this insight.

WALK WITH ANDREW MURRAY

"The world is the power that mankind has fallen under through sin. And the god
of this world, in order to deceive mankind, conceals himself under the form of
what God has created. The world surrounds the Christian with temptations, as
was the case in the Garden of Eden. We find in Genesis 3 the three characteristics
which John mentions:

"1. The lust of the flesh—'The woman saw that the fruit of the tree was good
for food.'

"2. The lust of the eyes—'... pleasing to the eyes.'

"3. The pride of life—'... desirable for gaining wisdom.'

"And the world still offers us desirable food and much to please the fleshly
appetites.

"Christian, you live in a dangerous world! Cleave fast to the Lord Jesus. But
remember: There must be daily fellowship with Jesus. His love alone can expel the
love of the world. Take time to be alone with your Lord."

WALK CLOSER TO GOD

Food, wealth, beauty, knowledge—none of these is, of itself, evil. The problem
comes when you—like Eve—shift your love and loyalty from the one who made
you to the things he made for you.

As Andrew Murray suggests, the cure for a misplaced love for the world is
deeper love for the Lord, a passion that grows with every hour you spend in his
presence. ❖

november**20**

WORTH THE WAIT AND WORTH THE CONFLICT

And this is what he promised us—eternal life.

1 JOHN 2:25

Studies show that all work and no rest make for a poor worker. And the promise of future rest for the Christian makes the struggle of this world easier to bear.

Sin and sorrow, death and tears will all be left behind when the child of God goes to be with his heavenly Father.

Thomas à Kempis shares this comforting glimpse of Christ's perspective on life—a view only visible from the standpoint of eternity.

WALK WITH THOMAS À KEMPIS

"Do not be worn out by the labors which you have undertaken for my sake, and do not let tribulations ever cast you down. Instead, let my promise strengthen and comfort you under every circumstance.

"I am well able to reward you above all measure and degree. You shall not toil here long, nor always be oppressed with griefs. A time will come when all labor and trouble will cease.

"Labor faithfully in my vineyard; I will be thy recompense. Life everlasting is worth all these conflicts, and greater than these. Are not all plentiful labors to be endured for the sake of life eternal?

"Lift your face therefore unto heaven; behold, I and all my saints with me—who in this world had great conflicts—are now comforted, now rejoicing, now secure, now at rest, and shall remain with me everlastingly in the kingdom of my Father."

WALK CLOSER TO GOD

Two verses speak volumes about the benefits of eternal life:

"For God so loved the world that he gave his one and only Son, that whoever believes in him shall not perish but have eternal life" (John 3:16).

"Now this is eternal life: that they know you, the only true God, and Jesus Christ, whom you have sent" (John 17:3).

Get to know Jesus Christ, and you will spend an eternity getting to know God. ❖

november21

SOULS THAT BEAR HIS IMAGE BRIGHT

Dear friends, now we are children of God, and what we will be has not yet been made known. But we know that when Christ appears, we shall be like him.

1 JOHN 3:2

Adopting a son is one way to ensure that the family name will be passed on. The family likeness, however, is not so easily transmitted!

Adoption into the family of God is different. There you receive both a new name and a new nature—the nature of God's Son. The nature of purity, holiness, godliness.

Being loved by him would be reason enough to rejoice. But John adds that "we shall be like him" when we see him face to face. Isaac Watts offers praise for that fact in these majestic stanzas.

WALK WITH ISAAC WATTS

> Behold, the amazing gift of love
>   The Father hath bestowed
> On us, the sinful sons of men,
>   To call us sons of God!
>
> Concealed as yet this honor lies
>   By this dark world unknown,
> A world that knew not when He came,
>   Even God's eternal Son.
>
> Our souls, we know, when He appears
>   Shall bear His image bright:
> For all His glory, full disclosed,
>   Shall open to His sight.
>
> A hope so great, and so divine,
>   May trials well endure;
> And purge the soul from carnal sin,
>   As Christ Himself is pure.

WALK CLOSER TO GOD

When you've received so much from the Father—life eternal in the family of God and all its accompanying blessings—the challenge to "well endure" trials doesn't sound so unreasonable.

Not when you have a Father to whom you can cry "Abba," one who cares for his own like a tender shepherd, one who knows each of his children by name. Now would be a good time to bow in gratitude for such an "amazing gift of love." ❖

november22

LIGHTEN THE BURDENS OF ANOTHER ALONG THE WAY

If anyone has material possessions and sees a brother or sister in need but has no pity on them, how can the love of God be in that person?

1 JOHN 3:17

Jesus, who walked the earth as love personified, is rarely pictured in the Gospels telling another individual, "I love you." He didn't have to; his actions spoke volumes—to the poor, the leper, the blind, the lame, the social outcast. By dealing with their physical need, Jesus set the stage for speaking to their spiritual need as well.

The world's calamity thus becomes the Christian's opportunity, a situation Jonathan Edwards addresses.

WALK WITH JONATHAN EDWARDS

"There are innumerable kinds of temporal calamities in which men and women need help. Many are hungry, or thirsty, or strangers, or naked, or sick, or in prison, or in suffering of some other kind; and to all such we may minister.

"By thus endeavoring to do good to them externally, we have a greater opportunity to do good to their souls. For when our preachings are accompanied with such outward kindness, it opens the way to give the preachings their full force.

"And we may thus contribute to the good of others in three ways: By giving to them those things that they need and which we possess; by doing for them and helping promote their welfare; and by suffering for them, aiding them to bear their burdens, and doing all in our power to make those burdens lighter."

WALK CLOSER TO GOD

In the final analysis, what every person needs is Jesus Christ. But if an empty stomach or a burdened heart or some other pressing need is clouding the message, perhaps it's time for sympathy rather than a sermon.

You can give that others might listen. You can help that others might hear. You can lift a burden that others might learn firsthand of your burden-bearer.

That kind of love is hard to resist. ❖

november23

TIME FOR A TEST

Dear friends, do not believe every spirit, but test the spirits to see whether they are from God.
1 JOHN 4:1

"It's time for a test." These words periodically send shockwaves through countless classrooms; but without the test, there's no assurance that you've learned the lesson. In 1 John 4, John gave his readers a series of tests to help them distinguish between false spirits, evil spirits and God's Spirit.

Testing your spiritual experiences against the timeless standard of God's Word is another "exam" you can't afford to miss, as A. W. Tozer comments.

WALK WITH A. W. TOZER

"The seeker after God's best is always eager to hear from anyone who offers a way by which he can obtain it. He longs for some new experience, some elevated view of truth, some operation of the Spirit that will raise him above the religious mediocrity he sees all around him.

"Our Lord has made it plain not only that there shall be false spirits abroad, endangering our Christian lives, but that they may be identified and known for what they are!

"The first test must be: 'What has this done to my relationship with and my attitude toward the Lord Jesus Christ?' Do I love God more? Is Jesus Christ still to me the center of all true doctrine?

"Again: 'How does it affect my attitude toward the Scriptures?' Did this new view of truth spring from the Word of God itself or was it the result of some stimulus that lay outside the Bible? Be assured that anything that comes to us from the God of the Word will deepen our love for the Word of God!"

WALK CLOSER TO GOD

Father, now is a good time to test myself and see if I am growing in my walk with you.

When seeking the truth, may I be quick to ask these two questions: "What will this do to my relationship with and attitude toward Jesus Christ?" and "How does this affect my attitude toward your Word?"

May my answers reflect my deep love for you, Father. Amen. ❖

november24

HEARTS AGLOW WITH RESPONSIVE LOVE

And so we know and rely on the love God has for us. God is love. Whoever lives in love lives in God, and God in them.

1 John 4:16

What does love look like?

Augustine pictured love this way: "It has the hands to help others. It has the feet to hasten to the poor and needy. It has eyes to see misery and want. It has the ears to hear the sighs of men."

Basically, love looks like Jesus!

Love talked about is easily turned aside. Love demonstrated is irresistible. And love modeled is the best way to learn how to love in return. "We love because he first loved us" (1 John 4:19). That's why John used the word "love" more than 30 times in his letter—and why this thought from A. B. Simpson is both appropriate and timely.

WALK WITH A. B. SIMPSON

"The secret of walking closely with Christ, and working successfully for him, is to fully realize that we are his beloved.

"Let us but feel that he has his heart set upon us, that he is watching us from those heavens with tender interest, that he is following us day by day as a mother follows her babe in his first attempt to walk alone, that he has set his love upon us, and in spite of ourselves is working out for us his highest will and blessing, as far as we will let him—and then nothing can discourage us.

"Our hearts will glow with responsive love. Our faith will spring to meet his mighty promises, and our sacrifices shall become the very luxuries of love for one so dear.

"This was the secret of John's spirit. 'And so we know and rely on the love God has for us.' The heart that has fully learned this has found the secret of unbounded faith and enthusiastic service."

WALK CLOSER TO GOD

How much does God love you? The evidences are obvious: Calvary's cross, the empty tomb, the indwelling Comforter.

How much do you love God? The evidences should also be obvious. Count them with gratitude for God's goodness to you. ❖

november25

CERTAIN BEYOND ALL DOUBT

And this is the testimony: God has given us eternal life, and this life is in his Son.

1 JOHN 5:11

Saying "I know" can either be a sign of bored resistance or an enthusiastic affirmation. It all depends on your attitude.

The child who responds, "I know, I know," to a parent's commands, probably doesn't. The believer who responds to his Lord's promises with a confident, "I know, I know," hopefully does.

A careful reading of 1 John will uncover many things God wants you to know (see 1 John 2:20–21,29; 3:2,5,14–15; 5:13,15,18–20).

Because of what God has done or said, you can know, without doubt, that you belong to him. When God makes a promise, you can stand upon it with confidence. Charles Spurgeon examines the promise of eternal life in Jesus Christ.

WALK WITH CHARLES SPURGEON

"Let us regard the promise as a thing so sure and certain that we act upon it and make it a chief figure in all our calculations.

"The Lord promises eternal life to those who believe in Jesus; therefore, if we really believe in Jesus, let us conclude that we have eternal life, and rejoice in this great privilege. The promise of God is our best ground of assurance; it is far more sure than dreams or visions, and fancied revelations; and it is far more to be trusted than feelings, either joy or sorrow.

"Nothing can be more certain than that which is declared by God himself; nothing more sure to happen than that which he has guaranteed by his own hand and seal."

WALK CLOSER TO GOD

John proclaims a powerful message: "God has given us eternal life, and this life is in his Son" (1 John 5:11). If you have the Son, you have life. And whether you need to invite him into your life for the first time, or you simply need to invite him into the complexities of your life today, you can act upon that verse right now.

Nothing can be more certain than what the Son himself declares. ❖

november26

THE SUPREME PLACE IN OUR AFFECTIONS

Dear children, keep yourselves from idols.

1 JOHN 5:21

While few people bow before tree stumps or stone pillars today, that doesn't mean idolatry is a thing of the past. As one commentator stated, "Most of the gods of this world are composed of tinted glass, baked-on enamel, chrome, Dacron, wool, silk, or alligator leather."

Albert Barnes examines some of the subtle ways in which devotion for God can be misdirected—with disastrous consequences.

WALK WITH ALBERT BARNES

"We are not in danger, indeed, of bowing down to idols. But we may be in danger of substituting other things in our affections in the place of God, and of devoting to them the time and the affection which are due to him. It is possible to love even our children with an attachment as shall effectually exclude the true God from the heart. And we may love the world with an attachment such as an idolator would his idol-gods.

"There is practical idolatry all over the world.

"God should have the supreme place in our affections. The love of everything else should be held in subordination to the love of him.

"He should reign in our hearts; be acknowledged in our families; be submitted to at all times as having a right to command and control us; be obeyed in all expressions of his will; and be so loved that we shall be willing to part without a murmur with the dearest object of affection when he takes it from us."

WALK CLOSER TO GOD

"God or_____"

Is there anything you might put in that blank that would cause you to think twice about the choice?

If so, now is the time to call it what it is—an idol—and to deal with it accordingly.

If not, ask God for an undivided and undiminishing love for him.

There's no better way to "keep yourselves from idols" than to keep yourself wholly his. ❖

november27

A LIFE THAT WILL LEAVE NO REGRETS

Watch out that you do not lose what we have worked for, but that you may be rewarded fully.

2 JOHN 8

Salvation in Christ is not a "paycheck" for good works but is instead the unmerited gift of God's love. As with any gift, a heartfelt "thank you" is appropriate.

And as H. A. Ironside points out, thankful service is a reasonable response when you have experienced the mercies of God and received by grace a gift you don't deserve.

WALK WITH H. A. IRONSIDE

"All who trust in the Lord Jesus are saved, and this totally apart from human merit.

"But all who profess to believe in him are responsible to serve him and to use whatever gift, ability, or means they have for his glory, and to further his interests in this world.

"There are those who profess to be servants who are not even born of the Spirit. But God holds people accountable for what they know and profess. It is incumbent on those who believe his Word to serve wholeheartedly in view of the day when every one of us shall give an account.

"In that solemn hour no one will regret having been too much concerned about living for him. But many will regret the hours spent in selfishness and folly which might have been used for his glory, and talents wasted or hidden away that if properly invested in the light of eternity would have earned Christ's 'well done.'

"He will reward all that is done in accordance with his Word."

WALK CLOSER TO GOD

Jesus Christ bore the cost of your salvation that you might reap the riches of his grace.

Because he willingly paid the price of sin, you are now free to serve him in "a new life" (Romans 6:4).

Riches in Christ now. Rewards for faithful service to Christ later.

What greater motivation could there be to turn your gratitude into good works — for his glory? ✤

november28

HAVING A SOUL THAT IS SATURATED WITH THE TRUTH

It gave me great joy when some believers came and testified about your faithfulness to the truth, telling how you continue to walk in it.

3 JOHN 3

Being in close proximity to truth is not enough; truth must be digested before it is of any real benefit in a life.

The apostle John had a deep concern for the role of truth in the lives of his readers. And he had a burden to protect them from destructive error.

The attitude he expressed toward truth in his third letter is explored by Charles Spurgeon.

WALK WITH CHARLES SPURGEON

"Truth must enter into the soul, penetrate and saturate it, or else it is of no value.

"Doctrines held as a matter of creed are like bread in the hand, which gives no nourishment to the frame; but doctrine accepted by the heart is as food digested, which by assimilation sustains and builds up the body.

"In us truth must be a living force, an active energy, an indwelling reality, a part of the woof and warp of our being.

"It is a rule of nature that the inward affects the outward as light shines from the center of the lantern through the glass. When therefore the truth is kindled within, its brightness soon beams forth in the outward life and conversation.

"To walk in the truth imparts a life of integrity, holiness, faithfulness, and simplicity—the natural products of those principles of truth which the gospel teaches, and which the Spirit of God enables us to receive."

WALK CLOSER TO GOD

Without food, it is impossible to sustain physical life. Without truth, it is impossible to sustain spiritual life.

The nourishing truth of God's Word will help you grow daily into the likeness of the one who is "the truth"—Jesus Christ (John 14:6).

The cleansing, strengthening truth of God: Feed on it daily, and watch how life-giving it can be for you! ❖

november29

ABUSING THE VALUABLE TREASURE OF GRACE

Contend for the faith ... For certain individuals ... have secretly slipped in among you. They are godless people, who pervert the grace of our God into a license for immorality and deny Jesus Christ.

JUDE 3−4

If a rich friend gave you a blank check, would you: return the check unused, buy something you needed, buy something you wanted, empty the account and then ask for more?

Unlike friends with finite resources, God's grace is infinite. But the riches of his grace aren't to be used contrary to his wishes.

Jude confronted this problem in his short, potent letter, and John Calvin comments on the author's admonition concerning the recipients' abuses.

WALK WITH JOHN CALVIN

"Jude's readers had abused the grace of God, leading themselves and others to take an impure and profane liberty in sinning.

"After being called by God, we ought not to glory carelessly in his grace, but instead walk watchfully; for if anyone trifles with God, the contempt of his grace will not be unpunished.

"Those whom God has honored with the greatest blessings, whom he had extolled to the same degree of honor as we enjoy at this day, he afterwards severely punished. In vain were they all proud of God's grace who did not live in a manner suitable to their calling."

WALK CLOSER TO GOD

Gifts tend to bring out the best—and worst—in people. Some respond with pride, as if they deserved what they received all along. Others respond with humility, acknowledging the goodness of the giver and the unworthiness of the recipient.

God's gift of grace shines brightly when you recall that you didn't deserve what you received—forgiveness and pardon. Nor did you receive what you deserved— condemnation and judgment.

Don't hesitate to receive God's grace with gladness. But be careful how you handle it—as befitting a treasure too valuable to trifle with. ✤

november30

O WORSHIP THE KING, ALL GLORIOUS ABOVE

To the only God our Savior be glory, majesty, power and authority, through Jesus Christ our Lord, before all ages, now and forevermore! Amen.

JUDE 25

If you received an invitation requesting your presence at the White House, chances are high that your initial excitement would soon dissolve into a mixture of fear, wonder and curiosity.

Fear at the power of the officeholder. Wonder over the grandeur of his office. Curiosity about why you were invited!

Attitudes change when God is in view. Thomas Manton describes the attitude of a Christian confronted with the greatness of God.

WALK WITH THOMAS MANTON

"It is a comfort to the soul to consider God's glory, majesty, dominion, and power; for this is the ground of our respect to him and that which encourages us in our service. We need not be ashamed to serve him to whom glory, and power, and majesty, and dominion belong.

"It heartens us against dangers. Surely the great and glorious God will bear us out in his work.

"It increases our awe and reverence. To whom should we go in our necessities but to him who has dominion over all things, and power to dispose of them for the glory of his majesty?

"God is glorious and will maintain the honor of his name and the truth of his promises. When we are dismayed by earthly rulers, it is a relief to think of God's majesty, in comparison to which all earthly grandeur is but the dream of a shadow."

WALK CLOSER TO GOD

If the thought of standing before your nation's president or prime minister causes your pulse to quicken and your vision to sharpen, how much more should standing before the omnipotent God of creation!

He "is able to keep you from stumbling and to present you before his glorious presence without fault and with great joy" (Jude 24).

And in addition to all the reasons Thomas Manton has suggested for glorifying God, that's one more good reason to live for him! ❖

december1

WORTH PRAISING WITH EXUBERANCE

To him who loves us and has freed us from our sins by his blood, and has made us to be a kingdom and priests to serve his God and Father—to him be glory and power for ever and ever! Amen.

REVELATION 1:5–6

If there is anything the book of Revelation reveals, it is that God is worthy to be praised. Amidst the imagery and action as God's plan is fulfilled, the language of praise and worship bursts forth with exuberance.

Even in his greetings to the churches, John cannot help but add a note of praise. H. A. Ironside explains the reason why.

WALK WITH H. A. IRONSIDE

"John's heart was full and could hold back no longer. Adoration and praise were the spontaneous result of Christ's person and offices as Prophet, Priest, and King.

"Then John heralds the glad news of his coming again. He is going to return—not as a babe, born of woman, but as the glorified one descending from heaven. John speaks for all the church when he cries with rapture, 'So shall it be! Amen' (Revelation 1:7).

"He is the Alpha and the Omega—the beginning and the ending; he created all things; he will wind up all things and will bring in the new heavens and the new earth. He is, and was, and is the coming one. May our hearts be occupied with him, and his return be ever for us 'the blessed hope' (Titus 2:13)!"

WALK CLOSER TO GOD

What better way to begin a month of praise than to sing Charles Wesley's great hymn:

> O for a thousand tongues to sing
>   My great Redeemer's praise,
> The glories of my God and King,
>   The triumphs of His grace!
>
> My gracious Master and my God,
>   Assist me to proclaim,
> To spread through all the earth abroad
>   The honors of Thy Name.
>
> Glory to God, and praise, and love
>   Be now and ever given
> By saints below and saints above,
>   The Church in earth and heaven. ✤

december2

FALL BEFORE HIM AND ADORE HIM

Among the lampstands was someone like a son of man ... When I saw him, I fell at his feet as though dead.

REVELATION 1:13,17

It is difficult to imagine a congregation of modern worshipers falling down on the ground in their Sunday best. But read John's description of what he saw in Revelation 1, and it's even harder to imagine anyone *not* falling down before the glorified Christ!

Humble worship is the only appropriate response when the King is in view. Charles Spurgeon explores the significance of John's action.

WALK WITH CHARLES SPURGEON

"Does death alarm you?

"We are never so much alive as when we are dead at his feet. We are never so truly living as when the creature dies away in the presence of the all-glorious, reigning King.

"I know this, that the death of all that is sinful in me is my soul's highest ambition, yes, and the death of all that is carnal. And all that savors of the old Adam. Oh, that it would die.

"And where can it die but at the feet of him who has the new life, and who by manifesting himself in all his glory is to purge away our dross and sin?

"I only desire that I had enough of the Spirit's might so to set forth my Master that I might contribute even in a humble measure to make you fall at his feet as dead, that he might be in us our All in All."

WALK CLOSER TO GOD

Put yourself in John's trembling sandals, listen to the thundering voice of the Alpha and Omega, fall before him as your Lord of hosts—then rise to serve him in holy consecration.

When Isaiah was confronted by the Lord of hosts, he responded in a way similar to John: "Woe to me!... I am ruined!" (Isaiah 6:5).

Confronted by the God of holiness and glory, Isaiah and John saw themselves worthy only of death. But God touched them and made them alive to serve him. He can touch you that way too. ✤

december3

THE EXCITEMENT OF YOUR FIRST LOVE

Yet I hold this against you: You have forsaken the love you had at first.

REVELATION 2:4

Love is more than a feeling of exhilaration in the presence of another. Rather, love is a commitment that grows deeper with the years.

In the case of the Ephesian church, the excitement of first love for God had faded into meaningless ritual, motions without enthusiasm, works without warmth.

G. Campbell Morgan illustrates the problem of losing your first love for God with this story.

WALK WITH G. CAMPBELL MORGAN

"A friend of mine had a daughter whom he dearly loved. They were great friends. One day his birthday came; and in the morning of that day she came into his room with her face wreathed in smiles and said, 'Father, I have brought you a present.' She handed him a box in which he found an exquisitely decorated pair of slippers.

"He said, 'Darling, it was very good of you to buy these for me.'

"'O Father,' she said, 'I did not buy them. I have made them for you.'

"Then looking at her he said, 'Oh, now I understand. Is this what you have been doing for the last three months?'

"She replied, 'Yes, Father. But how did you know how long I had been at work on them?'

"He said, 'Because for three months I have not had your company. You have been too busy. My darling, I like these slippers very much. But next time, buy the slippers, and let me have your company. I would rather have my child than anything she can make for me.'"

WALK CLOSER TO GOD

Father, I find it so much easier today to *work* for you than to *walk* with you.

Restore to me the freshness and vitality of first love. Let me sense again your touch in my life. In place of my meager labors, I offer you the one thing you desire most: myself. In the name of the one who gave himself in love. Amen. ✤

december**4**

STEPPING AHEAD IN THE WALK OF FAITH

I know your deeds, your love and faith, your service and perseverance, and that you are now doing more than you did at first.

REVELATION 2:19

Maintaining the status quo. That may sound like a commendable, if somewhat conservative, goal for life. But the Christian life calls for more than a "status quo" mentality. Rather, it calls for growth, maturity, fruit-bearing.

The believers at Thyatira belonged to a growing, pace-setting church. Albert Barnes uses their example to emphasize the importance of moving ahead in the walk of faith.

WALK WITH ALBERT BARNES

"The works which had been recently done at Thyatira were more commendable than those which had been done previously.

"They were making progress; they had been acting more and more in accordance with the nature and claims of the Christian profession.

"Religion of the soul, and in a community, is designed to be progressive. We always should seek to live so that we will have the commendation of the Savior; and we should regard it as something to be greatly desired if we are approved as making advances in knowledge and holiness; that as we grow in years we may grow alike in the disposition to do good, and in the ability to do it; that as we gain in experience, we may also gain in a readiness to apply the results of our experience in promoting the cause of religion."

WALK CLOSER TO GOD

The Christian life is rarely composed of giant steps of progress. "Three steps forward, two steps backward" might even be a more accurate description.

Keeping "in step" with the Father requires that you make small but significant decisions in concert with him every day. Decisions in matters of love, faith, service and perseverance.

It's important to know where you are—and where you are headed. But don't overlook the equally important question: How fast are you headed there? ❖

december5

SPLENDOR THAT SUITS THE DRESS CODE OF HEAVEN

Yet you have a few people in Sardis who have not soiled their clothes. They will walk with me, dressed in white, for they are worthy.

REVELATION 3:4

"How little people know who think that holiness is dull." C. S. Lewis wrote those words to counteract the notion that holiness is somehow drab and boring.

If that idea were true, then the saints of Revelation 3 ought to be wearing drab gray or dull black. Instead, they are adorned in dazzling white.

Matthew Henry shares this insight into what the faithful servant of God can expect to wear.

WALK WITH MATTHEW HENRY

"The small faithful remnant in Sardis had not given in to the prevailing corruptions of the day and place in which they lived.

"God notices the smallest number of those who abide with him and makes a very gracious promise to them: 'They will walk with me, dressed in white, for they are worthy'—in the white robes of justification, and adoption, and comfort, in the white robes of honor and glory in the next world.

"Their fidelity has prepared them for it.

"Those who walk with Christ in the clean garments of real, practical holiness here, and keep themselves unspotted from the world, shall walk with Christ in the white robes of honor and glory in the life to come: This is a suitable reward.

"The purity of grace shall be rewarded with the perfect purity of glory. Holiness, when perfected, shall be its own reward."

WALK CLOSER TO GOD

In heaven God's children will wear the reward of holiness. But for now, those around you may be wearing clothes more "in style" with the world. That's a style that will change and be discarded.

By contrast, God's "style" never varies: integrity, fidelity, purity. They are timeless as God himself.

Holiness. Wear it well, as befitting the beautiful bride of Christ of which you are a part. You needn't wait till heaven to begin to walk with him in white. ❖

FAITH: COURAGEOUS CONFIDENCE IN GOD

Since you have kept my command to endure patiently, I will also keep you from the hour of trial.

REVELATION 3:10

Near the end of a long run, the weary but determined jogger is sorely tempted to ease up, to quit a few steps early. But the mind has ways of overcoming the muscles, and a few dozen steps later he reaches the finish line. He has done what his body told him it was impossible to do.

Revelation 3 speaks of the goal of patience that seems unreachable to many believers. And yet it is a goal that God is committed to developing in the lives of his children.

Oswald Chambers gives insight into the relationships between patience, confidence and faith.

WALK WITH OSWALD CHAMBERS

"Patience is more than endurance. God is aiming at something the saint cannot see, and he stretches and strains, and every now and again the saint says, 'I can't stand anymore.'

"But trust yourself in God's hands. Maintain your confidence in Jesus Christ by the patience of faith. You cannot see him just now; you cannot understand all he is doing, but you know him.

"Shipwreck occurs where there is not that mental poise which comes from being established on the eternal truth that God is holy love. Faith is the heroic effort of your life, as you fling yourself in reckless confidence on God.

"God has ventured all in Jesus Christ to save us; now he wants us to venture our all in abandoned confidence in him."

WALK CLOSER TO GOD

God calls you to trust him even as you are being stretched to the limit. Patience comes when you look ahead and see God waiting at the finish line of life. He is the one who controls all the circumstances, knows the limits of your endurance and will reward you at the end.

You can be confident he'll finish the good work he has begun in you (see Philippians 1:6). ✤

december7

THE WEAKNESS THAT KILLS REPENTANCE

Those whom I love I rebuke and discipline. So be earnest and repent ... Whoever has ears, let them hear what the Spirit says to the churches.

REVELATION 3:19,22

The church at Laodicea suffered from a bad case of "the emperor's new clothes." Like that fabled emperor, their true condition was obvious to all but them.

A church in the same condition is no laughing matter. Appearances can't mask reality—especially from God. But how do you correct such a situation?

Charles Spurgeon offers the following suggestions for a well-dressed church.

WALK WITH CHARLES SPURGEON

"You may know of the faults of other people; and in watching a church, you may have observed weak points in many places. But have you wept or prayed over them?

"If not, you have not watched as you should for the good of your brothers and sisters, and perhaps have allowed evils to grow which ought to have been uprooted. You have been silent when you should have kindly and earnestly spoken to the offenders, or made your own example a warning.

"Do not judge your brother, but judge yourself; if you have any severity, use it on your own conduct and heart. We must pray the Lord to use this remedy, and make us know just where we are.

"We shall never get right as long as we are confident that we are so already. Self-complacency is the death of repentance."

WALK CLOSER TO GOD

In the first three chapters of Revelation, seven churches received personal messages from the Lord of the church. And within a few hundred years, all seven had disappeared. Perhaps, in Spurgeon's words, they were "confident" and full of "self-complacency," believing that they were well dressed already.

How about you? Are you satisfied with your walk with God? More important, is he satisfied with your walk with him? ❖

december8

LETTING GOD BE ALL IN ALL

You are worthy, our Lord and God, to receive glory and honor and power, for you created all things, and by your will they were created and have their being.

REVELATION 4:11

Humility has been called "the ability to withhold from others the high opinion you hold of yourself" and "the art of wearing greatness gently." More accurately, it is the result of a correct estimation of oneself.

The incomparable example of humility is, of course, Jesus. The Creator became the creature in order that "every tongue acknowledge that Jesus Christ is Lord" (Philippians 2:11). Andrew Murray shares this insight into the practice of humility.

WALK WITH ANDREW MURRAY

"The call to humility has been too little regarded in the church, because its true nature and importance have not been understood.

"It is not something we bring to God, or he bestows. It is simply the sense of entire nothingness, which comes when we see how truly God is all, and in which we make way for God to be all.

"When the creature realizes that this is the true nobility, and consents with his will, his mind, and his affections to be the form, the vessel in which the life and glory of God are to work and manifest themselves, then he sees that humility is simply acknowledging the truth of his position as creature, and yielding to God his rightful place."

WALK CLOSER TO GOD

The bigger your God becomes, the smaller will seem his creatures—including you!

Drawing near to God is the best way to gain a fresh view of his greatness and grandeur.

In C. S. Lewis's popular fantasy *The Chronicles of Narnia*, one of the characters provides this concise definition of what it meant for God to become a man: "A stable once held something inside that was bigger than our whole world."

Think of it: God residing in the lives of his believing creatures!

The question remains: How much room does he occupy in your life? ❖

SINGING THE WONDERFUL SONG OF THE LAMB

Then I heard every creature ... saying: "To him who sits on the throne and to the Lamb be praise and honor and glory and power, for ever and ever!".

REVELATION 5:13

The Lamb of God has inspired more songs than all other creatures combined, and many hymns owe their inspiration to the praise-filled verses of Revelation that extol the Lamb that was slain. Horatius Bonar builds this hymn of praise from the worshipful words sung in heaven.

WALK WITH HORATIUS BONAR

> Blessing and honor and glory and power,
> 　Wisdom and riches and strength evermore,
> Give ye to Him who our battle hath won,
> 　Whose are the Kingdom, the crown, and the throne.
>
> Soundeth the heaven of the heavens with His name;
> 　Ringeth the earth with His glory and fame;
> Ocean and mountain, stream, forest and flower
> 　Echo His praises and tell of His power.
>
> Ever ascendeth the song and the joy;
> 　Ever descendeth the love from on high;
> Blessing and honor and glory and praise—
> 　This is the theme of the hymns we raise.
>
> Give we the glory and praise to the Lamb;
> 　Take we the robe and the harp and the palm;
> Sing we the song of the Lamb that was slain,
> 　Dying in weakness, but rising to reign.

WALK CLOSER TO GOD

In 1432 Jan van Eyck painted his now famous *Adoration of the Lamb*. In the center of that painting Christ stands as the Lamb of God, blood pouring from his sacrificial wounds. All around are gathered worshipers of the Lamb. Yet the Lamb is not lying on the altar near death. Instead he stands tall and straight, in triumph and splendor. Death has been defeated.

It is no wonder he is worthy of praise. This Lamb is your Lord. ✤

december**10**

CHOOSING THE LAMB'S WRATH OR
THE LAMB'S LOVE

Fall on us and hide us from the face of him who sits on the throne and from the wrath of the Lamb! For the great day of their wrath has come, and who can withstand it?

REVELATION 6:16–17

By nature lambs are among the gentlest of creatures. How then is it possible that men and women flee in terror from the wrath of the Lamb?

It's not a pleasant picture. But as H. A. Ironside explains, the imagery is painfully appropriate.

WALK WITH H. A. IRONSIDE

"In that day there shall dawn upon multitudes the realization that the Lamb of God whom they had rejected and whose gentle rule they had spurned has visited their sins upon their own heads.

"Yet we read of no repentance, no true turning to God or trusting his Christ— just an awful realization that it is the rejected Lamb whom they must face, and whose wrath they cannot escape.

"Notice the solemnity of the expression 'the wrath of the Lamb.' We are not accustomed to linking the thought of wrath with the Lamb, which has always been the symbol of gentleness.

"But there is a terrible truth involved in this nevertheless. For if the grace of the Lamb of God is rejected, his indignation and wrath must be faced. It cannot be otherwise.

"But now grace is still reigning through righteousness, and a just God waits in lovingkindness to be the Justifier of everyone who believes in Jesus."

WALK CLOSER TO GOD

When confronted with your own sinfulness, you can respond in one of two ways: (1) You can seek to remove the symptoms (even in such radical ways as asking mountains to fall on you). (2) You can appropriate God's solution.

The blood of the Lamb will either be the covering or the condemnation for your sins.

Choose carefully your way of escape. And choose quickly. "Now is the time of God's favor, now is the day of salvation" (2 Corinthians 6:2). ❖

december11

THE WAY GOD LEADS THOSE HE LOVES

These are they who have come out of the great tribulation; they have washed their robes and made them white in the blood of the Lamb.

REVELATION 7:14

"Everyone who wants to live a godly life in Christ Jesus will be persecuted" (2 Timothy 3:12).

"Do not be surprised at the fiery ordeal that has come on you" (1 Peter 4:12).

Jesus warned his disciples, "If the world hates you, keep in mind that it hated me first" (John 15:18).

Robert Murray McCheyne, who himself suffered an early death, has this to say about the purpose behind the pain of suffering for the Savior.

WALK WITH ROBERT MURRAY MCCHEYNE

"Some believers are very surprised when they are called to suffer. They thought they would do some great thing for God, but all God permits them to do is to suffer.

"Just suppose you could speak with those who have gone to be with the Lord; everyone has a different story, yet everyone has a tale of suffering.

"One was persecuted by family and friends ... another was inflicted with pain and disease, neglected by the world ... another was bereaved of children ... another had all these afflictions.

"But you will notice that though the water was deep, they all have reached the other side. Not one of them blames God for the road he led them; 'Salvation' is their only cry.

"Are there any of you, dear children, murmuring at your lot? Do not sin against God. This is the way God leads all his redeemed ones."

WALK CLOSER TO GOD

This hymn expresses the hope of every heart that has suffered for Jesus:

> My soul, be on thy guard,
>   Ten thousand foes arise;
> The hosts of sin are pressing hard
>   To draw thee from the skies.
> Fight on, my soul, till death
>   Shall bring thee to thy God;
> He'll take thee at thy parting breath,
>   Up to His blest abode. ❖

december**12**

THE FRAGRANT AROMA OF THE SAINTS' PRAYERS

He [another angel] was given much incense to offer, with the prayers of all God's people, on the golden altar in front of the throne.

REVELATION 8:3

A young child, enamored with his teacher, gave her three daisies with this note attached:

> These flowers will fade and die,
> But you will smell forever.

In your prayer life, as in poetry, it's the thought—and the fragrance—that counts. John refers to the "golden bowls full of incense, which are the prayers of God's people" (Revelation 5:8). The angel in Revelation 8 is seen bringing those sweet offerings of adoration before the Father, as William R. Newell explains.

WALK WITH WILLIAM R. NEWELL
"This angel is publicly to bring before heaven three things:

"First, that the prayers of the saints are ever before God: a most blessed and solemn truth!

"Second, that the incense (ever in Scripture setting forth the power of Christ's atonement acting upon God), representing our Lord's person and work at Calvary, added in due time to the prayers of all the saints, makes them effectual before God.

"Third, that God's judgment is in a sense the answer to 'your kingdom come' (Matthew 6:10), which the saints of all ages have prayed. No other answer could be given, since earth has rejected the rightful King!"

WALK CLOSER TO GOD
Father, all too often I neglect my times of prayer, not realizing the eternal impact of those heavenly conversations.

To know that my prayers ascend to you as a fragrant aroma causes me to think more of what I pray and how I pray. To know that you hear and answer causes me to wonder at the relationship I enjoy with you. To know that my prayers help to usher in your kingdom makes me bolder to pray according to your will. Your kingdom come!

In the name of him who taught me to pray. Amen. ❖

december13

CREATED FOR IMMORTALITY

They were told not to harm the grass of the earth or any plant or tree, but only those people who did not have the seal of God on their foreheads.

REVELATION 9:4

Not all fears are bad. Some are wholesome, even necessary for life. For example, Jesus said this about fear: "Do not be afraid of those who kill the body but cannot kill the soul. Rather, be afraid of the One who can destroy both soul and body in hell" (Matthew 10:28).

In Revelation 9 those who deny God suffer an end far more dreadful than mere physical death. John Calvin explains why fearing God is a healthy idea for this life—and the next.

WALK WITH JOHN CALVIN

"If believers will consider for what purpose they were born, and what their condition is, they will have no reason to so earnestly desire an earthly life.

"God alone has the power of bestowing eternal life, or of inflicting eternal death. We forget God, because we are hurried away by the dread of men.

"Isn't it very evident that we set a higher value on the shadowy life of the body than on the eternal condition of the soul; or rather, that the heavenly kingdom of God is of little importance with us, in comparison with the fleeting shadow of the present life?

"How else is it that the dread of other people prevails in the struggle, but that the body is preferred to the soul, and immortality is less valued than a perishing life?"

WALK CLOSER TO GOD

When your body senses danger, it seeks an escape route. But where do you turn when your soul is in danger? Then no earthly refuge exists; there is no safety apart from God.

Eighty years in the body cannot compare with an eternity in heaven. But which takes priority in your decisions, your investments, your plans, your commitments?

Loving and serving God with your whole body and soul. There's no greater command, no higher calling in this life or the next! ✤

december14

THE BITTERSWEET BLESSING OF PAIN

I took the little scroll ... and ate it. It tasted as sweet as honey in my mouth, but when I had eaten it, my stomach turned sour.

REVELATION 10:10

What surgeon hasn't consoled a patient with the thought that the pain of the scalpel will promote healing and health? It's good news and bad news at the same time—much like the bittersweet news of the cross.

So often it's the same in our lives. We achieve maturity through the bitterness of suffering. Susannah Spurgeon, who suffered for over 25 years, understood the reward suffering brings.

WALK WITH SUSANNAH SPURGEON

"At the close of a gloomy day, I lay resting on my couch. Though all was bright within my cozy room, some of the external darkness seemed to have entered my soul and obscured its spiritual vision. In sorrow I asked, 'Why does my Lord so often send sharp and bitter pain to visit me?'

"Suddenly I heard a sweet, soft sound, a clear, musical note. It came from the oak log crackling on the fire! The fire was letting loose the imprisoned music from the old oak's inmost heart!

"'Ah,' I thought, 'when the fire of affliction draws songs of praise from us, then indeed we are purified, and our God is glorified!'

"Perhaps some of us are like this old oak log, cold, hard, insensible; we should give forth no melodious sounds were it not for the fire which kindles around us, and releases notes of trust in him and cheerful compliance with his will."

WALK CLOSER TO GOD

"This might hurt a little bit!" Those words bring scant comfort at the pediatrician's office. Only as the child matures will he realize that pain can sometimes lead to better health.

So too God's children must learn that "the Lord disciplines the one he loves" (Hebrews 12:6).

Why? "That we may share in his holiness ... a harvest of righteousness and peace" (Hebrews 12:10–11).

Bittersweet blessings. You may not enjoy them at first bite, but you'll love the aftertaste. ✤

december15

TAKING THE MEASURE OF A CHRISTLIKE CHARACTER

I was given a reed ... and was told, "Go and measure the temple of God and the altar, with its worshipers".

REVELATION 11:1

Trying to measure up to another's expectations can be nerve-racking. But when God is the evaluator, then you had better have help—the kind only to be found in a divine helper!

In Revelation 11 John was told to evaluate the place of worship and the worshipers there to see if they "measured up." Therein is a lesson for every true worshiper of God, as Albert Barnes explains.

WALK WITH ALBERT BARNES

"John is commanded to 'Go and measure the temple of God.' That is, ascertain its true dimensions.

"If the direction had been literally to measure the temple at Jerusalem, John would measure its length, and breadth, and height; he would measure its rooms, its doorways, its porticoes.

"If the direction is understood figuratively, as applicable to the Christian church, John's work would be to obtain an exact estimate or measurement of what the true church was.

"John has not preserved the measurement; for the idea here is not that he was to preserve such a model, but that its true character might be known.

"The obvious meaning is that he was to take a correct estimate of their character; of what they professed; of the reality of their piety; of their lives; and of the general state of the church professing to worship God."

WALK CLOSER TO GOD

When the yardstick of Christ's life is laid alongside your life, what does it reveal about

> the intensity of your worship?
> the level of your commitment?
> the purity of your attitudes and actions?
> the degree of your Christlikeness?

The measure of a person without Christ always comes up short. Only in Christ can you truly measure up, for " in Christ you have been brought to fullness. He is the head over every power and authority" (Colossians 2:10). ❖

december16

THE BLESSED HOPE OF CHRIST'S RETURN

The kingdom of the world has become the kingdom of our Lord and of his Messiah, and he will reign for ever and ever.

REVELATION 11:15

Christians today, like those of old, are prompted to ask, "Where is the promise of his coming?"

Patience, Christian. God is working out his purposes. Sometimes visibly, sometimes invisibly, he is patiently gathering the sons and daughters of the kingdom from every tongue, tribe and nation.

Hymn writer Charles Wesley knew this truth well. In one of his inspiring compositions he proclaims the hope of every Christian: "Christ the Lord returns to reign."

WALK WITH CHARLES WESLEY

> Lo! He comes, with clouds descending,
>   Once for our salvation slain;
> Thousand thousand saints attending
>   Swell the triumph of His train:
> Alleluia, alleluia!
>   Christ the Lord returns to reign.
>
> Every eye shall now behold Him,
>   Robed in dreadful majesty;
> Those who set at naught and sold Him,
>   Pierced and nailed Him to the tree,
> Deeply wailing, deeply wailing,
>   Shall the true Messiah see.
>
> Yes, Amen! let all adore Thee,
>   High on Thine eternal throne:
> Savior, take the power and glory;
>   Claim the kingdom for Thine own:
> Alleluia, alleluia!
>   Thou shalt reign, and Thou alone.

WALK CLOSER TO GOD

Someday the kingdom of God will come and God's Son will enjoy ultimate victory over the forces of evil. Every eye will see him, and every knee will bow before the one who shall reign for ever and ever.

Let the coming of his kingdom encourage you to readiness and expectancy. Someday you too will "swell the triumph of His train." ✤

december17

RESPOND WITH PRAISE TO THE PERFECTION OF GOD

Now have come the salvation and the power and the kingdom of our God, and the authority of his Messiah ... Therefore rejoice, you heavens and you who dwell in them!.

REVELATION 12:10,12

Clapping. Cheering. Cries of "Bravo!" All are appropriate responses when an audience enjoys talent displayed at the peak of perfection.

C. S. Lewis offers this intriguing suggestion as to why an eternal chorus of praise for a "performance" that is perfect in every way is such a satisfying activity for the Christian.

WALK WITH C. S. LEWIS

"I think we delight to praise what we enjoy because the praise not merely expresses but completes the enjoyment; it is its appointed consummation.

"If it were possible for a created soul fully to 'appreciate,' that is, to love and delight in, the worthiest object of all, and simultaneously at every moment to give this delight perfect expression, then that soul would be in supreme blessedness.

"To praise God fully we must suppose ourselves to be in perfect love with God, drowned in, dissolved by that delight which, far from remaining pent up within ourselves as incommunicable bliss, flows out from us incessantly again in effortless and perfect expression.

"Our joy is no more separable from the praise in which it liberates and utters itself than the brightness a mirror receives is separable from the brightness it sheds."

WALK CLOSER TO GOD

The quest for perfection. It's a worthy endeavor for any performer or musician.

And as C. S. Lewis has suggested, the Christian also has a quest: to love God perfectly, to respond with perfect praise to the one who perfectly deserves it — the one who perfectly loves you.

The more you behold him, the more appropriate — and enthusiastic — will be your response, until finally "we shall be like him, for we shall see him as he is" (1 John 3:2).

That's one performance you won't want to miss! ❖

december18

HIDING WITH CHRIST IS THE SAFEST PLACE TO BE

"If anyone is to go into captivity, into captivity they will go. If anyone is to be killed with the sword, with the sword they will be killed." This calls for patient endurance and faithfulness on the part of God's people.

REVELATION 13:10

To say that something "boomeranged" means that what you intended to send somewhere else has instead come back to haunt you.

In the case of the enemies of God and his people, all the enmity that they can muster against the forces of righteousness will "boomerang." They will suffer at the hands of their own weapons.

William Milligan offers these words of comfort for Christians threatened by suffering and opposition.

WALK WITH WILLIAM MILLIGAN

"Nothing can harm the life that is hidden with Christ in God. But the saints may still be troubled, persecuted and killed—as were the witnesses of chapter eleven—by the beast that was given power to make war and to conquer them.

"Such is the thought that leads to the words which we now consider: 'If anyone is to go into captivity, into captivity they will go. If anyone is to be killed with the sword, with the sword they will be killed.'

"In the great law of God, consolation is given to the persecuted. Their enemies would lead them into captivity, but a worse captivity awaits themselves. They would kill with the sword, but with a sharper sword than that of human power they shall themselves be killed. Is there not enough in that to inspire the saints with faith and patience?

"Well may they endure with unfailing hearts when they remember who is on their side, for 'God is just: He will pay back trouble to those who trouble you' (2 Thessalonians 1:6)."

WALK CLOSER TO GOD

"If God is for us"—and he is—"who can be against us?" (Romans 8:31).

The enemy's attempts at sabotage will boomerang to his own destruction; the believer in Christ will enjoy a well-deserved rest. So take heart!

Being "hidden with Christ in God" is the safest place to be. ✤

december19

SUFFERING FOR WHAT YOU VALUE

They could not buy or sell unless they had the mark, which is the name of the beast or the number of its name.

REVELATION 13:17

A world that ignores God is a world that rejects Christians. In the eyes of the world, the only thing worse than a Christian who lives like Christ is a Christian who doesn't live like Christ.

When John writes of the mark of the beast, he speaks of the unholy fraternity that confronts Christians. F. B. Meyer shares two resolutions for you to consider as a person devoted to Christ.

WALK WITH F. B. MEYER

"Christians are finding it increasingly difficult to carry on their businesses without adopting a lower standard than that of the sanctuary.

"Yet Christians must resolve that they will not trifle with their consciences, but will obey the law of Christ in all respects. For everyone there is an inevitable choice to be made and maintained, whether a clear conscience or a fortune is to hold first place in their business careers.

"Second, they must be content to bear poverty as part of the cross of Christ. We admire and canonize martyrs, but are strangely unwilling to face the disgrace of poverty, the dens and caves of the earth, which they endured for principle. Our religion will cost us something, or we may fairly question its vitality and worth. What one will not suffer for, one does not value."

WALK CLOSER TO GOD

If it might cost you your livelihood to take a stand for your living Lord, would you be swayed in your commitment? Consider:

"Whoever wants to be my disciple must deny themselves and take up their cross daily and follow me" (Luke 9:23).

"Whoever does not carry their cross and follow me cannot be my disciple" (Luke 14:27).

"Those of you who do not give up everything you have cannot be my disciples" (Luke 14:33).

Dare to obey Christ—regardless of the cost—and he will give you a contentment and confidence no earthly profession can supply. ❖

december**20**

SOULS THAT ARE SHAPED FOR LIFE IN HEAVEN

And I heard a sound from heaven ... The sound I heard was like that of harpists playing their harps. And they sang a new song before the throne.

REVELATION 14:2–3

Think of your life on earth as an opportunity to practice what you will be spending an eternity in heaven "performing": praising God.

Vocalists and violinists, actors and conductors, all strive for perfection in their respective disciplines. Jonathan Edwards exhorts you to practice your grand chorus of praise with the same enthusiasm and commitment to excellence.

WALK WITH JONATHAN EDWARDS

"We ought now to begin that work which will be the work of another world; for the purpose of this life is that we might prepare for a future life.

"Our present state is a state of preparation for the enjoyments and employments of the eternal state; and no one is ever admitted to those enjoyments and employments but those who have prepared spiritually for them here.

"We must be fitted for heaven; we must here have our souls molded and fashioned for that work and that happiness. They must be formed for praise, and they must begin their work here.

"If our hearts are not tuned to praise in this world, we shall never do anything in the world hereafter.

"As we hope to be of that blessed company which praises God in heaven, we should now accustom ourselves to the work."

WALK CLOSER TO GOD

After a particularly moving performance by a musician, one member of the audience was overheard to say, "Genius! Sheer genius!" To which the musician responded, "For 26 years I practice ten hours a day ... and now they call me a genius!"

You have only a handful of years to practice what will be your eternal preoccupation.

So if you know you're going to be singing a "new song" of praise before the throne, now would be a good time to start. ✤

december21

OUTWARD ENERGY REGULATED BY INWARD PEACE

I saw what looked like a sea of glass glowing with fire.

REVELATION 15:2

Before the seven last bowls of judgment are poured, John pictures an unusual scene: a "sea of glass glowing with fire"—images evoking both peace and judgment. In the same seemingly contradictory way, Jesus is called both the "Lion" and the "Lamb" (Revelation 5:5–6). Contradictions? No—balance.

Out of John's description of peace and judgment, W. Graham Scroggie gleans a lesson on the powerful possibilities of a balanced life.

WALK WITH W. GRAHAM SCROGGIE

"Peace and energy do not always go together, though they should. Peace without energy may be only stagnation; and energy without peace may be but a form of panic.

"What we need is that our glassy sea be mixed with fire, and that our fire shall have for its home a glassy sea.

"Why should peace exclude passion, and why should passion destroy peace? Why should one moral quality triumph at the expense of another?

"Yet too often it is so. Sometimes our sea is not glass, but tempest-tossed, and sometimes our fire burns low. Sometimes it is all calm and no energy, and sometimes it is all energy and no calm.

"But what is possible and right is that the glassy sea be mixed with fire, that our outward energy be regulated by inward peace, and that our inward peace find expression in outward energy. Then shall there be power in balance."

WALK CLOSER TO GOD

Power out of control (such as an earthquake or volcanic eruption) can endanger many. Power under control (an internal combustion engine or a hydroelectric plant) can benefit many. And a power outage accomplishes nothing for anyone!

Which of the three power levels best characterizes your life?

If the answer is unsettling, look to the one who can help you catch—and keep—the balanced walk of a child of God. ❖

december**22**

YOUR CHANCE TO CHOOSE THE RIGHT SIDE

Then I heard the angel in charge of the waters say: "You are just in these judgments, O Holy One, you who are and who were; for ... you have given them ... as they deserve".
Revelation 16:5–6

Someone facing an unpleasant task often goes through three phases: contemplating how to do it, contemplating when to do it, and contemplating.

That formula may be humorous for mundane chores, but in eternal matters, procrastination can be lethal. When God's judgment comes, it will come with finality. No postponements. No excuses.

C. S. Lewis paints this word picture of what that day might be like.

WALK WITH C. S. LEWIS

"When the author walks onto the stage, the play is over. God is going to invade, all right; but what is the good of saying you are on his side then, when you see the whole natural universe melting away like a dream and something else comes crashing in?

"This time it will be God without disguise; something so overwhelming that it will strike either irresistible love or irresistible horror into every creature.

"It will be too late then to choose your side. That will not be the time for choosing: It will be the time when we discover which side we really have chosen, whether we realized it before or not.

"Now, today, this moment, is our chance to choose the right side."

WALK CLOSER TO GOD

Today you face a choice; tomorrow you will face the consequences of the choice you made. Today you may choose your path; tomorrow you will discover just where the path has led you.

"Then the King will say to those on his right, 'Come, you who are blessed by my Father; take your inheritance, the kingdom prepared for you' ... Then he will say to those on his left, 'Depart from me, you who are cursed, into the eternal fire prepared for the devil and his angels'" (Matthew 25:34,41).

Which will it be: getting "right" with God ... or getting "left"? ✤

december23

CROWN HIM WITH MANY CROWNS!

They will wage war against the Lamb, but the Lamb will triumph over them because he is Lord of lords and King of kings.

REVELATION 17:14

In Revelation the Lamb of God triumphs over his enemies as King of kings.

Perhaps you find it easy to envision Jesus as the "Lamb of God, who takes away the sin of the world" (John 1:29) — but hard to view him as the Lord of lords vanquishing the forces of evil.

If so, Abraham Kuyper will help you with this timely description of Christ, the victorious Lamb.

WALK WITH ABRAHAM KUYPER

"Christ is your King! Does this title of honor tend merely to have you think of Christ as in a distant hamlet the man behind his plow thinks of his sovereign in the royal residence?

"Is the kingly image of the earthly prince, applied to your Savior purely by way of comparison, a way to express his power and honor?

"The Lamb, so it is proclaimed unto you in Revelation, is not merely your Reconciliation and your Surety, not alone your Redeemer and Savior, nor yet alone your Shepherd and your Guide.

"No, the Lamb of God—and in this contrast you feel what amazes and inspires—the Lamb of God is at the same time the Lord of lords and King of kings.

"The Lamb with the crown, the high, the holy union of self-effacement and dominion—your King!"

WALK CLOSER TO GOD

Lamb and Lord. Shepherd and Savior. It's a twin theme echoed in this familiar hymn. Use it right now to exalt your God and Guide:

> Crown Him the Lord of years,
> > The Potentate of time;
> Creator of the rolling spheres,
> > Ineffably sublime:
> All hail, Redeemer, hail!
> > For Thou hast died for me:
> Thy praise shall never, never fail
> > Throughout eternity. ❖

december24

LEAVING BEHIND THE FORTRESS OF DARKNESS

Then I heard another voice from heaven say: "Come out of her, my people, so that you will not share in her sins".

REVELATION 18:4

There is a time to take a stand, and a time to take your leave. And woe to the believer who fails to discern which time is which.

Paul's question is timely: "What do righteousness and wickedness have in common? Or what fellowship can light have with darkness?" (2 Corinthians 6:14).

Even the prophet Isaiah—certainly no stranger to the evils of his day—urged his readers, "Come out ... and be pure" (Isaiah 52:11).

F. B. Meyer uses Old Testament examples to show when and how to separate from the fortresses of darkness.

WALK WITH F. B. MEYER

"It is often argued that we should stay in the midst of churches and bodies whose sins and follies we deplore, in the hope of saving them for God and mankind. Such reasoning has a good deal of force in the first stages of decline. A strong protest may arrest error and stop the gangrene.

"But as time advances, and the whole body becomes diseased; when the protests have been disregarded, and the arguments trampled underfoot; when the majority have clearly taken up their position against the truth—we have no alternative but to come out and be pure.

"The place from which we can exert the strongest influence for good is not from within, but from without.

"Lot lost all influence in his life in Sodom; but Abraham, from the heights of Mamre, was able to exert a mighty influence on its history."

WALK CLOSER TO GOD

You may find yourself resembling a "speck of saintliness" in a "sea of sin." If so, the question to ask may not be "What sort of impact can I make?" but "How long can I maintain an effective witness here?"

Answer carefully; your spiritual health may well be at stake. ✣

december25

THE MARRIAGE SUPPER OF THE LAMB

Let us rejoice and be glad and give him glory! For the wedding of the Lamb has come, and his bride has made herself ready.

REVELATION 19:7

Revelation 19 describes the marriage supper of the Lamb—and you're invited! In preparation for that gala event, your deeds, your conduct, your life of service on earth—they all help weave the fine linen for the wedding dress Christ's bride will wear.

While you're waiting, don't lose heart wondering why God is waiting to deal with evil and the enemies who oppose him. Take careful note of Clarence Macartney's wise observations.

WALK WITH CLARENCE MACARTNEY

"We find comfort in the thought that God is able to bring good out of evil, but still we ask: Is God not omnipotent? Is not God all good? If so, why did He permit evil? Why doesn't He destroy it now?

"The great answer that the Bible gives us, and the answer of this vision, is the certainty of the overthrow of evil. When Robinson Crusoe's man Friday wanted to know why God did not destroy the devil, the answer that Crusoe finally gave him was the right answer, and the only answer, and the great answer: 'God *will* destroy him.'

"We see the unfolding of the long and bloody panorama of history, humanity's aspiration of the best and its doing of the worst. We also see the church in ceaseless battle with the beast. But that is not all we see. 'Then the end will come' (1 Corinthians 15:24). We see the Lamb of God standing upon Mount Zion."

WALK CLOSER TO GOD

The wonderful marriage celebration Revelation 19 describes will take place. God has promised. And you'll be there to join in the festivities!

But it's not an event to be taken lightly. "'His bride has made herself ready. Fine linen, bright and clean, was given her to wear.' (Fine linen stands for the righteous acts of God's people.)" (Revelation 19:7–8).

Only those properly attired in righteousness will be ready to meet the bridegroom, the Lamb of God. Is your wardrobe "pressed and ready"? ❖

december**26**

THE THRILL OF VICTORY

On his robe and on his thigh he has this name written: KING OF KINGS AND LORD OF LORDS.

REVELATION 19:16

Things certainly have changed in the last 50 years: God has been expelled from the public schools, abortion is a legal "choice," pornography is viewed as harmless and homosexuality as healthy, and Christianity is grossly misrepresented and ridiculed in the media.

In times like these, the temptation is to withdraw in silence—become a "secret agent" for Jesus. But do you know how God reacts to those who conspire against him? He laughs (see Psalm 2:4). We can laugh too, even when God's enemies laugh at us, for we know the one who is going to laugh last. B. B. Warfield encourages us to take comfort in this: Christ is going to win.

WALK WITH B. B. WARFIELD

"The section opens with a vision of the victory of the Word of God, the King of kings and Lord of lords over all his enemies. We see him come forth from heaven girded for war, followed by the armies of heaven. The birds of the air are summoned to the feast of corpses that shall be prepared for them. The armies of the enemy—the beasts and the kings of the earth—are gathered against him and are totally destroyed.

"It is a vivid picture of a complete victory, an entire conquest, that we have here; and all the imagery of war and battle is employed to give it life. This is the symbol. The thing symbolized obviously is the complete victory of the Son of God over all the hosts of wickedness. Christ is to conquer the earth: He is to overcome all his enemies."

WALK CLOSER TO GOD

Our times are not unique. God's people have often been surrounded by wickedness. The psalmist asked, "Why, LORD, do you stand far off?" (Psalm 10:1), but he took courage in God's coming victory: "The LORD is King for ever and ever; the nations will perish from his land" (Psalm 10:16).

Likewise, the apostle Paul wrote: "God is just: He will pay back trouble to those who trouble you ... when the Lord Jesus is revealed from heaven in blazing fire" (2 Thessalonians 1:6–7).

Do you have this same confidence? Make a habit of meditating on Christ's victory, and you will be thrilled! ❖

december**27**

THE GLORY THAT MAKES BURDENS BEARABLE

They came to life and reigned with Christ a thousand years.

REVELATION 20:4

Although some passages of the book of Revelation are difficult to understand, many verses—like small diamonds of encouragement—shine brightly with comfort.

As John's focus switched from the present to the future, from this world to the next, he discovered encouragement to face each fresh challenge to his faith. Martin Luther has these encouraging observations for those facing unjust suffering.

WALK WITH MARTIN LUTHER

"If we consider the great glory of the future life, it would not be at all difficult for us to bear the vexations of this world. But when Christ comes to judge the living and the dead and we experience these blessings, everyone will have to say for himself: 'Shame on me!'

"If I believe the Word, I shall on the last day not only gladly have suffered ordinary temptations, insults, imprisonment, but I shall also say: 'Oh, if I had only thrown myself under the feet of all the godless for the sake of the great glory which I now see revealed and which has come to me through the merit of Christ.'

"Paul well says, 'I consider that our present sufferings are not worth comparing with the glory that will be revealed in us' (Romans 8:18)."

WALK CLOSER TO GOD

Remember Stephen, perhaps the first martyr of the New Testament church. Even as the rocks were hurtling toward him, Stephen looked up to heaven and saw Jesus at God's right hand. Then, like his Lord, Stephen died praying for those who were taking his life.

Chances are you won't be stoned for your faith, but don't be surprised if you feel the heat as you live out your faith.

One message permeates nearly every chapter of Revelation: victory is certain. So take heart, look up, wait patiently. The glory to be revealed in us makes any burden bearable. ❖

december28

ADMITTED TO THE REALM OF HIDDEN TREASURE

And books were opened. Another book was opened, which is the book of life.

REVELATION 20:12

You heard the Good News; you believed the Good News; but you have yet to see all that the Good News holds in store.

Hoped for, yet not seen. John Calvin explores some of the reasons why you still have some surprises to come.

WALK WITH JOHN CALVIN

"Until the last day when the books will be opened, there is no possible way in which the things pertaining to our salvation can be possessed by us, unless we can transcend the reach of our own intellect and raise our eye above all worldly objects; in short, unless we surpass ourselves.

"Such mysteries of God cannot be discerned in themselves, but we behold them only in his Word. But how can the mind rise to such a perception of the divine goodness without at the same time being wholly inflamed with love to God?

"The abundance of joy which God has treasured up for those who fear him cannot be truly known without making a most powerful impression.

"Hence it is not strange that no sinister, perverse heart ever experiences this feeling—a feeling by which we are admitted to the most hidden treasures of God and the holiest recesses of his kingdom, which must not be profaned by the entrance of a heart that is impure."

WALK CLOSER TO GOD

To realize fully the wonders of salvation would be more than your finite mind could comprehend. Now you experience only a taste of the banquet you'll enjoy forever.

Peter described it this way: "Praise be to the God and Father of our Lord Jesus Christ! In his great mercy he has given us new birth into a living hope ... an inheritance ... kept in heaven for you, who through faith are shielded by God's power until the coming of the salvation that is ready to be revealed in the last time" (1 Peter 1:3–5).

God will one day reveal the full scope and grandeur of salvation. And you can be certain it will be well worth the wait. ✤

december29

HE WHO IS WORTHY OF FIRST PLACE IN YOUR HEART

He said to me: "It is done. I am the Alpha and Omega, the Beginning and the End".
REVELATION 21:6

God at the beginning. God at the end. And God at work in between.

The Bible speaks clearly of the Creator intimately involved in his world—preserving it, redeeming it. It also speaks of a Father who cares for each of his children, looking after their concerns from A to Z.

Clarence Macartney calls you to consider your commitment to the one who is your all in all.

WALK WITH CLARENCE MACARTNEY

"Christ is the Alpha and Omega of the believer. He is the Author and Finisher of our faith.

"His Word is our rule and law, his life our example and pattern, his death on the cross our salvation, his presence our joy, his smile our reward, and to be with him in glory is our eternal hope.

"What place does Christ take in your life? To what degree can you say, 'He is for me the Alpha and the Omega, the First and the Last, the Beginning and the End'?

"He who is the Lord of the ages, the King of time, and the Adored of the angels, is worthy of the first place in your life. Will you give that place to him?

"No one ever did that and lived to regret it. On the contrary, you will be able to say, as John Bunyan did: 'His love to me has been most sweet, and his countenance I have more desired than they that have most desired the light of the sun.'"

WALK CLOSER TO GOD

Ask a real estate agent for the three keys to good investments, and you'll hear this response: "Location, location, location."

Ask a coach for the three reasons for his winning season, and he'll tell you, "Practice, practice, practice."

Ask a Christian for the top three priorities in his life, and you should hear, "Jesus, Jesus, Jesus!"

Christ is Lord over birth; he is Lord over death. And he is Lord over everything in between. He wants to do more than fit in among your priorities; he wants to set your priorities. ✤

december**30**

CITIZENS OF THE HOLY CITY

I did not see a temple in the city, because the Lord God Almighty and the Lamb are its temple.
REVELATION 21:22

For some, city life evokes the excitement and challenge of being in a fast-paced beehive of business and opportunity. For others, it represents crime, squalor, poverty, unfulfilled dreams, dashed hopes, terrible loneliness. But one city will change all that—the Holy City, the new Jerusalem—the great city of God described in Revelation 21.

To understand the uniqueness of this city, says Alexander Maclaren, you must reverse the miseries of earth.

WALK WITH ALEXANDER MACLAREN

"All turns on two great thoughts—the blessed closeness of perfect and eternal union between God and men, and the consequent dawning of a new day in which all human ills shall be swept away.

"When the church was on the old earth, God dwelt with his people in reality, but, alas, with many breaks in their relationship caused by his people defiling the temple. But in the future everything that was symbolic shall be spiritual reality, and there will be no separation between the God who tabernacles among his people and the people in whom he dwells.

"His presence drives away all evils, as the risen moon clears the sky of clouds. How can sorrow, or crying, or pain, or death live where he is?

"Reverse the miseries of earth, and you know something of the joys of heaven. But begin with God's presence, or you will know nothing of its most joyful joy."

WALK CLOSER TO GOD

Think of John's description as a travelogue of the heavenly Jerusalem:

A city in which there is no temple, for the Lamb is personally present.
No sun or moon, for the Lamb is its light.
No night, for the Son always shines there.
No defilement, for holiness is its hallmark.

Best of all, there is no waiting list to become one of its citizens. Now, wouldn't you agree that's a city you'll enjoy living in—forever? ✤

december**31**

HOME AT LAST IN GOD'S BEAUTIFUL GARDEN

Then the angel showed me the river of the water of life, as clear as crystal, flowing from the throne of God and of the Lamb.

REVELATION 22:1

Throughout history gardens have been the scenes of significant life-and-death struggles. In a garden Eve made a decision that bore the fruit of death. In a garden the Savior agonized over a decision that would mean life eternal for all who believed.

John Henry Jowett probes the significance of that fateful night in a garden called Gethsemane.

WALK WITH JOHN HENRY JOWETT

"The Bible opens with a garden. It closes with a garden. The first is the Paradise that was lost. The last is paradise regained.

"Between the two there is a third, the garden of Gethsemane. And it is through the unspeakable bitterness and desolation of Gethsemane that we find again the glorious garden through which flows 'the river of the water of life' (Revelation 22:1).

"Without Gethsemane, no new Jerusalem! Without its mysterious and unfathomable night, no blessed sunrise of eternal hope!

"Can I forget Gethsemane? Yes, I can; and in the forgetfulness I lose the sacred awe of my redemption, and I miss the real glory of 'paradise regained.'

"'You are not your own; you were bought at a price' (1 Corinthians 6:19–20). That is the remembrance that keeps the spirit lowly, and that fills the heart with love for him 'whose I am,' and whom I ought to serve."

WALK CLOSER TO GOD

Eden ... Gethsemane ... the new Jerusalem. The journey has been costly and difficult. Yet through it all, God's purposes triumph.

His grace, his goodness, his Gethsemane have made it possible for you to dwell in the garden of God—forever. A garden in which there is no curse or darkness, only face-to-face fellowship with the Creator.

To forget such a gift might seem unthinkable. To understand fully such a gift— unfathomable. To spend this day thanking him for it—unbeatable!